I0810571

Images of Modern America

STERLING HEIGHTS

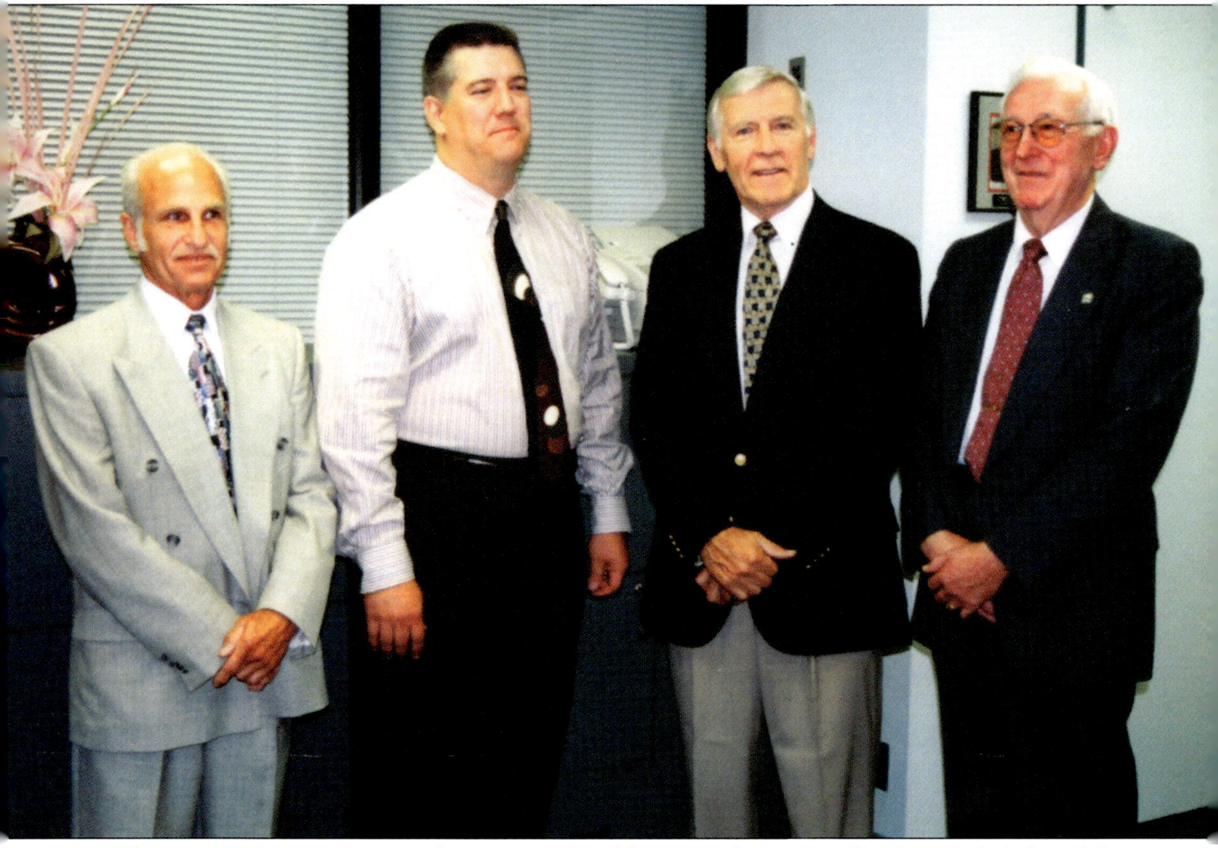

The city's 30th anniversary gathering in 1998 of former and current officials included, from left to right, Mayor Richard Notte and City Manager Steve Duchane standing with their counterparts from the past, the city's first mayor, Gerald Donovan, and the city's first city manager, Leonard Hendricks. (Courtesy of the Sterling Heights Community Relations Department.)

Front Cover: Dodge Park Bridge (Courtesy of Sterling Heights Community Relations Department, photograph taken by Steve Guitar; see page 67)

Upper Back Cover: Sterlingfest balloon crowd (Courtesy of Sterling Heights Community Relations Department; see page 78)

Lower Back Cover (from left to right): Teen strawberry pickers (Courtesy of Eileen Haff Herr; see page 22), City Center clock (Courtesy of Sterling Heights Community Relations Department; see page 76), Boys on bench (Courtesy of Sterling Heights Community Relations Department; see page 92)

Images of Modern America

STERLING HEIGHTS

Sterling Heights Public Library
and Historical Commission

ARCADIA
PUBLISHING

ISBN 978-1-4671-2777-6

Published by Arcadia Publishing
Charleston, South Carolina

Printed in the United States of America

Library of Congress Control Number: 2017946400

For all general information, please contact Arcadia Publishing:
Telephone 843-853-2070
Fax 843-853-0044
E-mail sales@arcadiapublishing.com

Visit us on the Internet at www.arcadiapublishing.com

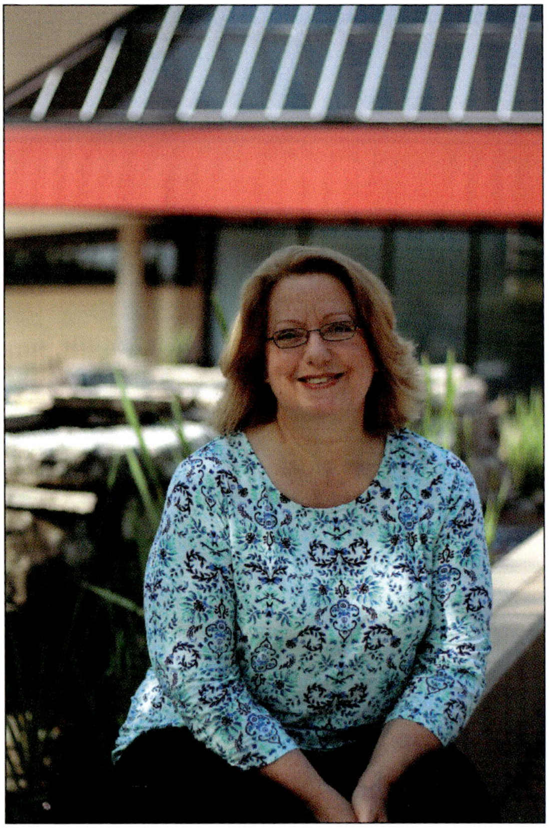

For this volume, librarian Debra Vercellone wrote the captions on behalf of the Sterling Heights Public Library. (Courtesy of Joe Vitale.)

Contents

ACKNOWLEDGMENTS

This work consists of images from the Local History Collection of the Sterling Heights Public Library. Most were taken by the employees of Sterling Township and the Sterling Heights Community Relations Department, while some were donated by residents. We would like to recognize the generosity of Chris Frezza, Steve Guitar, Alan and Linda Haggerty, Doug Harvey, Eileen Haff Herr, Charles Kosarek, Deanna Koski, Mary Marcinak, Diane McCauley, Colleen Miller Pawl, Gloria Pierce, Randy, Cheryl, and Sarah, Shank, Teresa Taylor, Pashko Ujkic, and John Urquhart for their generous donations of photographs, time, research, and support.

Thanks also to my coworkers and to the staff at the Sterling Heights Public Library, particularly Tammy Turgeon, Karen Stine, and Joe Vitale, whose patience and assistance are unmatched. Thanks also to my fellow City of Sterling Heights employees, past and present, who have been willing to help find information and more.

The extensive newspaper clipping collection begun by librarian Ruth Baker in the 1970s was invaluable. The majority of the information supporting the captions comes from reporting from the *Macomb Daily*, the *Advisor/Source* newspapers, the *Utica Sentinel*, and the *Sterling Heights Sentry*.

Special thanks also go to Jerry Sieja, for his support and efforts to spread the word on our need for information and donations, and to Janice Mulligan, for helping identify people in photographs.

Big hugs go to my family, Chuck, Allison, and Lauren, for putting up with my research addictions and making me smile, and to the late Ruth Baker, local history expert and retired librarian, who years ago gave me a solid start in my research on the area and whose interests and enthusiasm I shared.

Unless otherwise noted, all images appear courtesy of the Sterling Heights Community Relations Department.

—Debra Vercellone

Introduction

The City of Sterling Heights, Macomb County, Michigan, has a long and rich history.

From the earliest settlement nearly 9,000 years ago, to the native tribes who fished in our rivers and walked through our trails, to the western influence that started with the French in the late 1600s, and finally to the American influence that started with the surveying of land in 1817, the area that now makes up Sterling Heights has been serving and sustaining human populations for over 400 generations.

In our first volume (*Sterling Township: 1875–1968*), we detailed the transition of Sterling Township from a stopping off point between two villages to a vast farming community to a township in transition.

This book is dedicated to that transition.

On May 25, 1968, following a vote by the residents of Sterling Township, a charter was adopted to change Sterling Township into the City of Sterling Heights. On July 1, 1968, the City of Sterling Heights was incorporated. The city is governed by the council-manager system of local government that combines the political leadership of elected officials in the form of a governing body (the city council) with the managerial experience of an appointed manager. The first city council worked tirelessly to adopt ordinances, policies, and procedures for the new city. They hired their first city manager, Leonard G. Hendricks, on July 26, 1968, and they immediately began to construct master plans for development, roads, sidewalks, and water/sewer lines. They also had to establish city departments for police, fire, public works, parks and recreation, and a library.

The city's first mayor, Gerald N. Donovan, stated, "With that one vote in 1968, we no longer lived out in the country. We suddenly had become the second largest city in size in the state and had to grow and develop." Within that first year, a new Sterling Heights City Hall was dedicated on May 25, 1969.

In the 50 years since becoming a city, our population has grown from 61,365 in 1970, to 108,999 in 1980 (a 177 percent increase), up to 129,699 in 2010, and is now estimated to be approximately 132,000. Sterling Heights is currently the second-largest suburb in Metropolitan Detroit and the fourth-largest city in Michigan. It is 36.8 square miles and, according to the 2010 census, has 52,190 housing units with 78.8 percent home ownership.

Our city has become an important hub in the defense and automotive industries, and we have taken our place as one of the great cities of Michigan. The city's largest employers include Ford and Chrysler (also known as Fiat Chrysler) as well as BAE Systems and General Dynamics Land Systems, which have all brought jobs and opportunity to the area.

Over the years, the city has been recognized for many accomplishments. This includes receiving the Tree City USA Award from the National Association of State Foresters and the USDA Forest Service for the 32nd year in a row. In 2001, the *Detroit Free Press* named Sterling Heights the best city with high quality of life and low taxes. The Certificate of Achievement for Excellence in Financial Reporting has been awarded to the city from the Government Finance Officers

Association for many years as well. Sterling Heights was also named a Michigan Green Community in 2014. The city has consistently been named one of the safest cities in the state as well.

The city has much to be proud of, not only of its own accomplishments but also those of its partners. The city's residents are served by two award-winning school districts—Utica Community Schools and Warren Consolidated Schools. Students attending these schools have achieved recognition for academics, music, art, theater, robotics, and journalism.

Over the past 50 years, the Lakeside Shopping Center and various retail establishments have provided conveniences for the increasing number of residents. Local and chain restaurants have thrived here, as well as the development of golf courses and multiplex movie theaters. Businesses have flourished, and the residents have enjoyed quality city services.

Citywide events have also been a part of the city's tradition. In 2018, the city will hold its 39th consecutive year of the Memorial Day Parade/Ceremony, its 38th consecutive year of Sterlingfest (the city's main festival that includes art, music, food and a carnival), and the 17th consecutive year of the Cultural Exchange (a celebration of the various cultures represented in the city with food, music, dance, and information).

In 2014, the city went through a strategic planning process with input from residents, business owners, city leadership, and city staff and developed the 2030 Vision Statement: A vibrant, inclusive community for residents and businesses that is safe, active, progressive, and distinctive; Sterling Heights—a bold vision for an exceptional quality of life. This vision has laid the foundation for formal plan updates, service delivery plans, and enhanced outcomes.

In this book, you will see the city as it was then and the city as it is now. In this book, as in our community, the echoes of history are still seen in the midst of modern development. New construction casts its shadow on homes built 100 years ago, and vast commercial and industrial developments still share the outline of their original farm boundaries.

As time marches on, the city is slowly losing the visible signs of its township farming roots. Little by little, the old homes and farms have disappeared, and the landscape is wiped of the physical evidence of what was once a small sleepy community. During the year 2018, the City of Sterling Heights will be hosting a series of events to commemorate its 50th anniversary. Included will be the honoring of past city council members and mayors as well as a city celebration in Dodge Park. This book has been published to honor that anniversary.

As Sterling Heights moves forward into the next 50 years of its life, it is important to pause and reflect on the lives, struggles, successes, and hopes of the men and women who helped to build this innovative modern city. We hope you enjoy the memories that we have shared and will make new ones in this city we call home.

—Former Sterling Heights historical commissioner Michael Lombardini
and Sterling Heights Public Library director Tammy Turgeon

One

Business

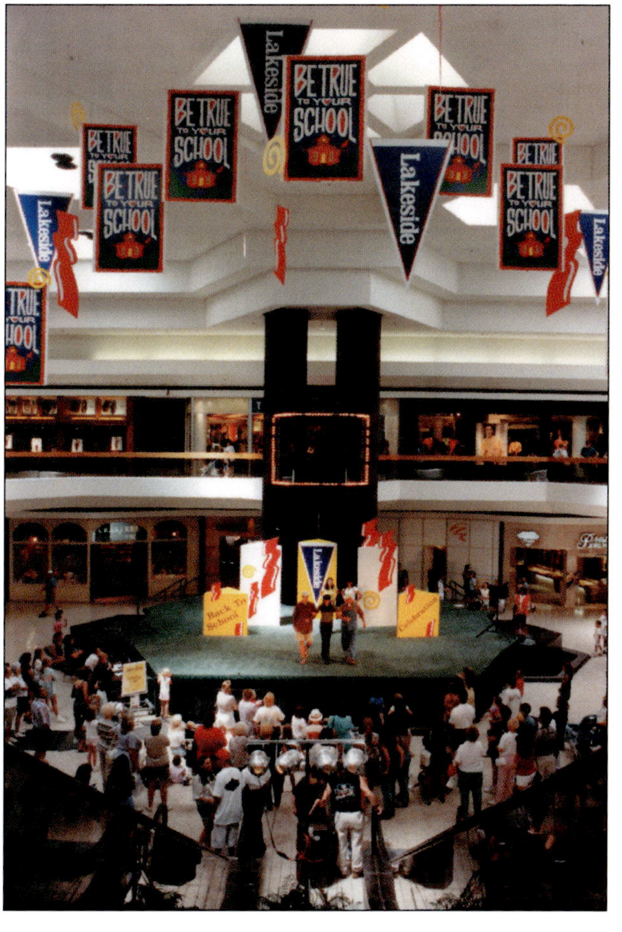

Lakeside Mall's main stage is seen in this undated photograph, possibly from the late 1990s. The store hosted many special events and became almost like a community center for the suburban area. The memorable glass elevator is seen behind the stage. There seemed to be no better fun for teens than to spend a Saturday afternoon at the mall.

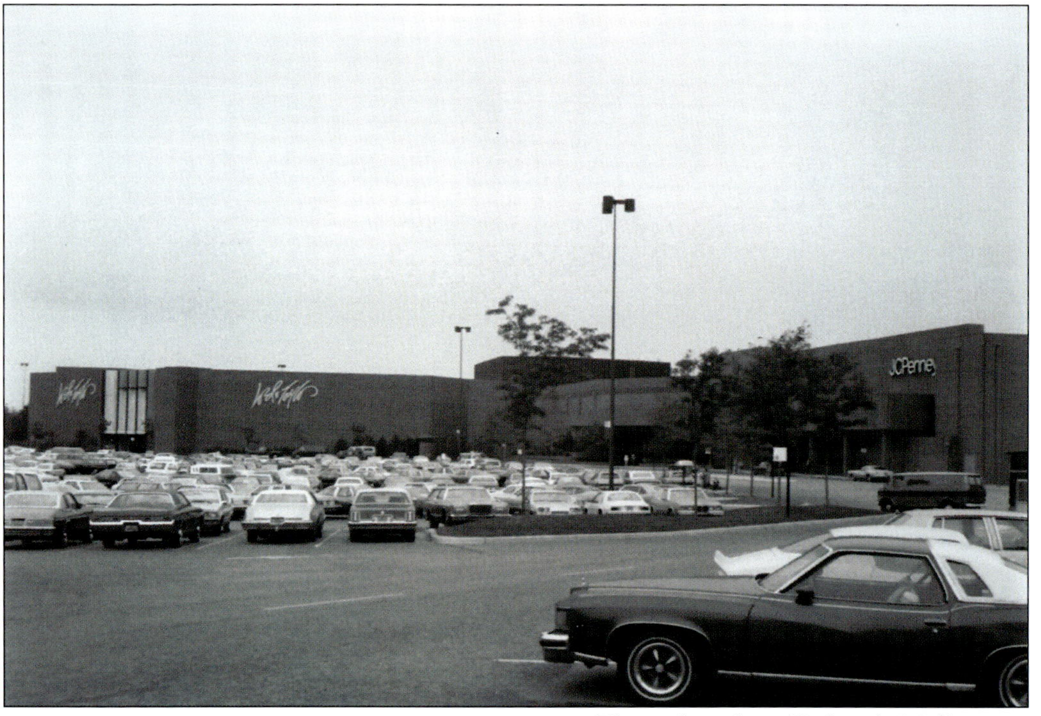

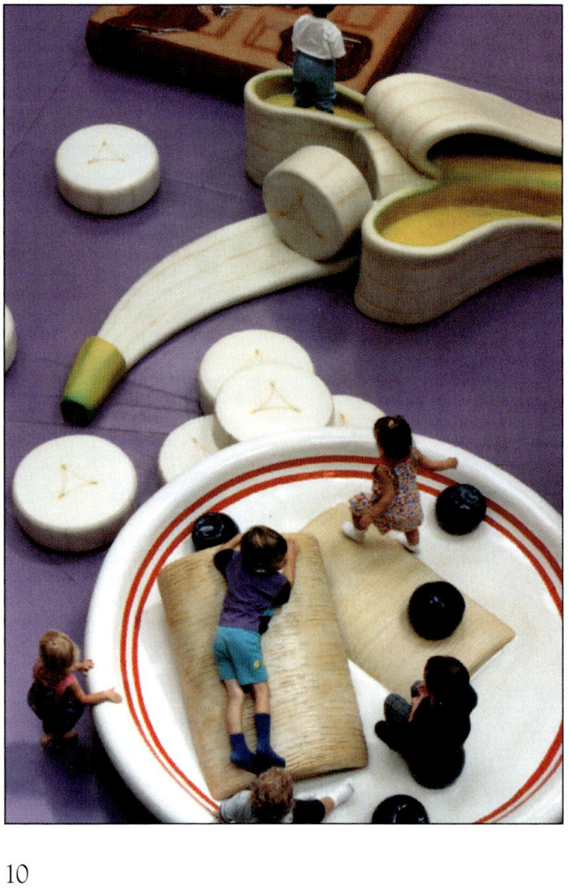

The parking lot of Lakeside Mall is seen in 1980, with anchor stores in the background. Lakeside, when developed out of 300 acres of farmland, changed the way of life for Sterling Heights. When it first opened, it was like an island in a sea of farmland, but it did not take long for the entire M-59 corridor to blow up with retail development, with housing following. Life was never the same again.

Lakeside's play area, seen here possibly in the 1990s, featured large-scale breakfast food to climb on. Other unique offerings of the mall over the years were an ice skating rink and a water slide, which is gone now. Interesting things that remain are a beautiful carousel and giant modern art sculptures scattered throughout the mall. The mall was developed by Al Taubman and opened in 1976.

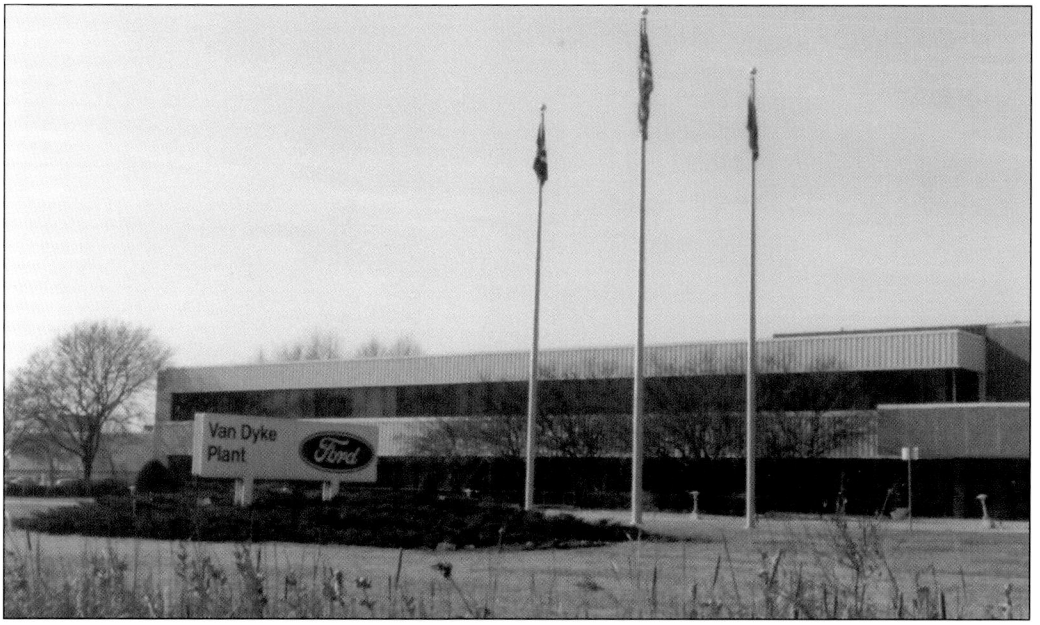

The Ford Van Dyke Plant, located on the northwest corner of 18 Mile Road and Van Dyke Avenue, opened in 1968, about 12 years after the Ford plant on Mound Road. Albert Kahn was the architect. Township officials noted it was a tremendous tax boost to the area and to Utica Community Schools. Since the first Ford plant opened, it has been one of the largest taxpayers in the city.

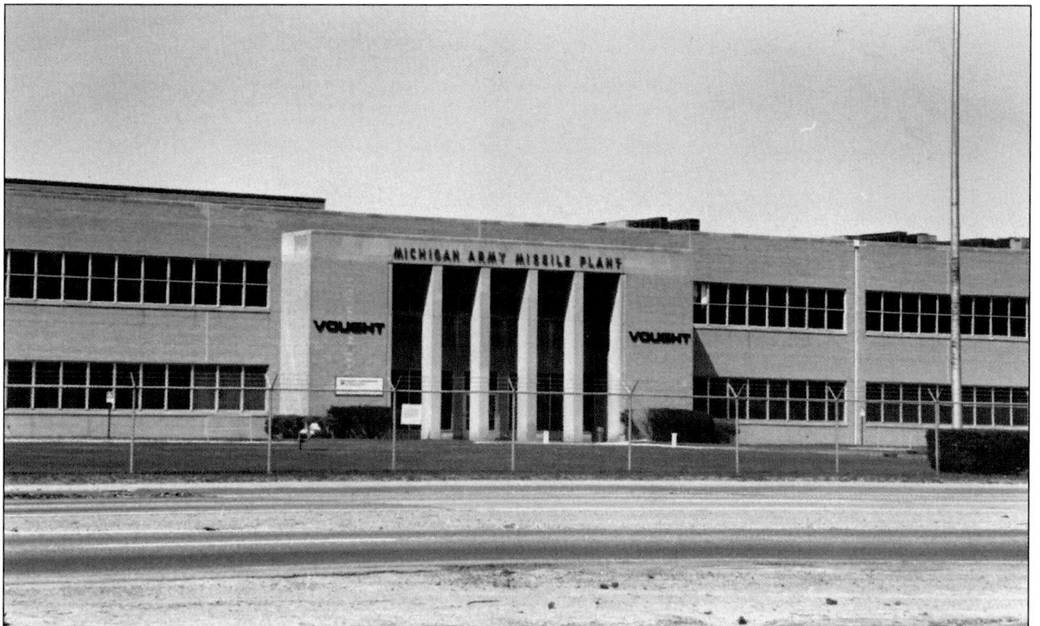

This closer view shows the front formal entrance of the plant, at the time the Vought Missile Plant. By 1983, it became Chrysler's Sterling Heights Assembly Plant (SHAP). During its time as Vought, there were missiles and rockets on display on the front lawn, located on Van Dyke Avenue north of Metro Parkway.

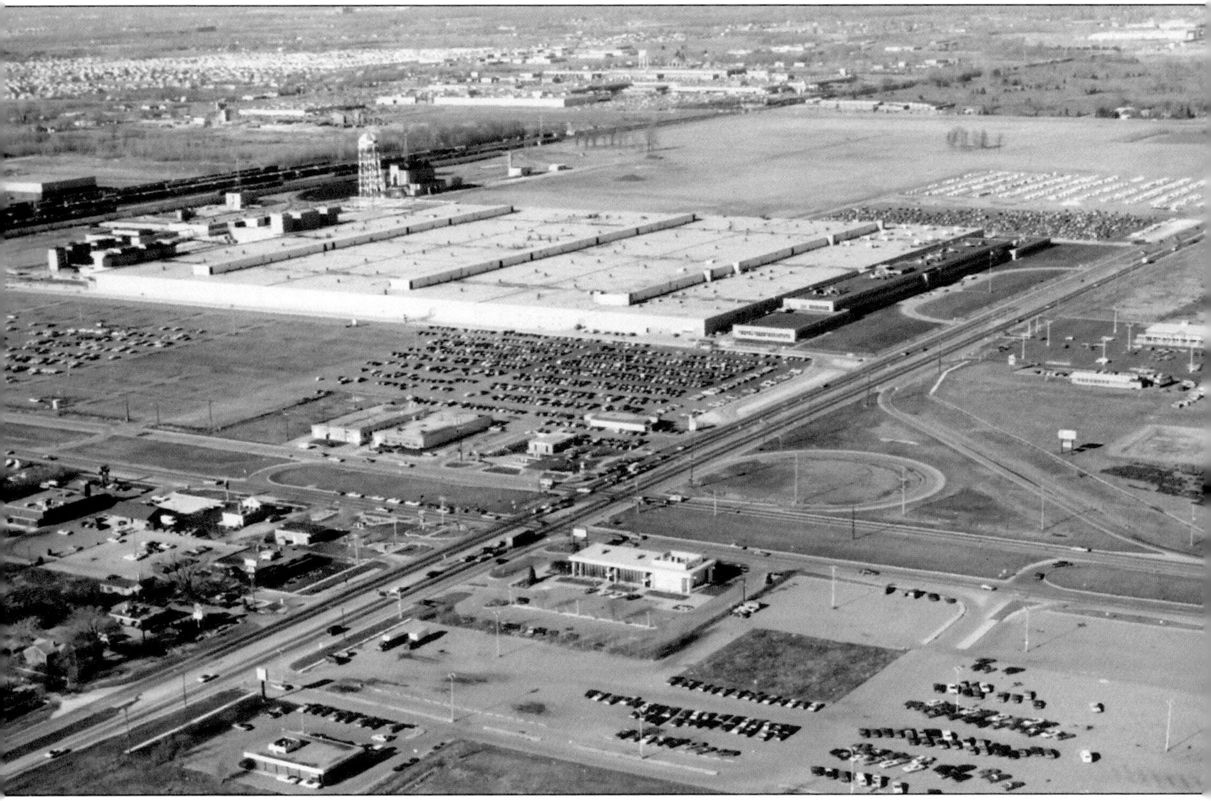

This photograph of the Chrysler Sterling Heights Assembly Plant (SHAP) was taken sometime in the early 1980s. The plant, on Van Dyke Avenue north of Metro Parkway, was originally owned by the US government in the 1950s; missiles were built here. In 1981, Volkswagen bought the building but never used it before selling it to Chrysler in 1983. Under Chrysler, it was a high tech pioneer plant using robotics and computer technology. Lee Iacocca drove the first Dodge Lancer ES off the line in 1984. The plant has been through many challenges and threats of closure due to the troubled auto industry but after the efforts of many has always persevered. The city's other Chrysler plant, the Chrysler Sterling Stamping Plant, on 15 Mile Road, is the largest stamping plant in the world. Chrysler is one of the city's biggest taxpayers.

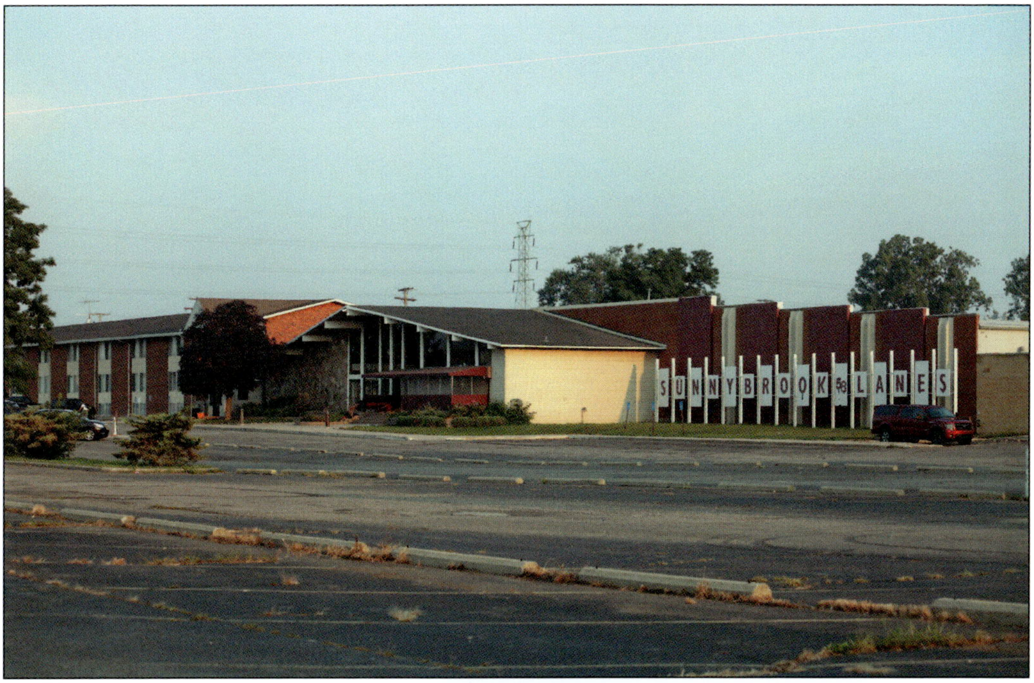

Sunnybrook Golf and Bowl first opened in 1936 on 17 Mile Road, between Mound Road and Van Dyke Avenue. Another nine-hole course and a bowling alley were added in 1962, and the hotel was built in 1968. Randy Shank; his wife, Cheryl; and daughter Sarah bought the complex in 1998; it consisted of 140 acres, 27 holes, 58 lanes, a charity poker room, and the hotel. Sunnybrook was one of a number of golf courses in Sterling Heights dating back to the 1920s and 1930s. It closed in 2015, was demolished, and the acreage was redeveloped as industrial. (Courtesy of Sunnybrook.)

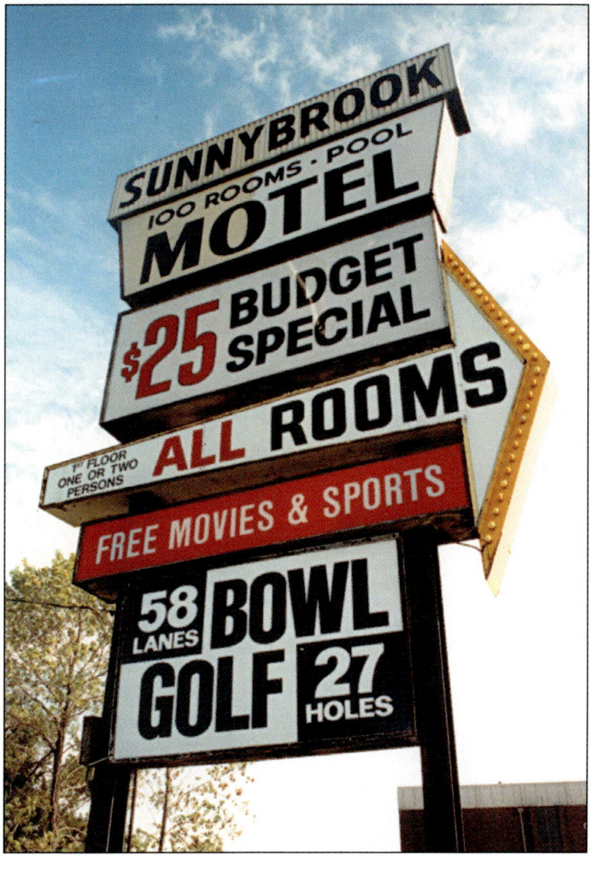

The Sunnybrook sign was a landmark for the southeast corner of 17 Mile Road and Van Dyke Avenue for many years. It was an off-site sign, which caused some trouble with city rules, but it existed for decades on that corner, alerting drivers to the Sunnybrook Golf and Bowl farther west on 17 Mile Road.

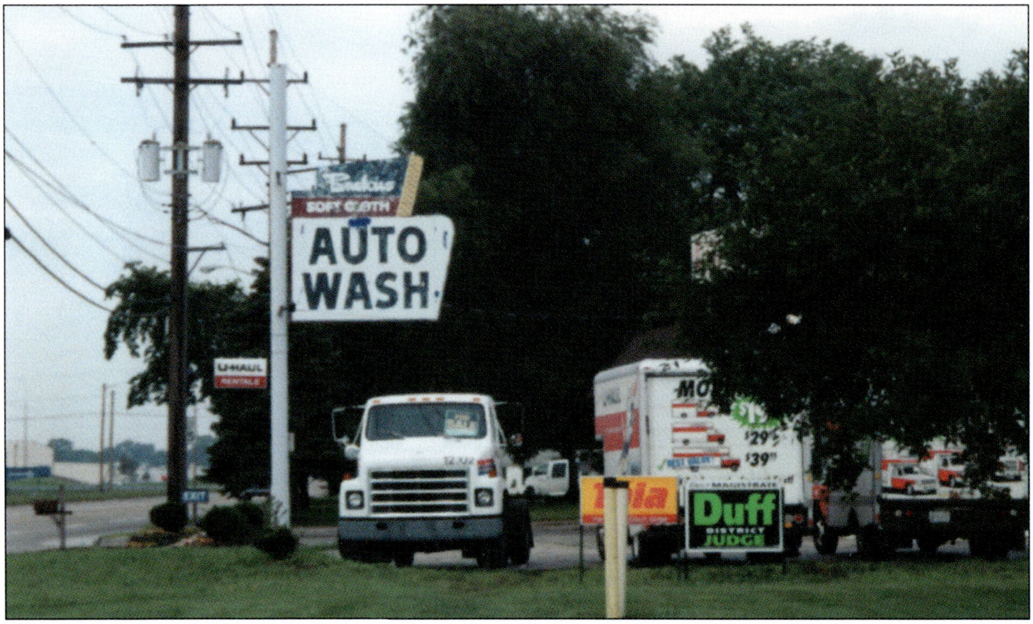

The sign for Backus Auto Wash, on 17 Mile Road, has become somewhat iconic. The Backus family emigrated from the Middle East to Detroit many years ago and eventually bought a farm on 17 Mile Road, west of Van Dyke Avenue, in 1936. In 1963, their sons opened an auto wash next door, and the family has operated it ever since. The family has always been very involved in civic affairs and public service.

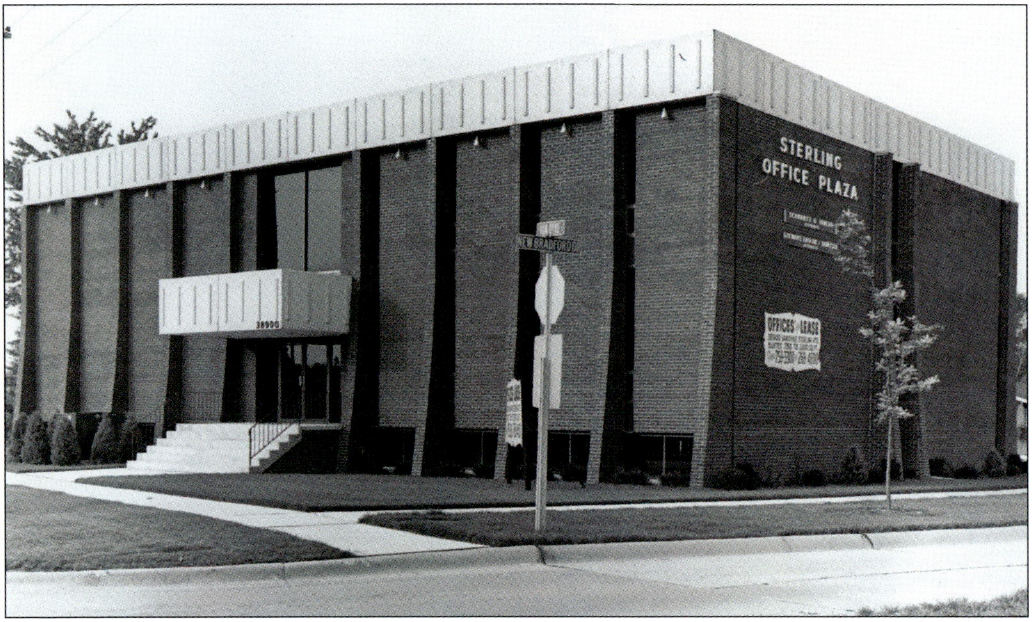

Sterling Office Plaza, located on Van Dyke Avenue just south of 17 Mile Road, was the first office building in Sterling Heights. Constructed in 1968 by attorneys Michael D. Schwartz and Albert Lopatin, the building was designed to house professional offices on three levels. As the city grew, the need for professional office space grew with it, and newly built facilities stepped up to fill the need.

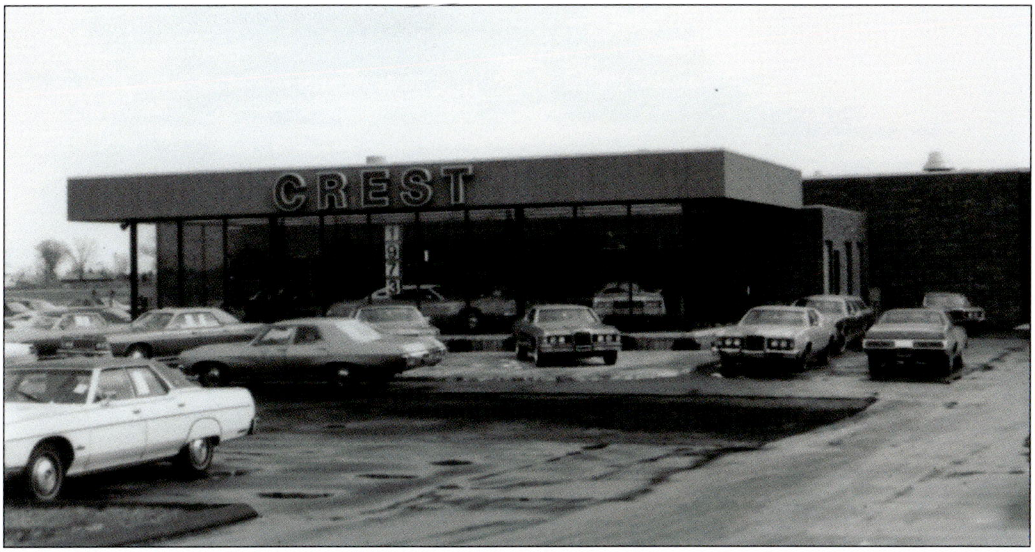

Crest Lincoln-Mercury, on Van Dyke Avenue between 15 Mile Road and Metro Parkway, is one of many automobile dealerships along Van Dyke Avenue in Sterling Heights that have been around for decades. Crest was owned by Bill Ritchie (the father of singer Kid Rock) until he sold in 1999. This 1972 photograph shows the company advertising 1973 models in the window.

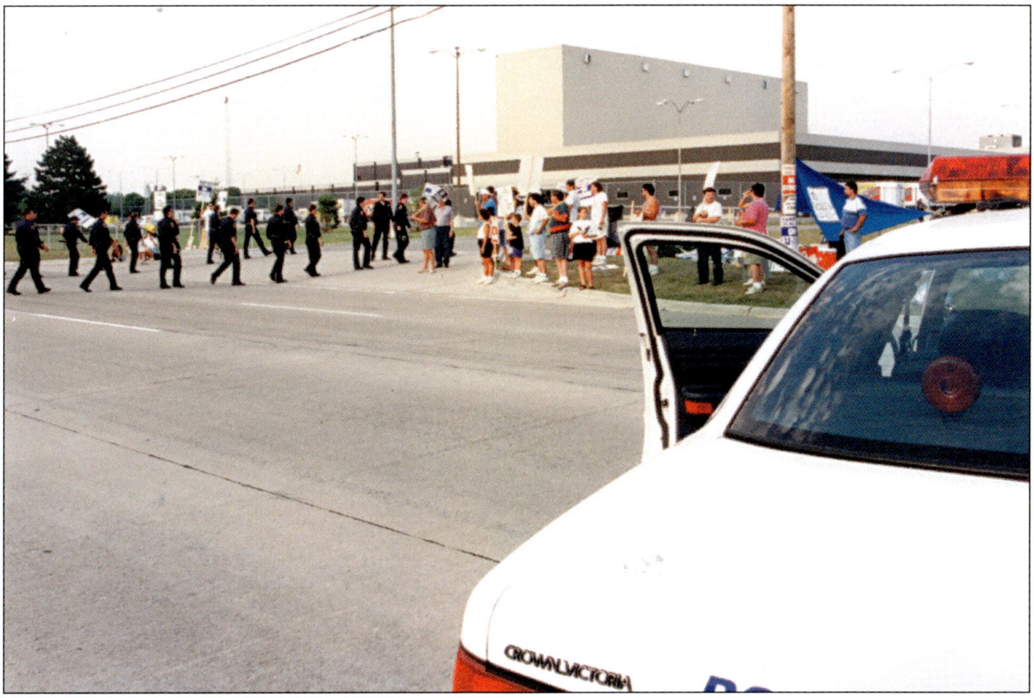

The Detroit Newspaper Strike was strongly felt at the corner of Mound Road and Metro Parkway. Workers from six labor unions went on strike against the two Detroit newspapers, the *Detroit Free Press* and the *Detroit News*, in this costly, contentious event that began in 1995 and ended in 1997. This location was the North Printing Plant, where major picketing and police presence occurred. The plant is seen in the background.

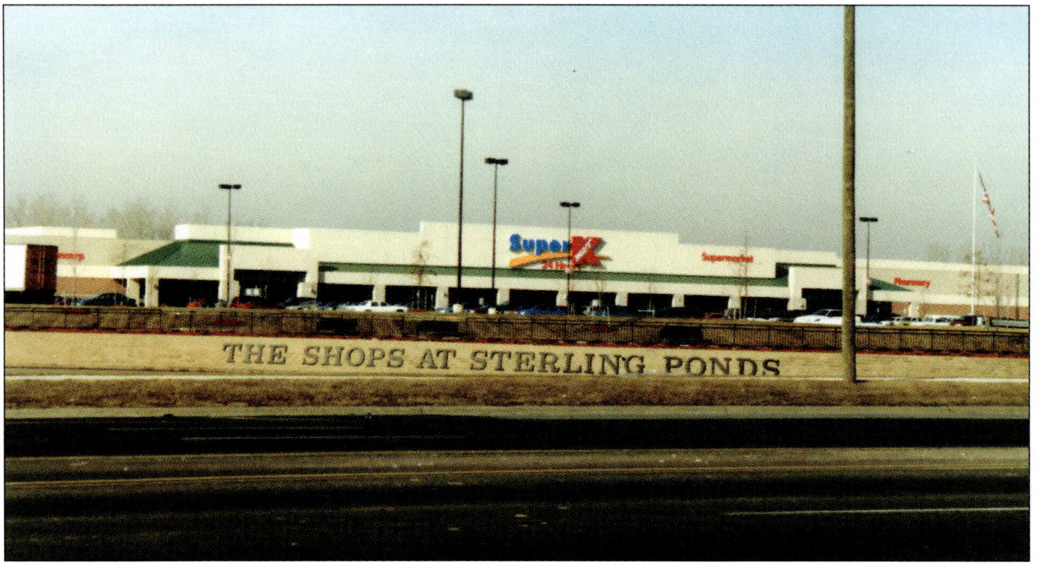

Super Kmart anchored the Shops at Sterling Ponds when it first opened in 1996 on the northwest corner of Van Dyke Avenue and 14 Mile Road. After the closure of the store in 2003, the structure was eventually torn down and rebuilt as a Super Walmart.

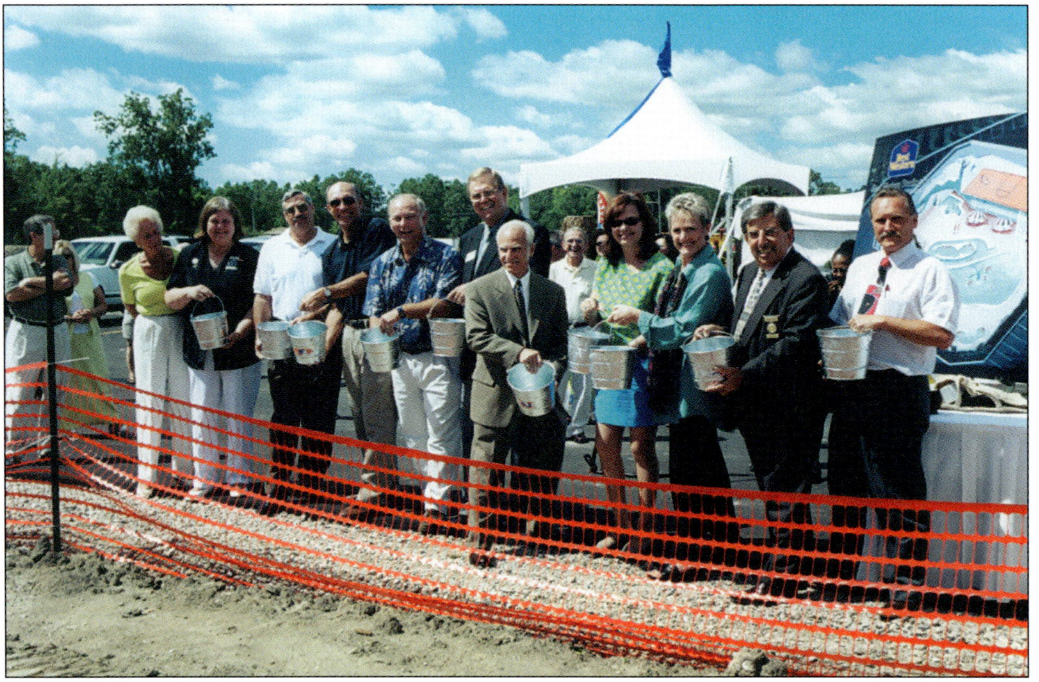

Celebrating the onset of construction of the new Sterling Inn Waterpark, owners and city officials get ready to throw buckets of water. The hotel, on the southwest corner of Van Dyke Avenue and 15 Mile Road, was purchased by Victor Martin and John Urquhart in 1973. The year 2001 saw the opening of the water park and a five-story hotel addition. Victor Martin is in the print shirt, and John Urquhart is on the far right. The hotel complex was recently sold and is now a Wyndham Garden hotel.

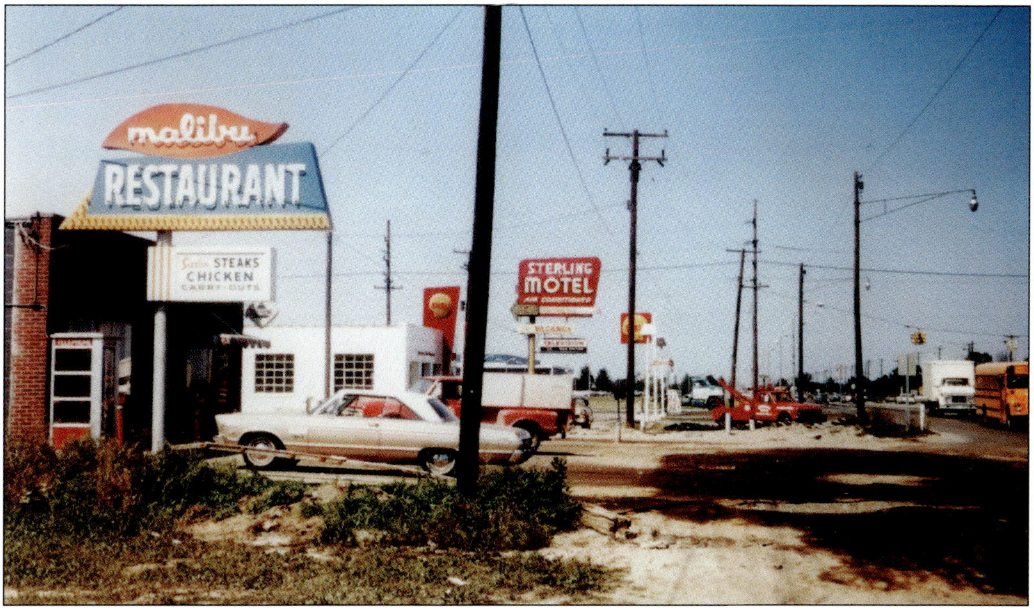

This was the view looking north on Van Dyke Avenue just south of 15 Mile Road in 1969. The Malibu Restaurant, now gone, was advertising steaks and chicken; the Sterling Motel changed into the Best Western Sterling Inn and Conference Center and then a Wyndham Garden hotel; and a Shell gas station, now run by another oil company, was pumping gasoline. Beyond the intersection on the far left would be the Chrysler Sterling Stamping Plant. (Courtesy of John Urquhart.)

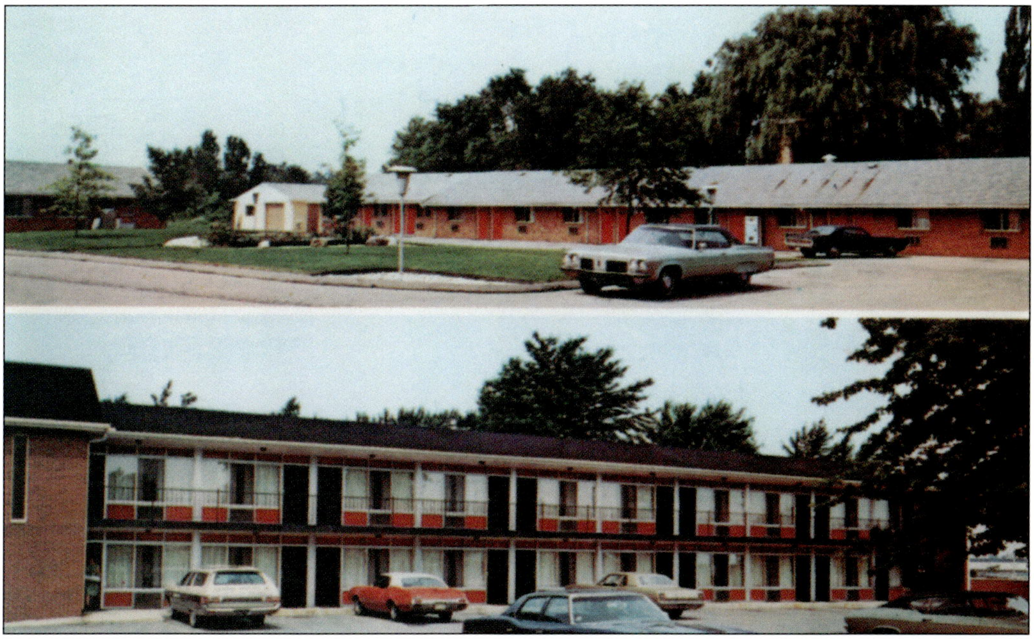

The original Sterling Motel, located on the southwest corner of Van Dyke Avenue and 15 Mile Road, is pictured here around 1970. It grew and evolved over the years to become the Best Western Sterling Inn and Conference Center, with a water park and a restaurant run by award-winning chef Ray Hollingsworth running the restaurant. John Urquhart and Victor Martin owned the hotel for years, selling to Wyndham Garden around 2015. (Courtesy of John Urquhart.)

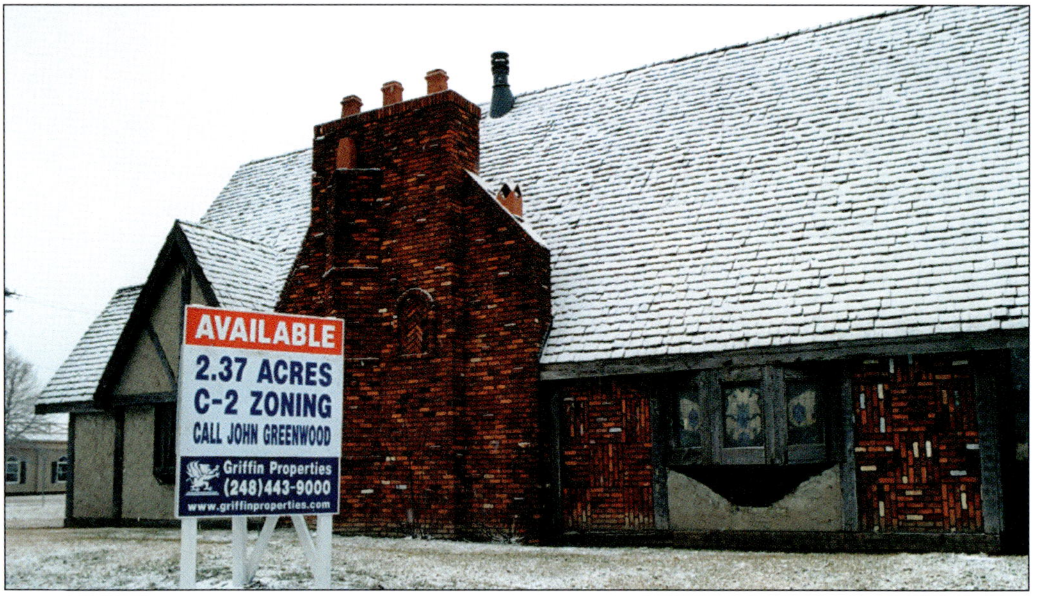

The Sixpence Restaurant, on Van Dyke Avenue at Plumbrook Road, opened in 1977. It was owned by partners in Mount Clemens who opened it after their first Sixpence location in Warren was successful. The building was designed in a brick Tudor style, using imported stained glass and woodwork. The interior had cozy booths made to look like an old English country inn. Area residents have many memories of this unique restaurant, but it was troubled. It closed, sat vacant, and was eventually demolished.

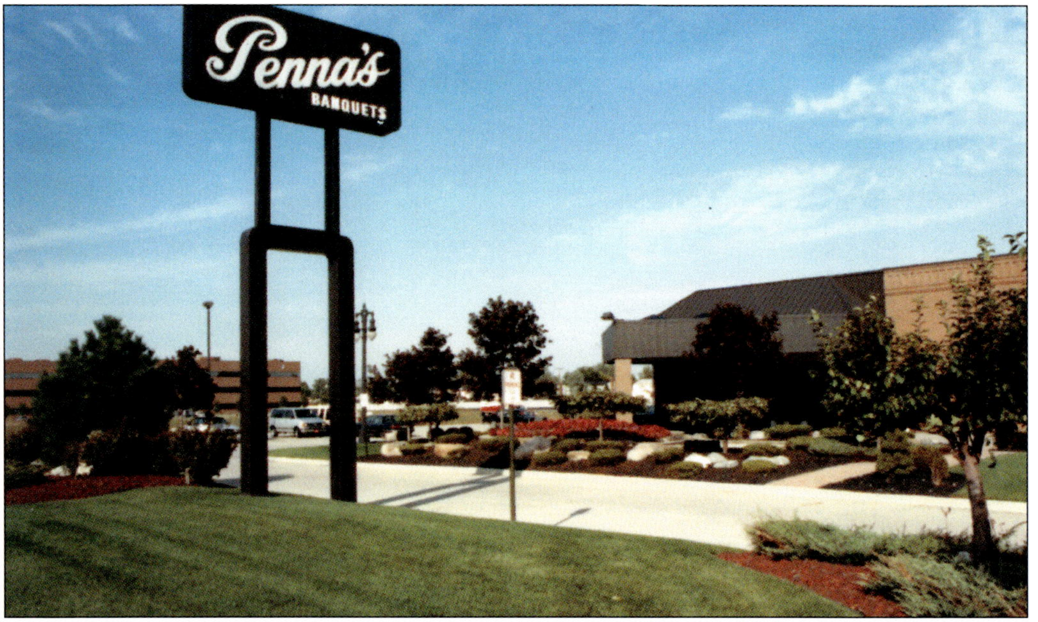

Penna's Banquet Center, on Van Dyke Avenue south of 17 Mile Road, is one of two banquet centers owned and managed by the Penna family. Villa Penna is located on Hayes Road in Sterling Heights. The Penna family began their restaurant and banquet business in Detroit, moved to Warren, and then to Sterling Heights, opening the pictured location in 1984. Countless area weddings and proms have been held at these two very successful locations.

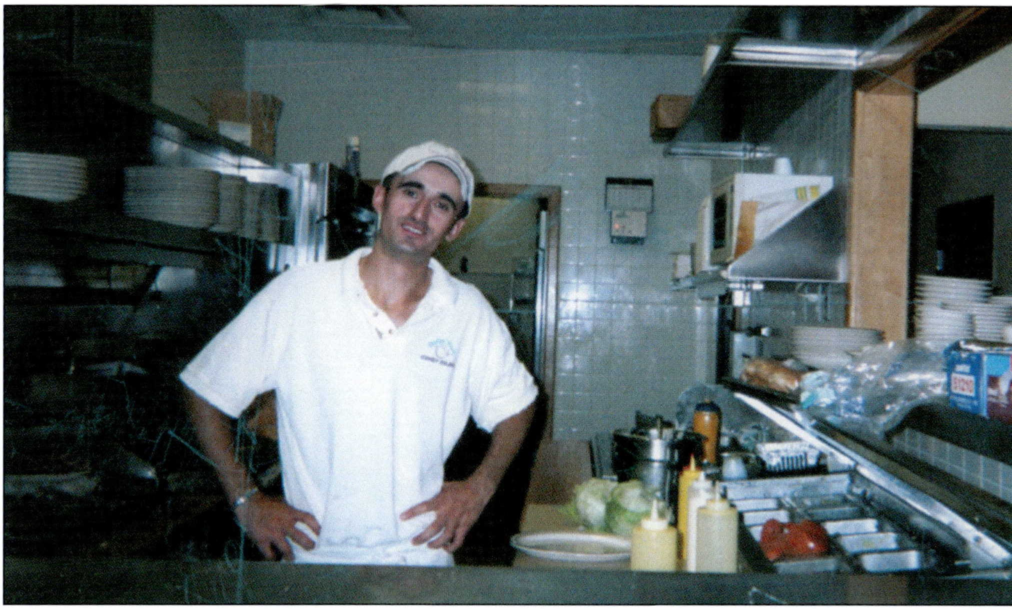

Pashko Ujkic, owner of Dodge Park Coney Island, is a success story. From Albania and Montenegro, he immigrated to the United States as a young child. By the age of 23, he opened this family restaurant at 15 Mile Road and Dodge Park Road. His work ethic and generosity to the community have earned him a reputation as a community leader. Mayor Notte was quoted as saying, "He is what Sterling Heights is all about." (Courtesy of Pashko Ujkic.)

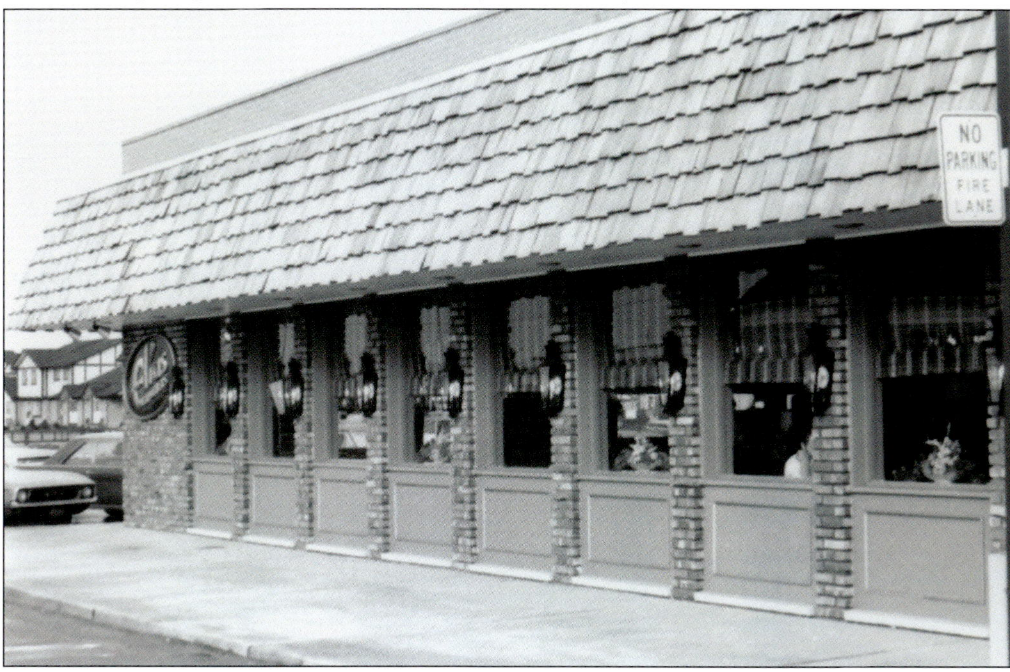

This Big Boy restaurant, on the corner of 18 Mile Road and Van Dyke Avenue, opened in the early 1970s. The chain fell on hard times, and all three Big Boy restaurants in Sterling Heights have now closed; the last one, pictured here, in 2016. The Andover Heights Condominium complex can be seen across the street in this photograph from the 1970s.

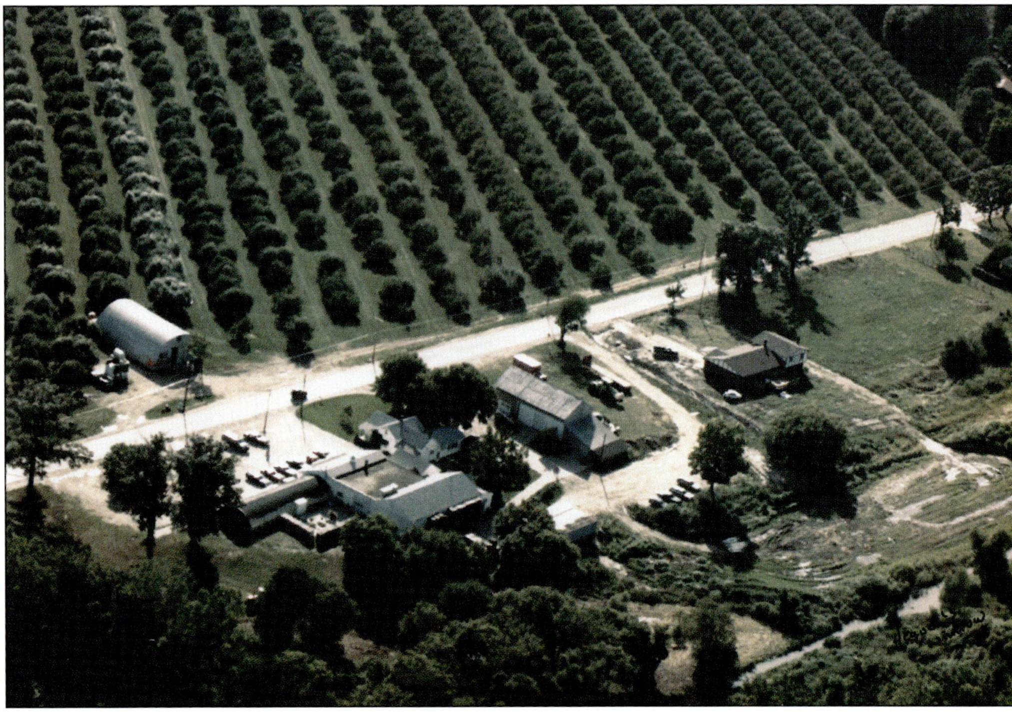

The actual orchard that used to supply Miller's Orchard market was across the street from the store on Clinton River Road. The orchard was begun around 1935 and was a fixture in the area until it was sold in 1989 and cleared and developed into a subdivision around 1990. The market is now supplied by its farm property in northern Macomb County. (Courtesy of Colleen Miller Pawl.)

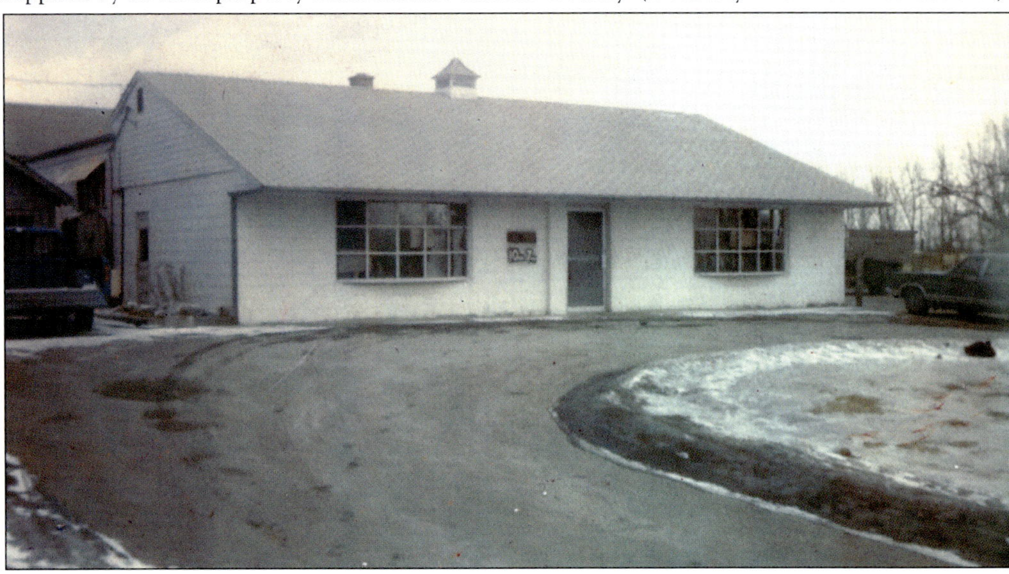

Miller's Orchard market, on Clinton River Road between Saal and Hayes Roads, started as a produce farm and apple orchard in 1935. In the 1960s, the owners added a roadside stand to sell their wares to the locals, and that grew into this store pictured here. The market has become very cute, clean, and homey and a handy place to pick up deli meats, produce, and the market's famous pies. (Courtesy of Colleen Miller Pawl.)

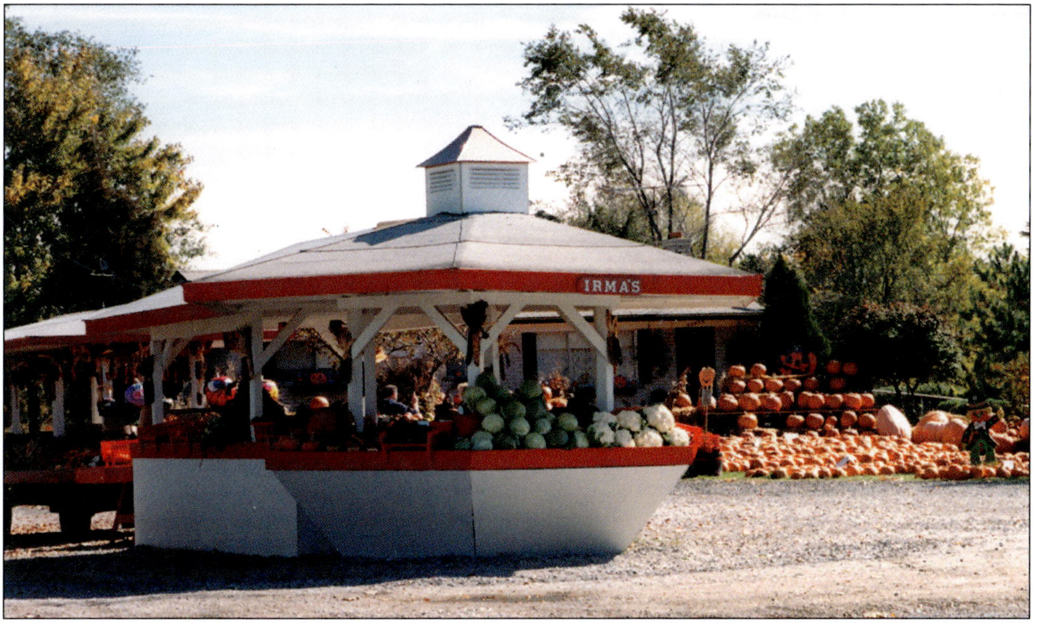

Irma's Family Farm Fresh Vegetables stand, on Dequindre Road, has been selling wonderful produce since 1958. What they do not grow themselves, they get from area farmers, and in the off-season, they do a nice business in greenery grave blankets. Irma's daughter Diane McCauley has been running the stand since Irma's death. Kathy's Produce, right next door to Irma's, offers some friendly competition.

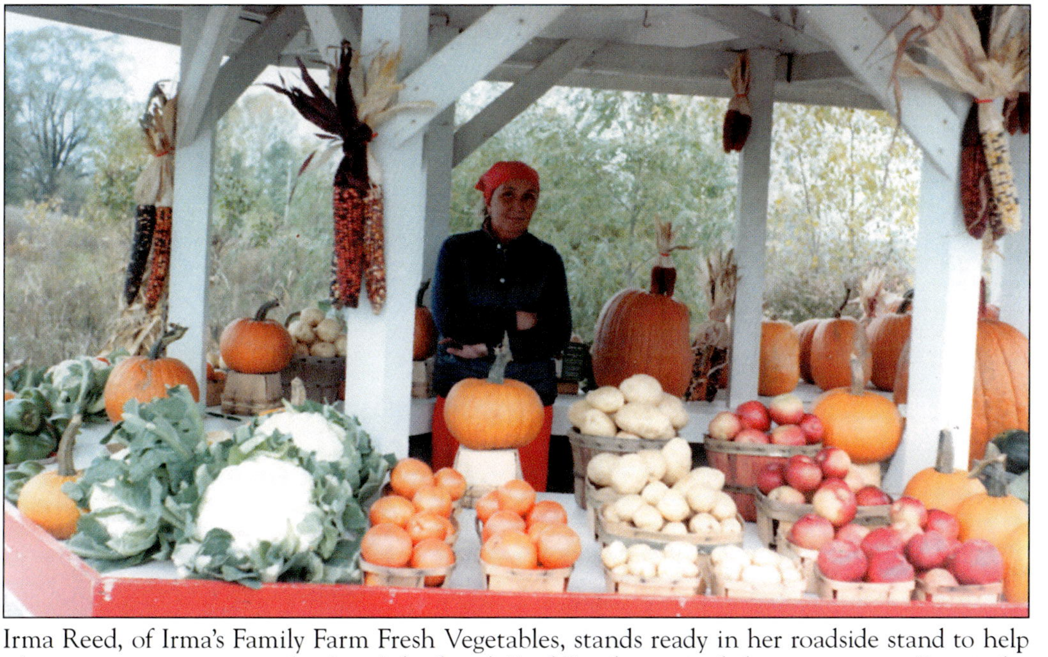

Irma Reed, of Irma's Family Farm Fresh Vegetables, stands ready in her roadside stand to help whatever customers come by. Irma's husband, Fred Reed, acquired the property on Dequindre Road, south of 19 Mile Road, in 1958. Irma came from Berlin, Germany, not long after to join him. They liked to farm, and selling fresh produce on the side of the road continued an area tradition of roadside stands. Irma passed away in 1997. (Courtesy of Diane McCauley.)

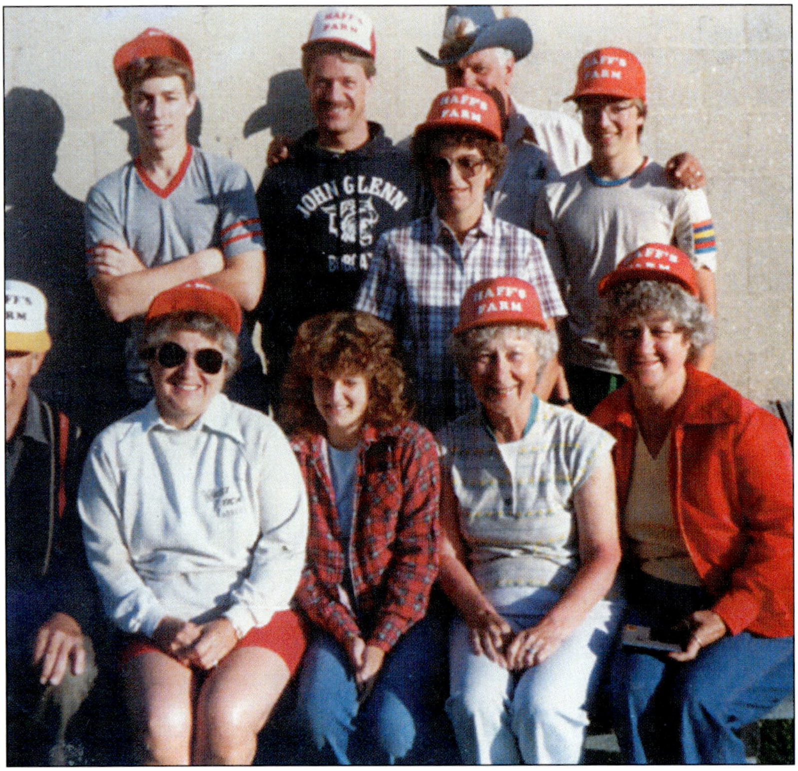

The Haff family had worked their farm, located on Dequindre Road north of 19 Mile Road, since 1839. The big white house with the large red barn has been a landmark for generations. It was a dairy farm until 1956. More modern years saw the farm offering eggs and U-pick strawberries. This photograph includes much of the family, which consisted of siblings Vera, Gladys, Lawrence, Violet, and Eileen. (Courtesy of Eileen Haff Herr.)

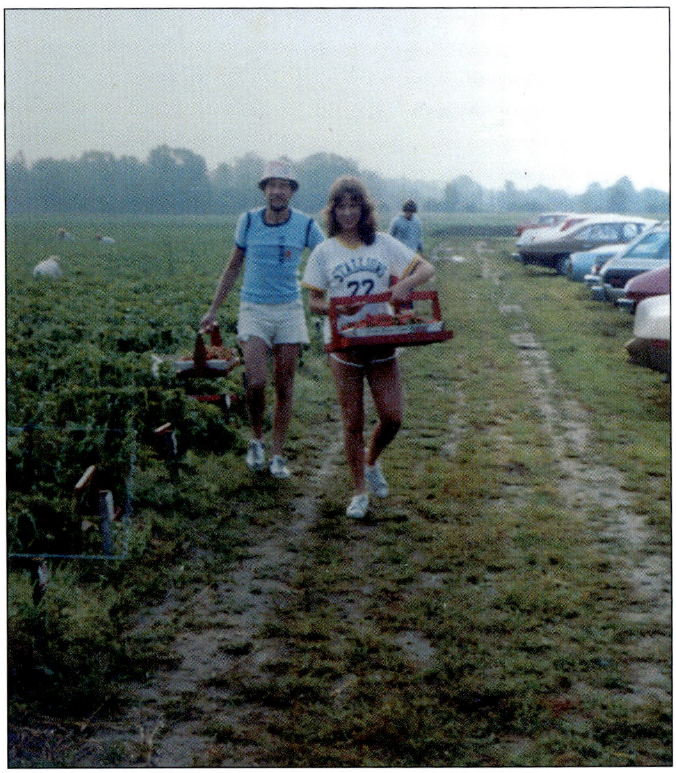

Picking strawberries at the Haff Farm seems to have been a success for these young people. The young woman is wearing a Sterling Heights High School Stallions shirt as they walk up to the often long lines to pay for their produce. The Haff Farm offered U-pick strawberries during the late 1970s to around 1980 and was a very popular outing for families. (Courtesy of Eileen Haff Herr.)

Two

Government

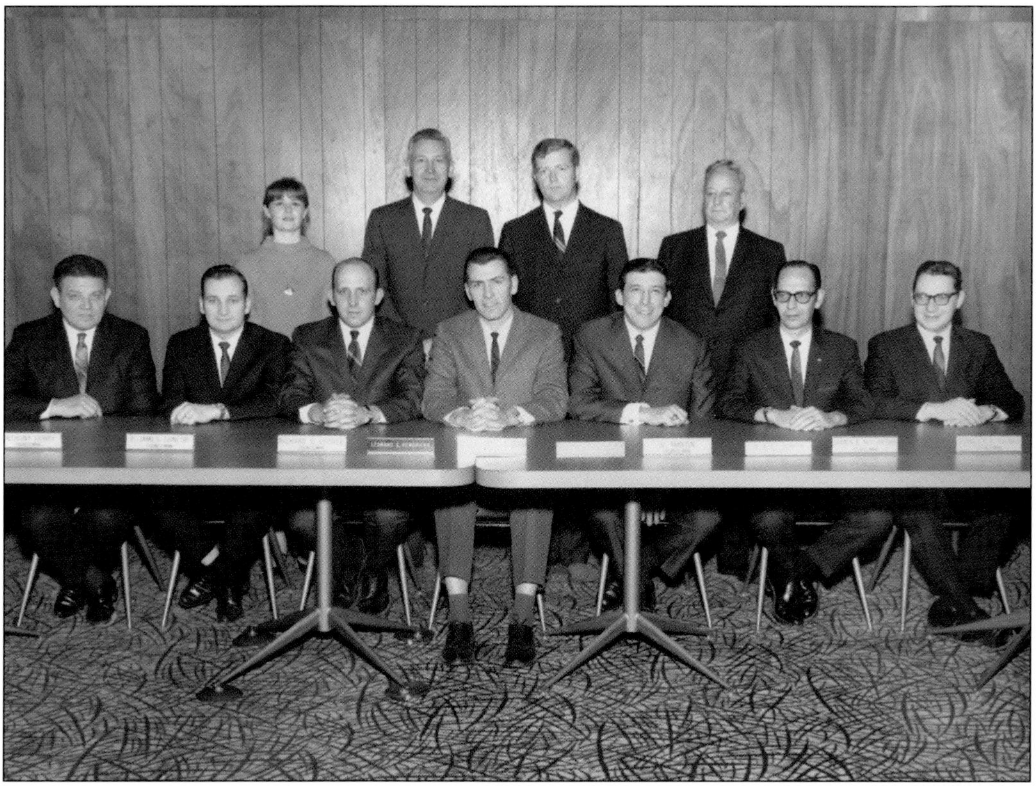

Pictured here is the very first city council along with other officials elected from the brand-new city of Sterling Heights. From left to right are (first row) Anthony Dobry, F. James Dunlop (mayor pro tem), Richard D. George, Gerald Donovan (mayor), Al Martin, James E. McCarthy, and Stanley Rainko; (second row) Barbara Yager (recording secretary), Leonard Hendricks (city manager), Paul O'Reilly (city attorney), and George Bunker (city clerk). This group represented a changing of the guard in local government.

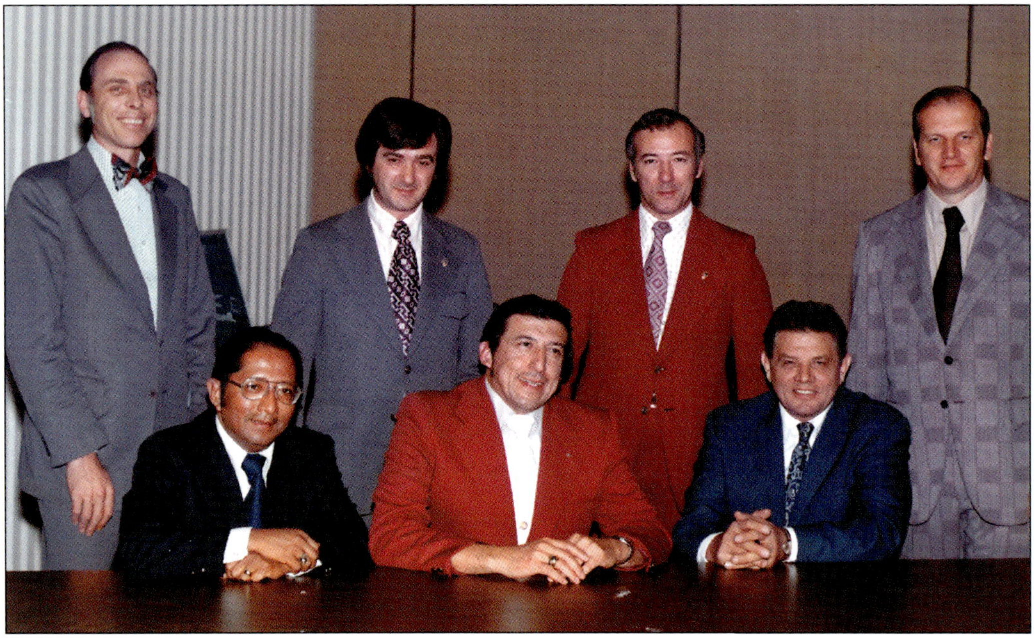

The city council is pictured here around 1973. From left to right are (seated) Jose Benavides, Al Martin, and Mayor Anthony Dobry; (standing) Lyle Robertson, Richard O. Brown, Daniel J. McCarthy, and Edward Janis.

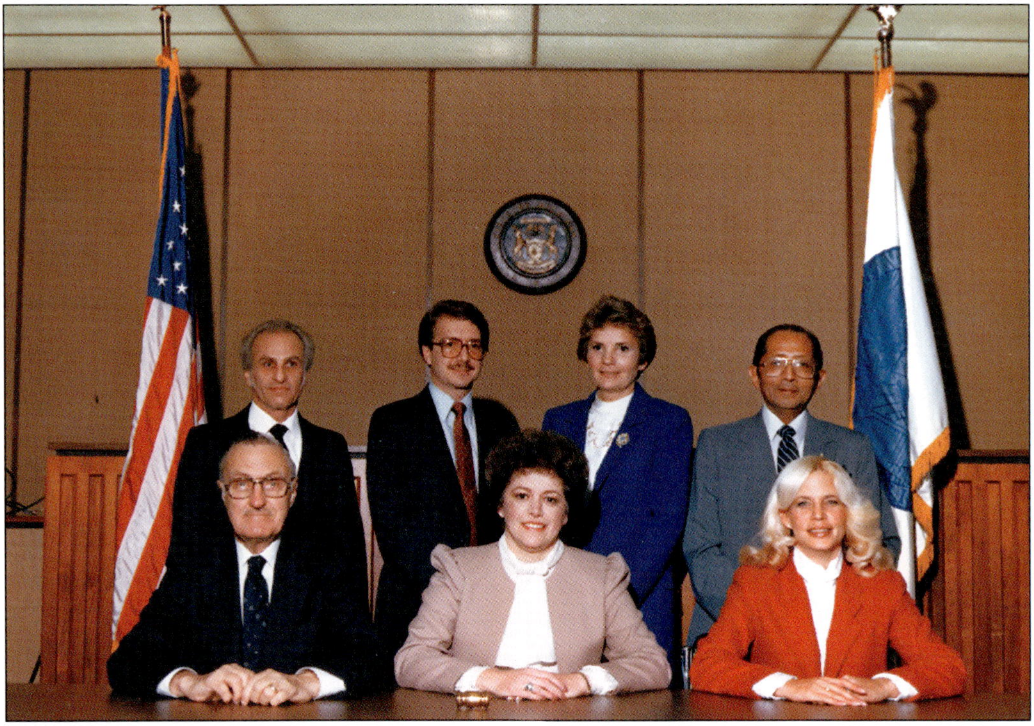

City council members, pictured around 1986 are, from left to right, (seated) Charles Marling, Mayor Jean DiRezze-Gush, and Linda Godfrey; (standing) Richard Notte, Stephen Rice, Joan Carpenter, and Jose Benavides. Richard Ives (not pictured) was city manager at this time.

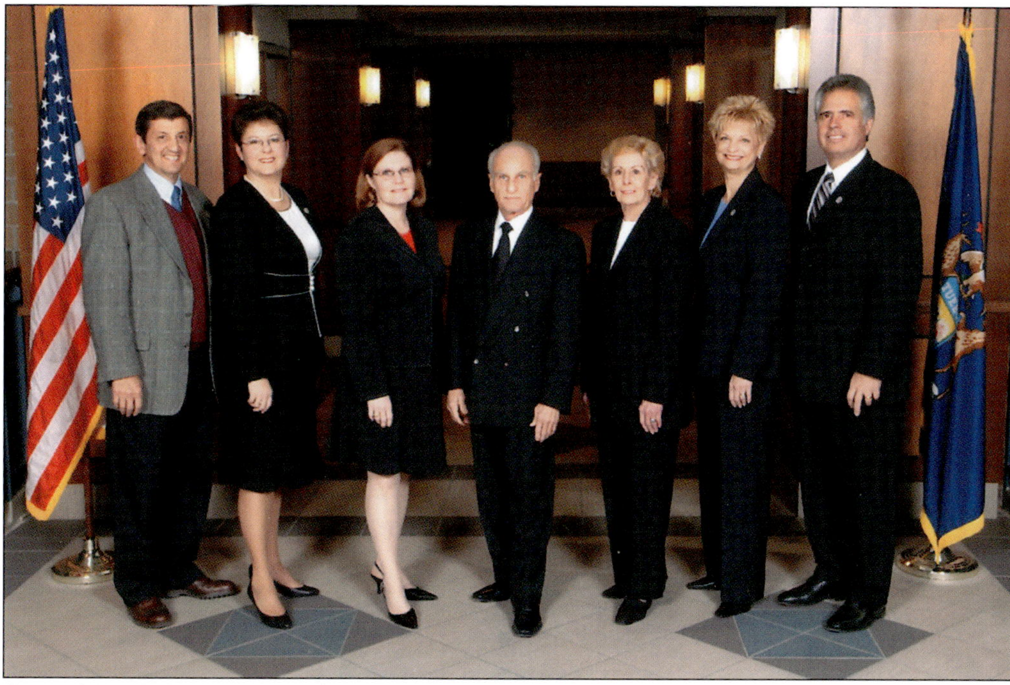

Around 2005, the city council consisted of, from left to right, Joseph Romano, Maria Schmidt, Yvonne Kniaz, Mayor Richard Notte, Deanna Koski, Barbara Ziarko, and Richard Bracci. Mark Vanderpool (not pictured) was city manager at this time.

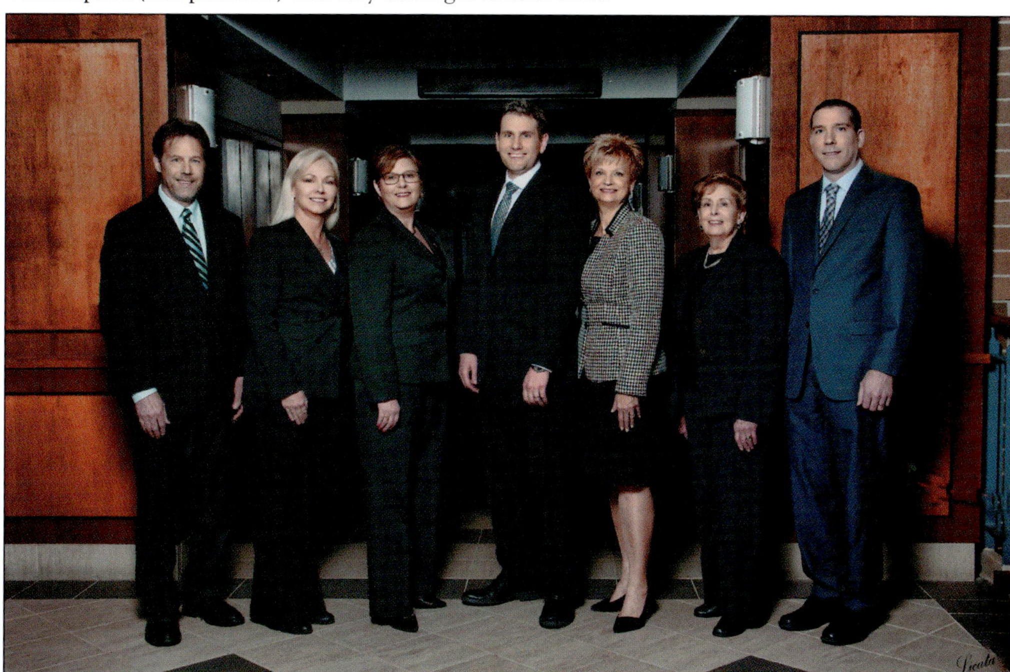

The Sterling Heights City Council in 2017 consisted of, from left to right, Gary Lusk, Liz Sierawski, Maria Schmidt, Mayor Michael Taylor, Mayor Pro Tem Barbara Ziarko, Deanna Koski, and Nate Shannon, all standing in front of the new council chambers in city hall.

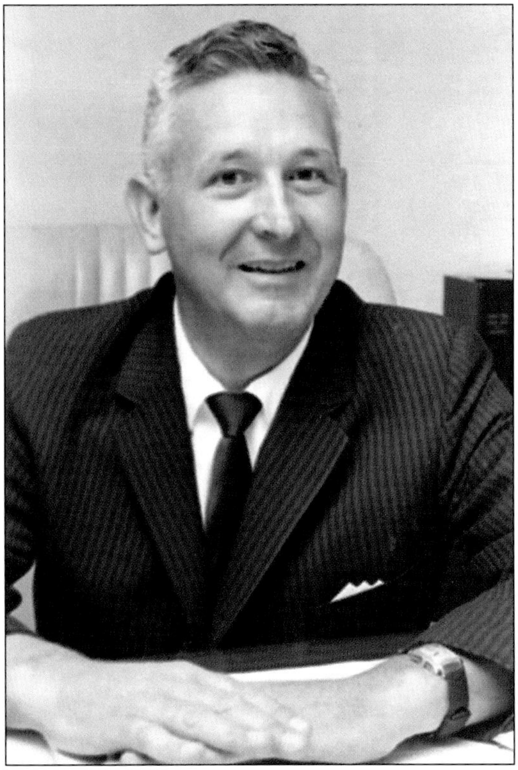

Leonard Hendricks was hired by council to guide the young city as its first city manager in 1968 and held the job until 1982, except for an 18-month period starting in 1974. The soft-spoken man was born in Mississippi and educated in the Detroit area; served as the city manager of Clawson, Michigan, prior to Sterling Heights; and worked for Auburn Hills later in his career.

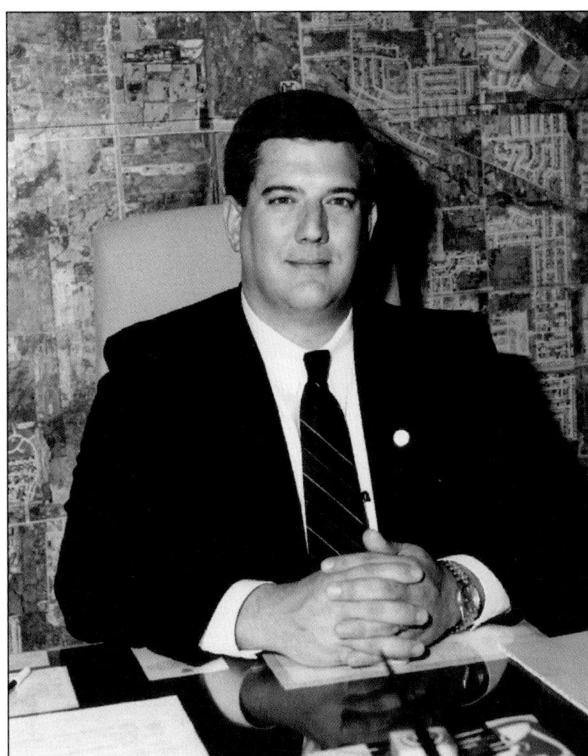

Steve Duchane held the position of city manager for many years in Sterling Heights, beginning in 1988, following Richard Ives. He was known for being the youngest city manager in Macomb County at the time, 32 years old when hired. During his tenure, he oversaw the building of a new Sterling Heights Senior Center and two new fire stations and massive renovations on the City Center. He left the city in 2003 amid controversy and went on to become the city manager of Lincoln Park and later Eastpointe, Michigan.

Gerald Donovan was the first mayor of Sterling Heights. At that time, the mayor was elected by the city council members from among themselves, usually the highest vote getter of the public city council election. A teacher and a recreation director in Centerline, Donovan had served on the Sterling Township Parks Commission. He declined to run again in 1971 in order to spend time with his family and pursue other community interests. (Courtesy of the *Utica Sentinel* newspaper.)

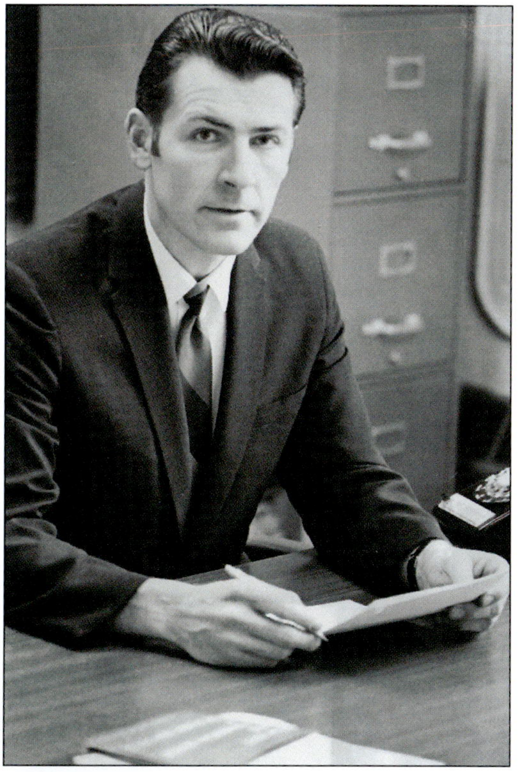

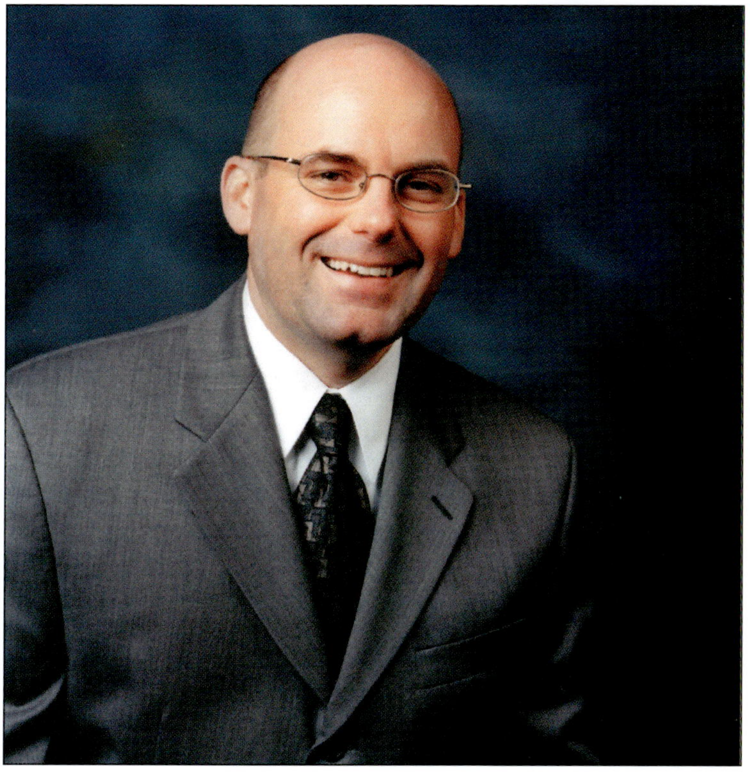

Mark Vanderpool was hired in 2004 by the city council as city manager after Steve Duchane left. He had been the assistant city manager in Skokie, Illinois, prior to coming to Sterling Heights and was highly recommended. He has held his position for quite a long time, weathering the economic downturn in Michigan and the trying times for the city's main taxpayers, the automobile companies. He, and the city, has come through.

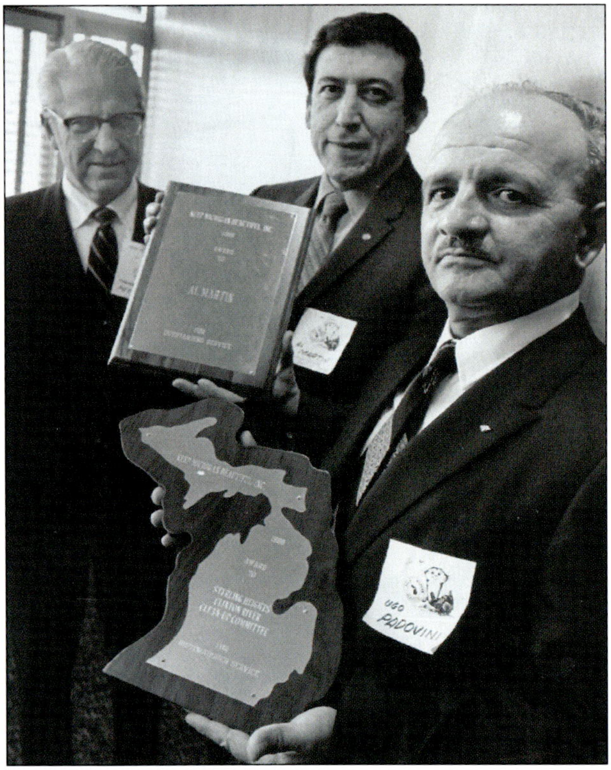

Al Martin and Ugo Padovini received awards from the Keep Michigan Beautiful organization, which recognized their Clinton River Clean Up activities in 1969. Martin was a Sterling Heights city councilman, former mayor, president of the Rotary, spearheaded the new Clinton River Watershed Council, and ran a number of Clinton River cleanups using volunteers. Padovini was the chairman of the Zoning Board of Appeals and a Rotarian.

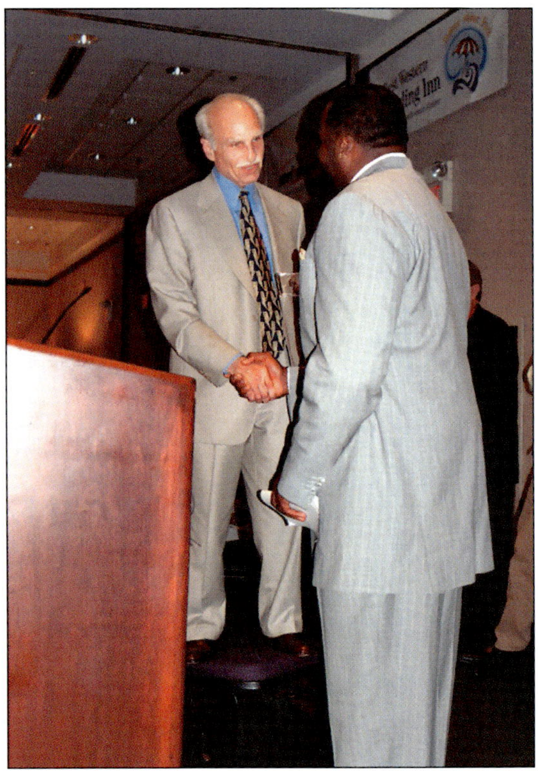

The now infamous former mayor of Detroit, Kwame Kilpatrick, was the guest speaker at the city's 2004 Spirit Award luncheon held at the Sterling Inn. As a joke, Mayor Richard Notte stood on a chair to be equal in height to Mayor Kilpatrick, a very tall man.

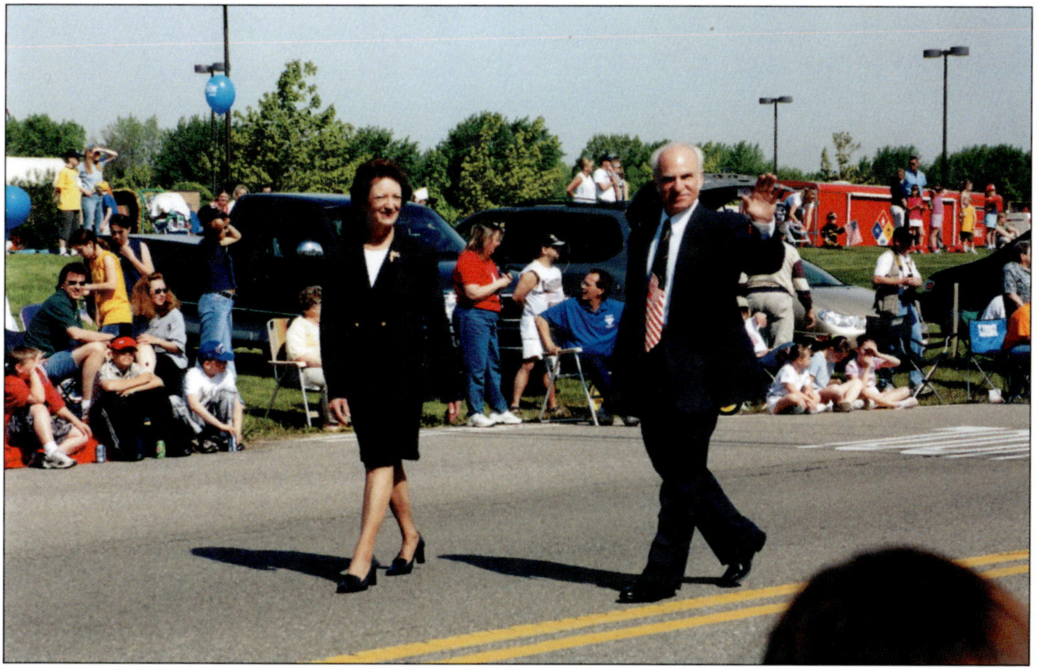

Mayor Richard Notte and his wife, Margaret, walk the Memorial Day Parade down Dodge Park Road while waving to the crowd. Notte was known as "the people's mayor" for being accessible and was a spokesperson for the middle class and American manufacturing. Margaret Notte passed away in 2004.

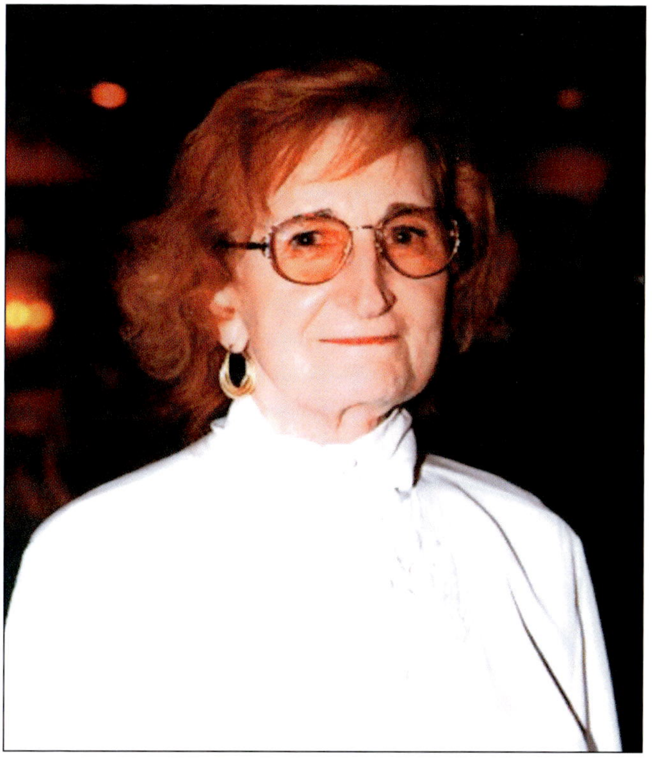

Mary Zander became Sterling Heights city clerk in 1976 and held the position for 21 years. She was president of the Michigan Municipal Clerks Association, earned professional awards, and was known as "The Keeper of the Records." A colorful personality, most who knew her will not forget Mary Zander.

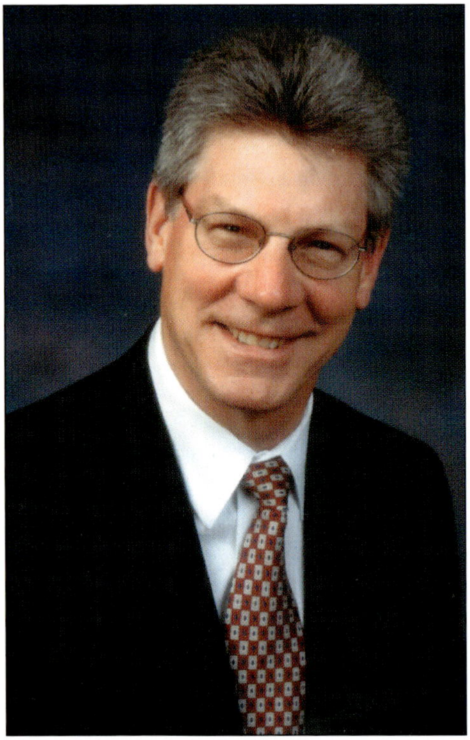

Norm Birr came to the city of Sterling Heights as a deputy planning director in 1977 and was promoted to city planner in 1983. Working in that position until his retirement in 2003 put him in the middle of the action for the city's development boom. He was quoted as saying when he started that the city was only 35 percent developed. By 2003, it was near full capacity.

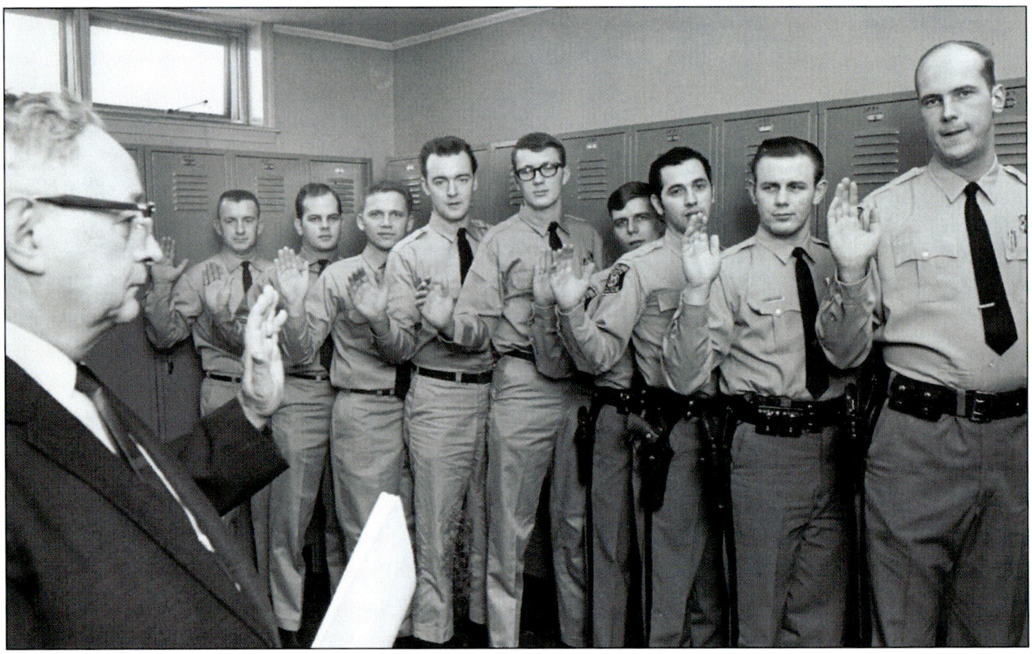

It was 1969 and time for the growing city to beef up its police force. George F. Bunker, the city clerk, swears in new officers and cadets. From left to right are cadets Bobby Collins, Dennis Baril, Jerry Myny, and Ken McNichol and officers Al Zielinski, Paul Palazolla, Joe Dreslinski, and Ralph Goode. A street in the Sterling Commons Apartments complex has been named to honor longtime public servant George F. Bunker.

John Childs was hired as a firefighter in the young city of Sterling Heights in 1971, later becoming a fire instructor and awarded the 1984 Michigan Fire Service Instructor of the Year. He became chief and retired in 2007 after 14 years in that position where his noted accomplishments were building two new fire halls, commissioning the fireman statue, and renovating three more fire halls, as well as earning the ISO certification for the fire department.

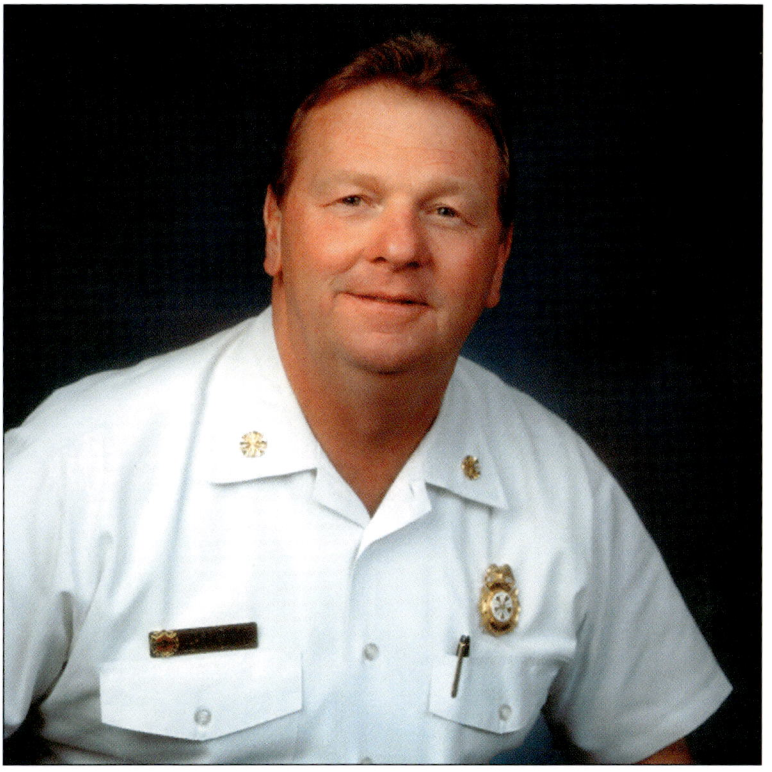

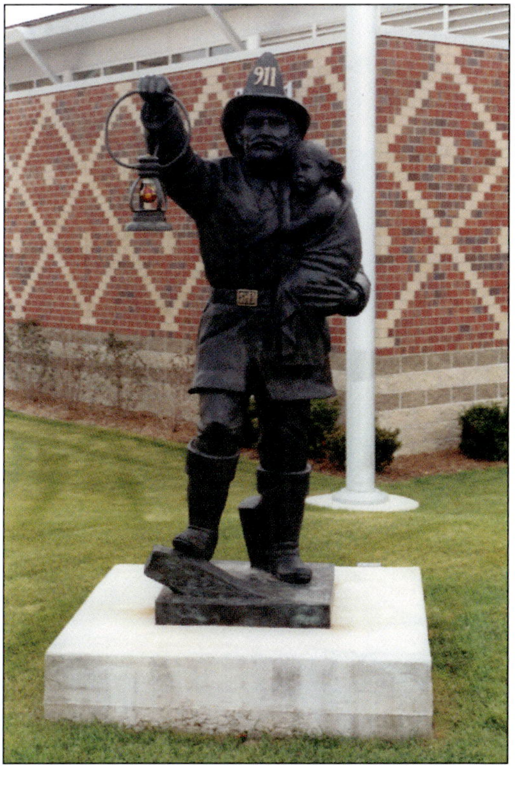

Fire Station No. 1, on the corner of Van Dyke Avenue and 17 Mile Road, boasts this Fireman Statue, which was unveiled at the dedication of the newly built station in 2002. Adapted from the Fireman's Memorial in Roscommon, Michigan, the statue was designed by sculptor Edward Chesney and retired Sterling Heights assistant fire chief Barney Calka in 1982.

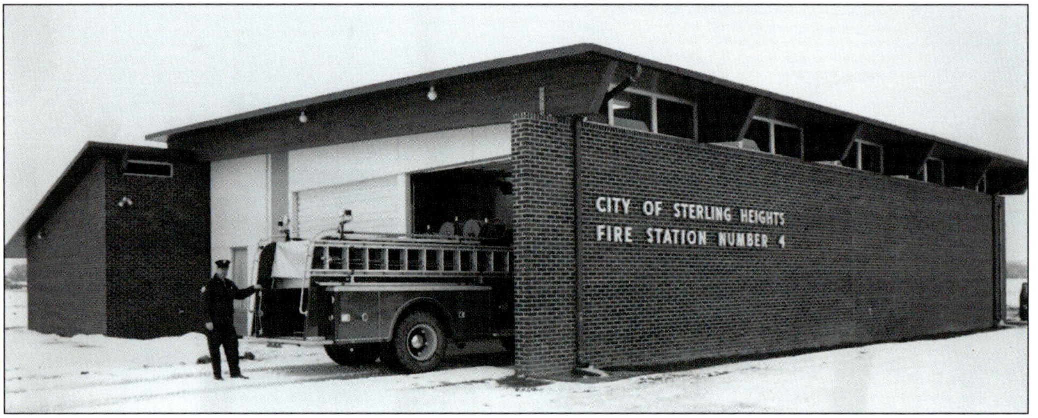

Fire Station No. 4, located on 15 Mile Road, west of Schoenherr Road, was originally built in 1973. As the stations aged and new technologies became available, the older stations in the city, Fire Stations No. 2 and No. 3, were demolished and rebuilt using a new plan. Fire Station No. 4, pictured, was rebuilt on the original footprint with a new design. By 2010, the new, improved stations were up and running.

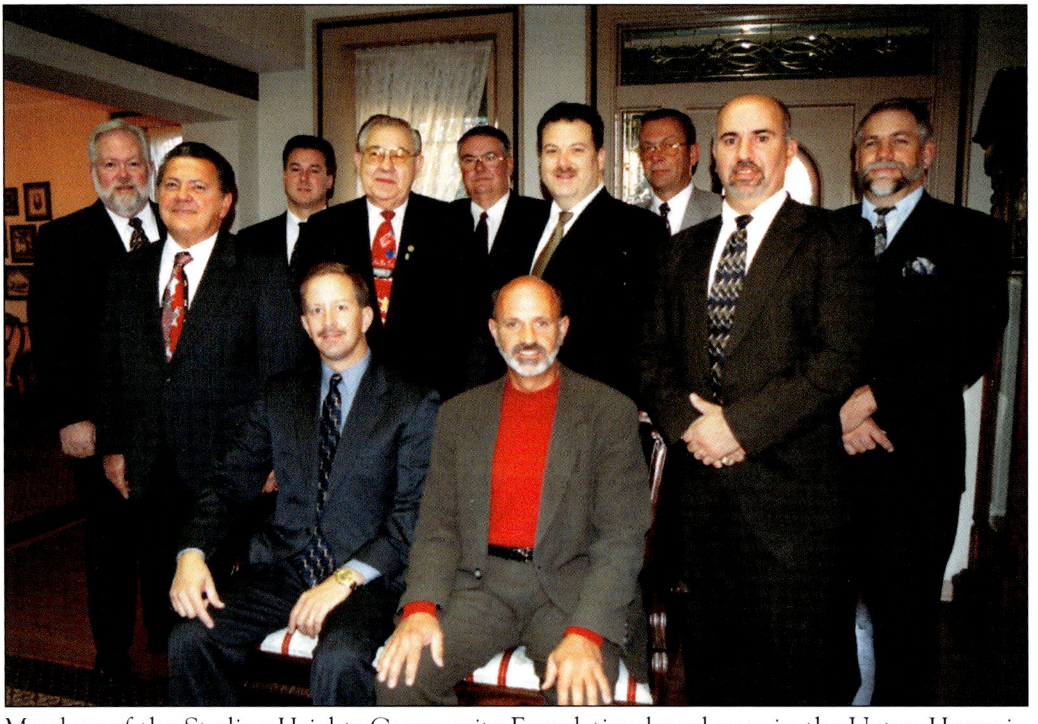

Members of the Sterling Heights Community Foundation board pose in the Upton House in this undated photograph. The Sterling Heights Community Foundation offers scholarships and grants, enabled by fundraising events, gifts, and endowments, to improve the quality of life for area residents. Longtime president of the foundation, Karl Oskoian, is seated at right. The foundation was created in 1991.

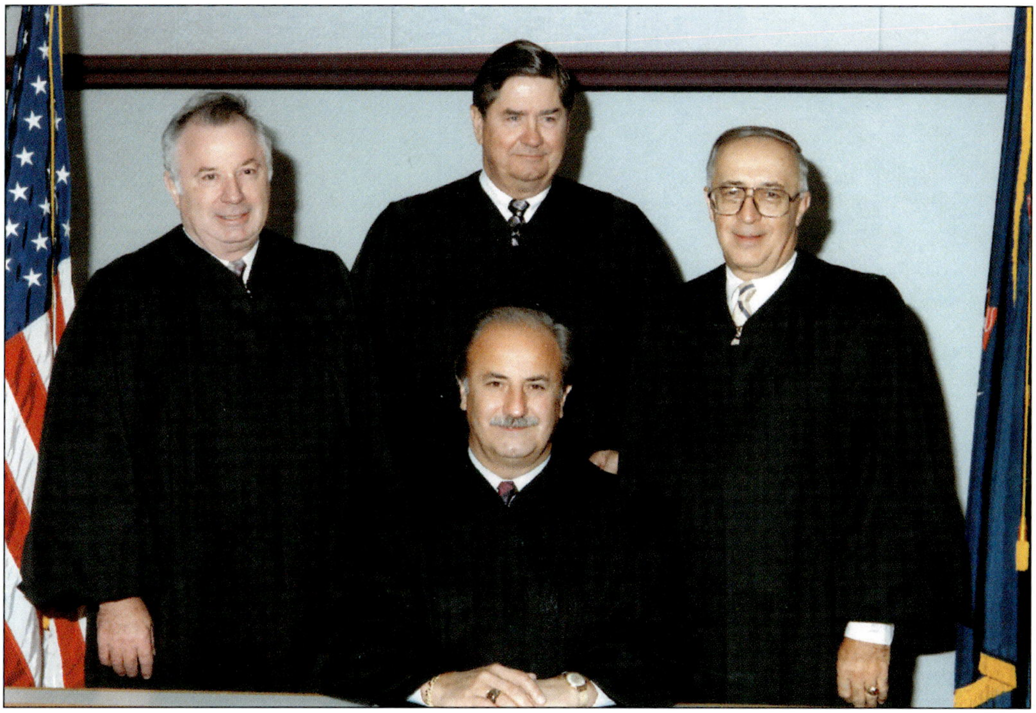

Judges of the 41A District Court are pictured here in the early 1990s. Chief District Judge Kenneth Kosnic is seated, while Judge Herman Campbell, Chief Judge Pro Tempore Thomas McDonell, and Judge Andrew Dranchak stand behind. The 41A District Court was originally operated out of the city council chambers, then moved to the upper level of the new police/justice building, and finally to the new district court structure located just south of the public library.

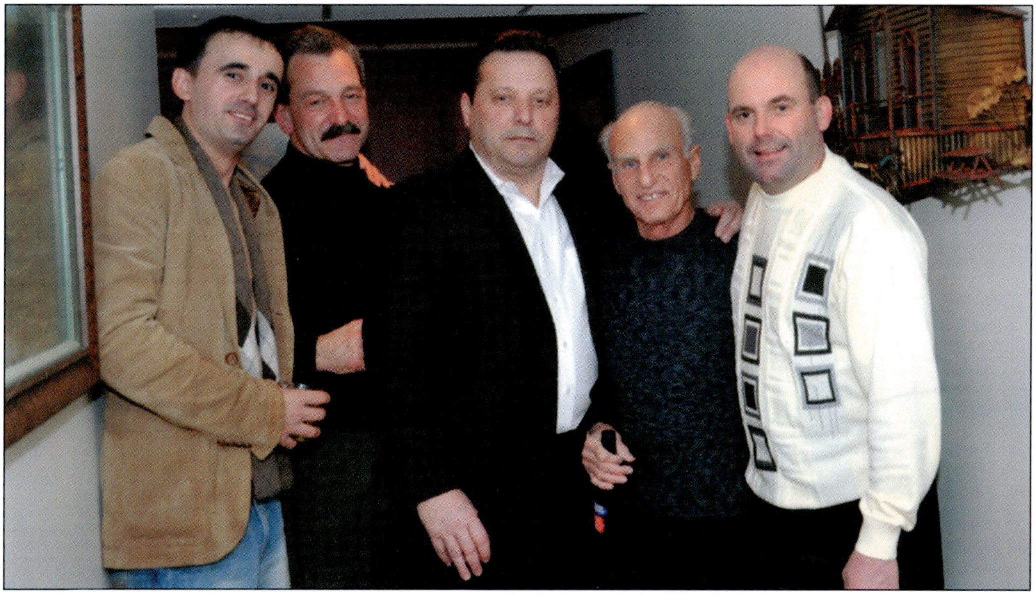

A social gathering brought these friends together for a good time. From left to right are Pashko Ujkic (owner of Dodge Park Coney Island), unidentified, Sterling Heights police chief Michael Reese, Mayor Richard Notte, and City Manager Mark Vanderpool. (Courtesy of Pashko Ujkic.)

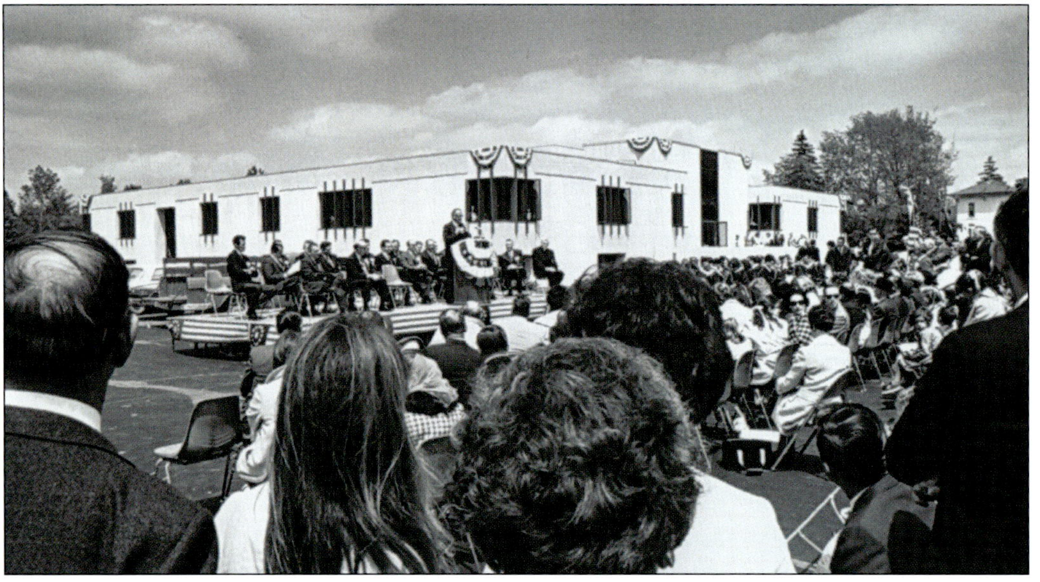

The dedication of the new city hall on May 25, 1969, was attended by over 500 people who heard Congressman James G. O'Hara deliver the main address. The structure was designed to carry five additional floors to accommodate the offices of a strong mayor government, but when a city manager form of government was voted in, the future building expansion plan was abandoned.

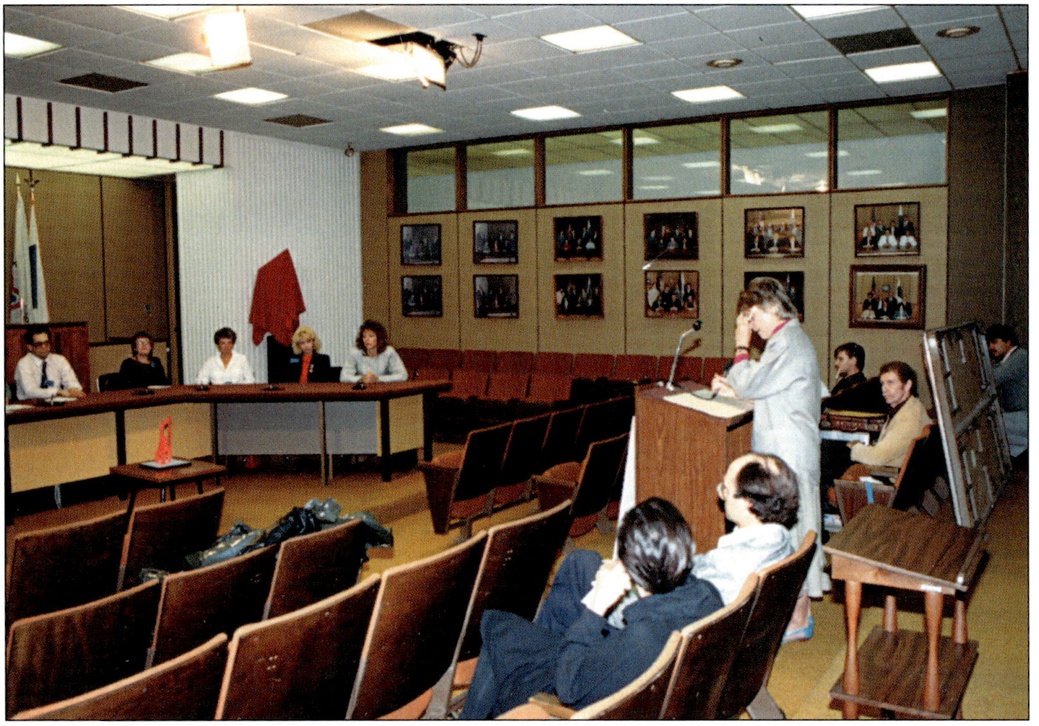

This photograph shows what the council chambers looked like as originally constructed in the 1969 building. The walls were lined with photographs of former city council member groups. In this photograph, artists are making presentations to the Sterling Heights Cultural Commission in hopes of getting approval to have their work installed on city grounds.

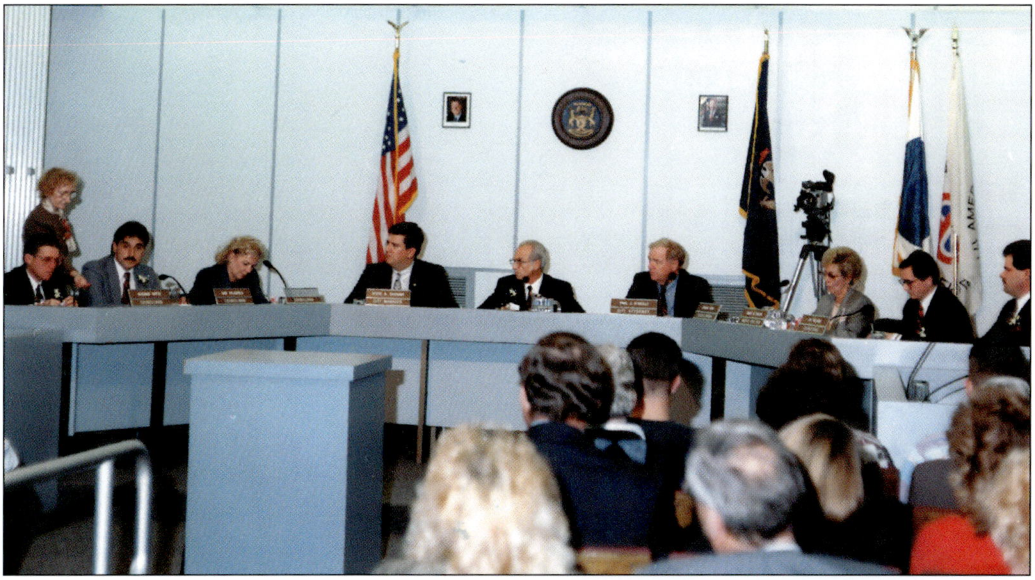

Here, a city council meeting is in progress around 1994. From left to right are (seated) council members Eugene Zaniewski, Sam Palazzolo, and Elaine Arnold; City Manager Steve Duchane; Mayor Richard Notte; City Attorney Paul O'Reilly; and council members Deanna Koski, Andy Zaczek, and Jay Pollard. The city clerk, Mary Zander, is standing at left. The video camera behind them was used by Community Relations, which filmed the meeting for local cable viewing.

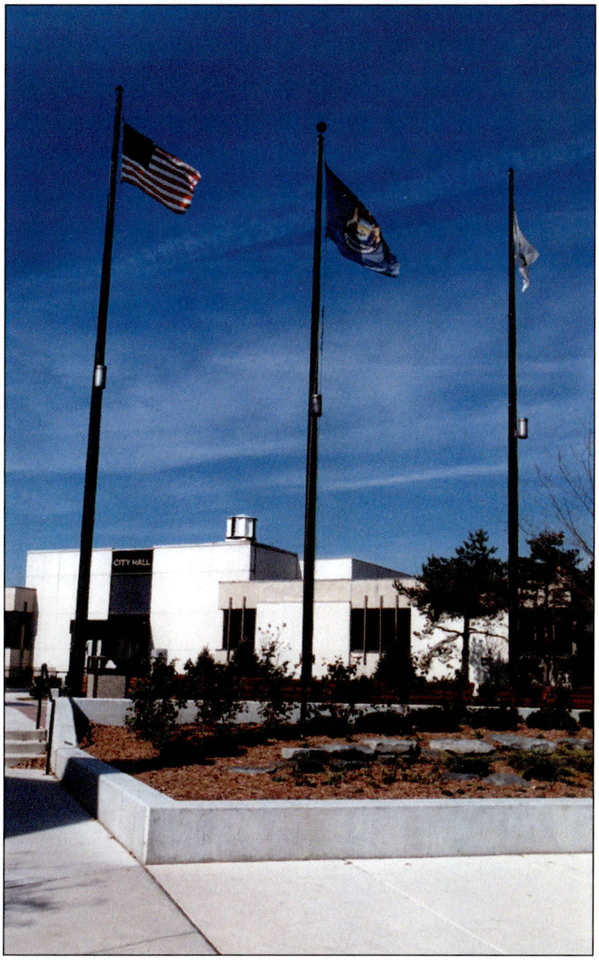

This is city hall as it looked sometime in the 1990s. It was built in 1969, one year after the city was formed. Prior to the construction, city business was spread between the old town hall building on Van Dyke Avenue at Plumbrook Road and the old Clinton Valley Country Club on Utica Road, which continued to be used as the police department until 1978. Both buildings have been demolished.

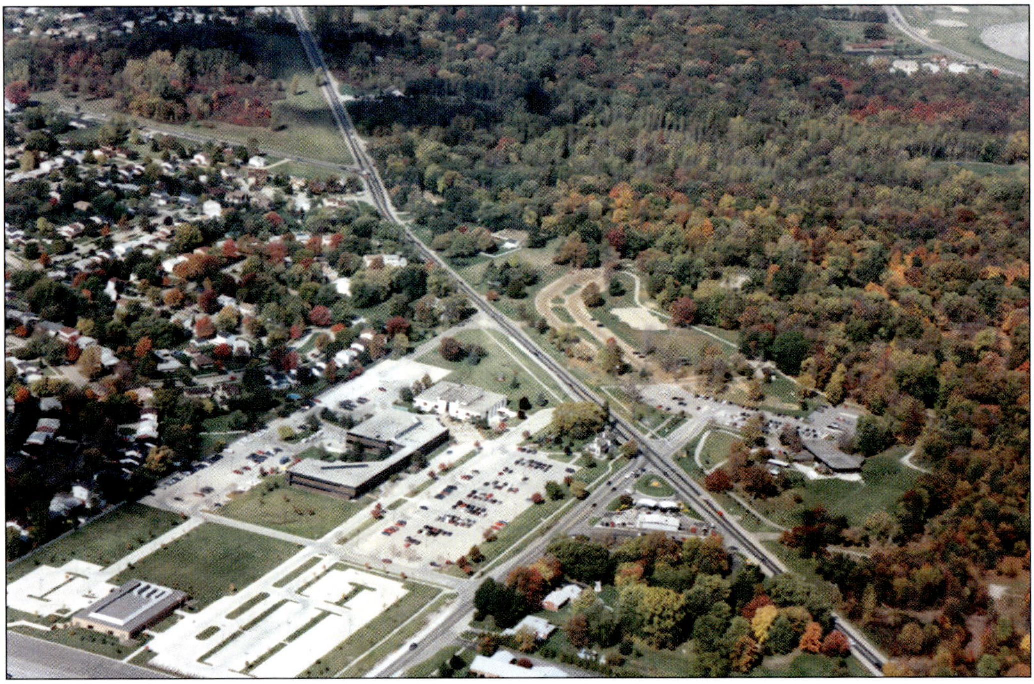

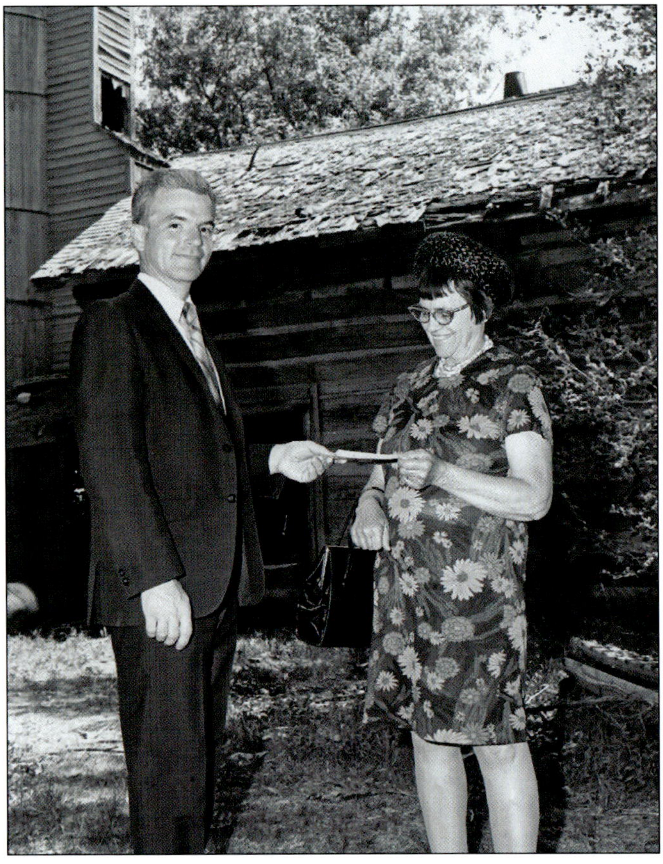

This aerial view of the corner of Utica and Dodge Park Roads features the 41A District Court, the public library, police station, city hall, and Dodge Park on the north side of Utica Road. This view was taken in the 1990s before the additions to city hall and the library. The Clinton River runs through the wooded area parallel to Utica Road.

This abandoned log cabin was once located on Maple Lane, just north of 14 Mile Road. Believed to be the oldest home standing at the time, possibly built in the 1840s or earlier, it was slated to be restored by the newly formed Historical Commission. Pictured are Dr. James Olson and Agnes Sheff holding a donation check from developer Graham Orley toward the effort. The cabin was burned by vandals not long after.

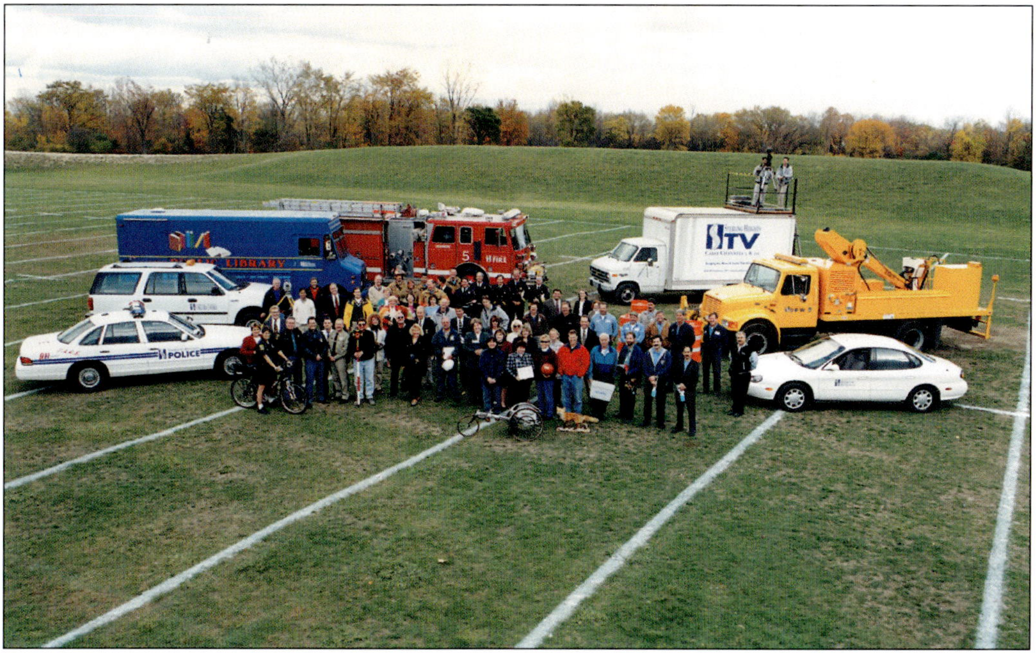

City employees pose with their vehicles on a soccer field around 1999. Noteworthy are the library's bookmobile van and the taxidermy fox from the Sterling Heights Nature Center.

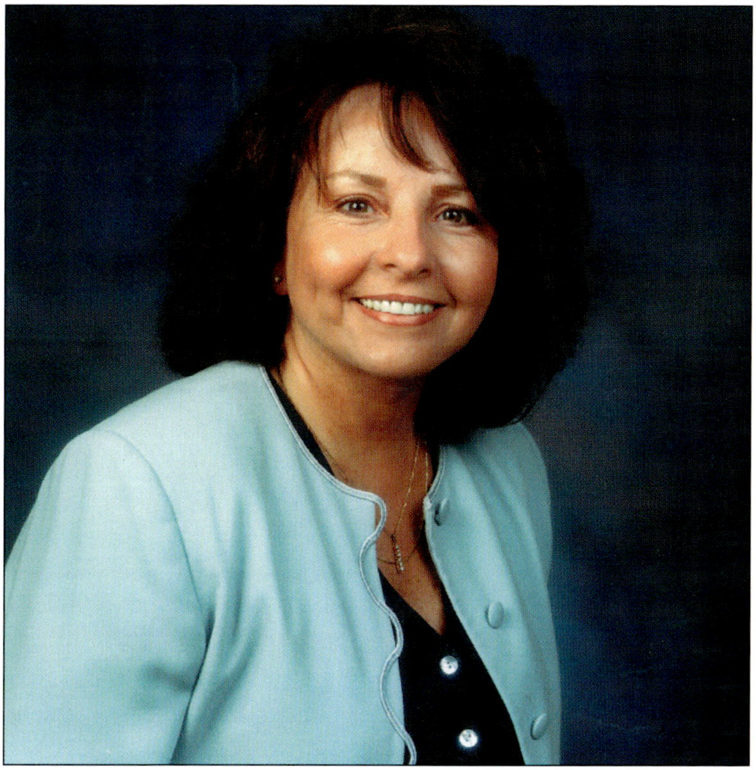

Community Relations director Pat Lehman was the city's voice, in good times and in bad. She started with the city in 1981 and retired in 2005. Running the cable television production department, doing the city calendar and newsletters, and being a large part of the management of the Memorial Day Parade and Sterlingfest all added to an ever-changing challenge. Longtime employee Steve Guitar took over upon her retirement.

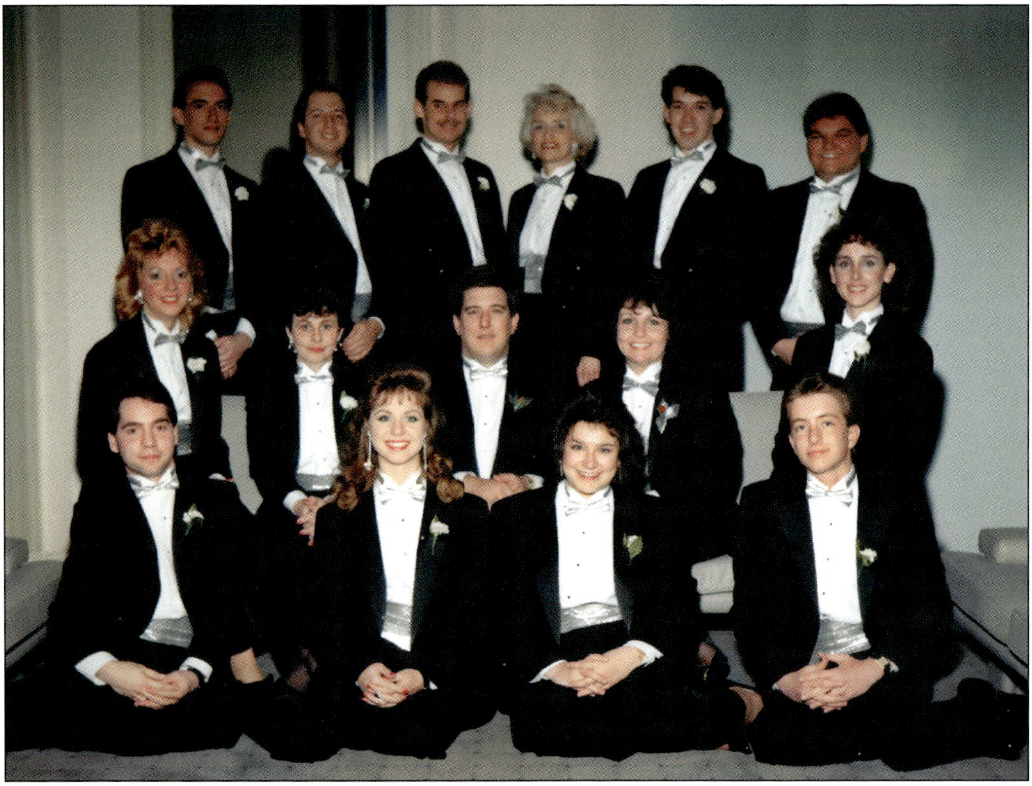

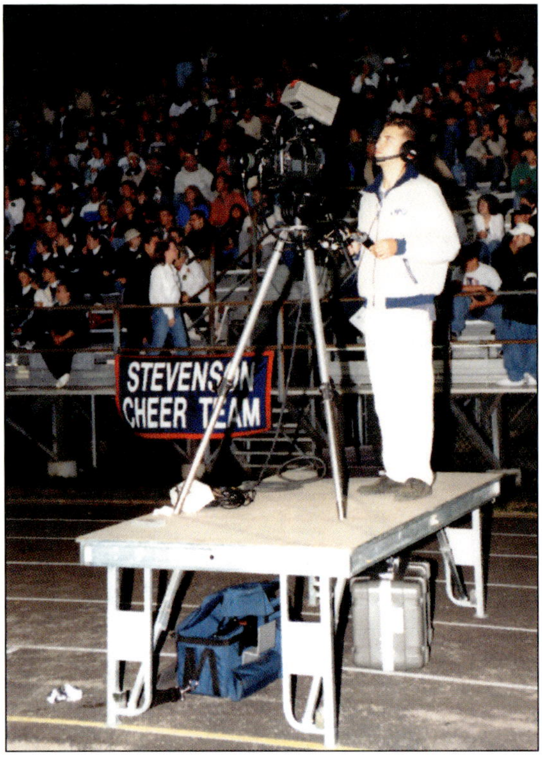

The Community Relations staff and its director, Pat Lehman, plus the city manager, Steve Duchane (center), are dressed up in tuxedos for a special city event. The photograph includes Steve Guitar (standing at far right), who went on to become the head of the department until his retirement in 2014.

SHTV, part of the Community Relations Department, is seen here broadcasting a Stevenson High School football game. Many local sporting events were made available on the city's local cable channels, allowing fans and family to watch from the comfort of their homes.

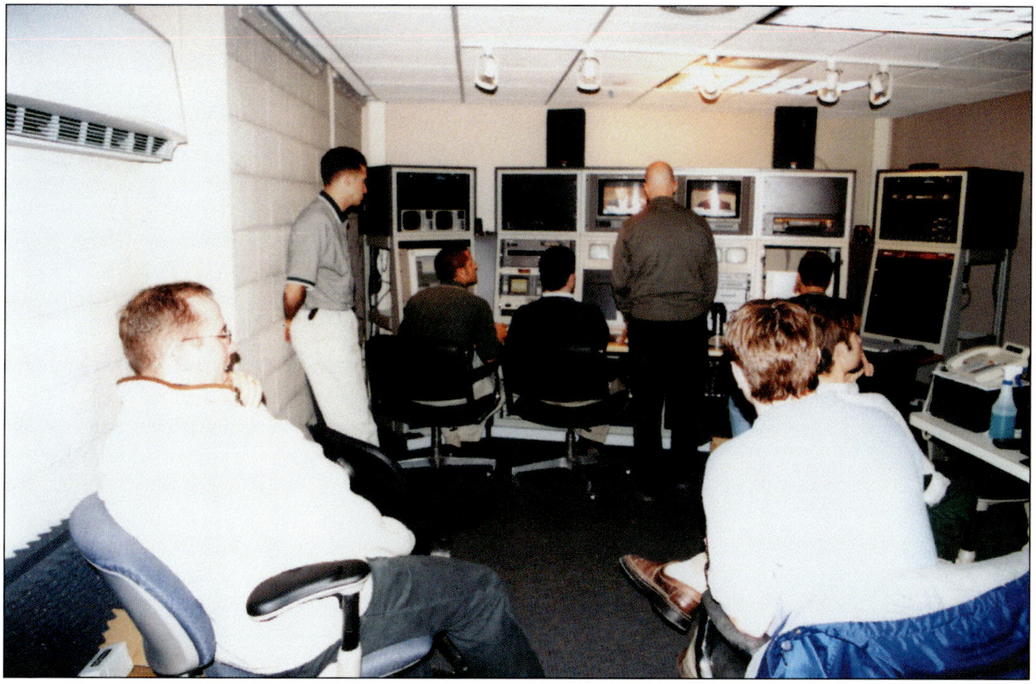

In the control room in the basement of city hall, award-winning SHTV technicians monitor a video production of a city council or commission meeting. One of the main functions of the broadcast services division is to make meeting footage available. The department also produces news reports, interviews, and informational segments.

Mike Kostrzeba, left, and Tom Chappelle, right, leaders in the Parks and Recreation Department, pose in the Upton House parks and recreation offices around 1990. The award-winning Chappelle supervised the department for many years, developed 22 city parks, initiated the Special Recreation program (among others), and was honored with a city park in his name.

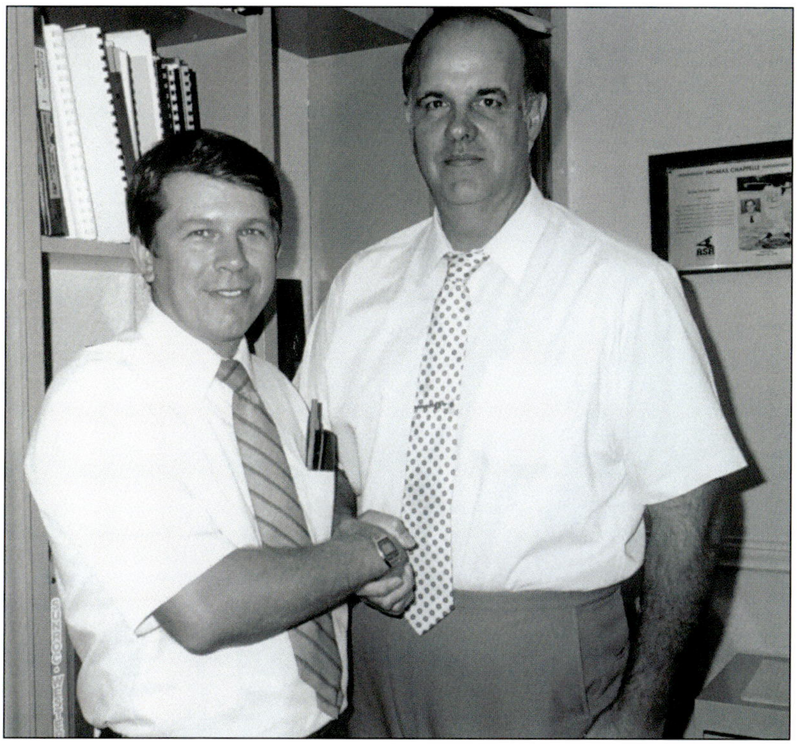

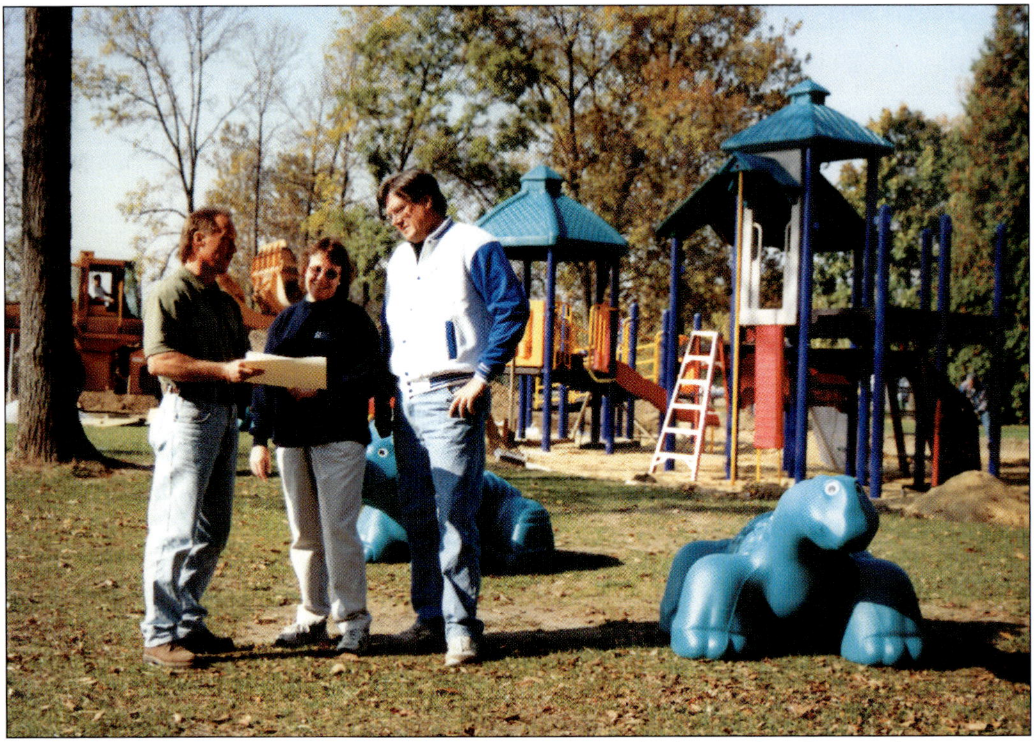

Parks and recreation employees Debbie Bozich and Joel Casey look over plans for new play structures with the installer. Almost all the city parks have play structures, and they are replaced every so often to keep them in safe, usable condition in line with industry standards and to be appropriate for all different ages and abilities. The pictured structure is in Dodge Park.

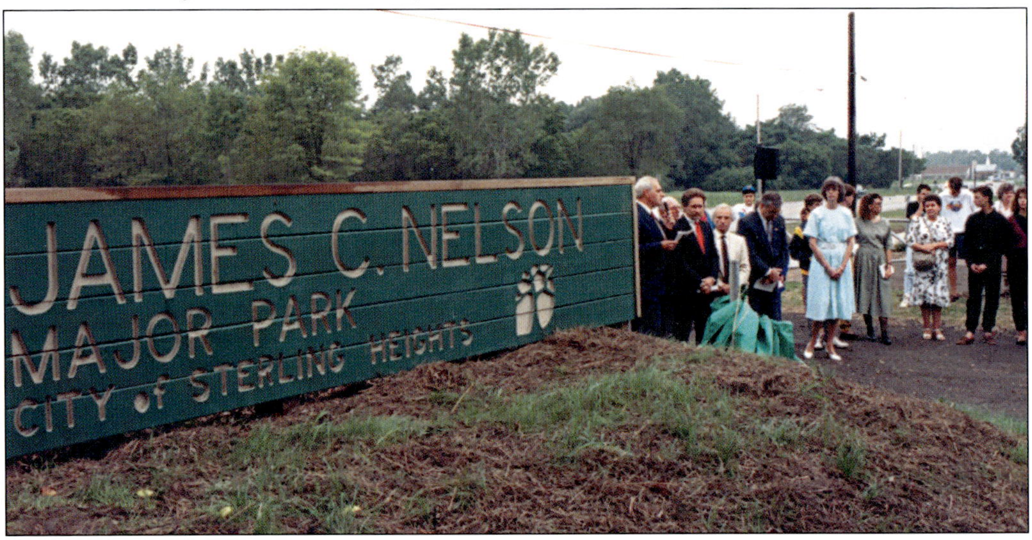

James C. Nelson was the first Sterling Heights firefighter killed in the line of duty. Responding to a 1983 arson fire at Sterling Junior High School (now named Bemis), he sustained a head injury and passed away. A new major park on 15 Mile Road, west of Ryan, was named in his honor during this ceremony in August 1990. His widow, children, and city officials were among those attending.

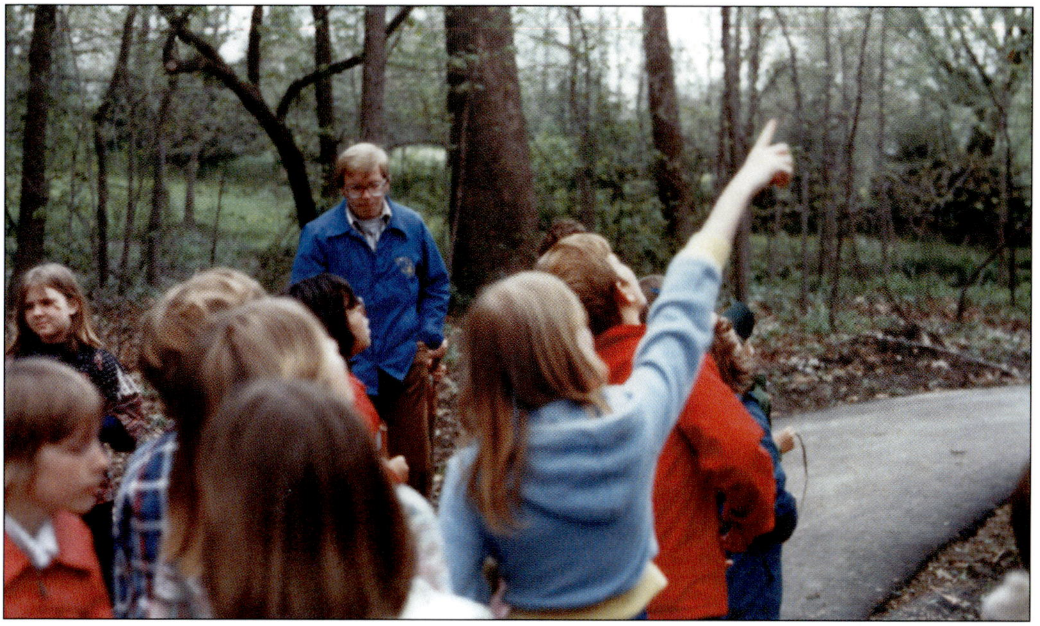

Marty Piepenbrok, of the Parks and Recreation Department, offers local children a guided tour of the nature trails in Dodge Park. The park features over 20 species of trees, including the paw paw and Kentucky coffee tree, which are rare for this part of the state. A wide variety of wildflowers can be found, if one looks closely. The dirt trails were paved in 1978, making nature much more accessible.

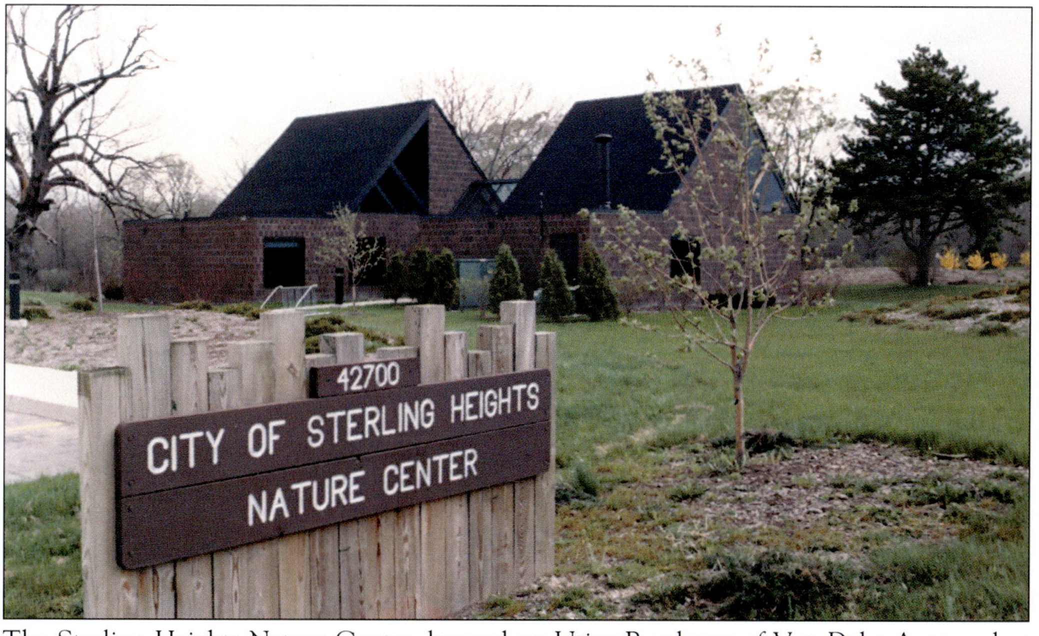

The Sterling Heights Nature Center, located on Utica Road east of Van Dyke Avenue, has been a family favorite since it first opened in 1982. The center has offered nature film viewings, tours, hands-on displays, taxidermy mounts, and tours of the Clinton River Park to families and school groups, while an addition in 2002 increased its size and added an aquarium, atrium, and expansion of the auditorium.

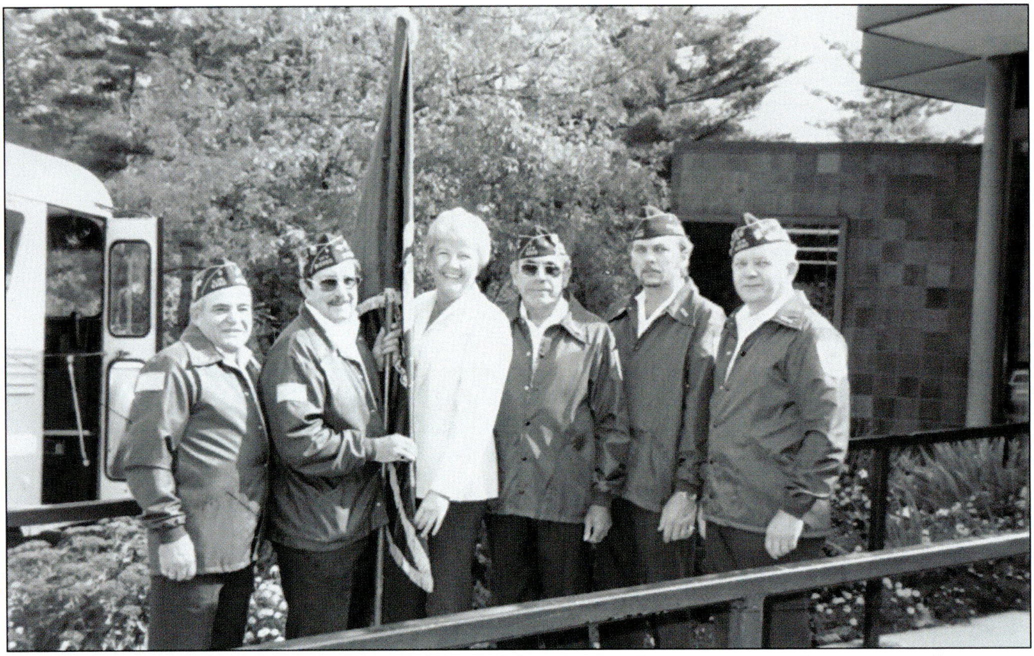

Helen Cerny, senior supervisor at the Sterling Heights Senior Center, poses with some proud veterans in front of the senior center. From left to right are Phil Colosi, Mike Adragna, Helen Cerny, Pete Lupo, unidentified, and Barney Calka. This photograph was taken in the early 1980s.

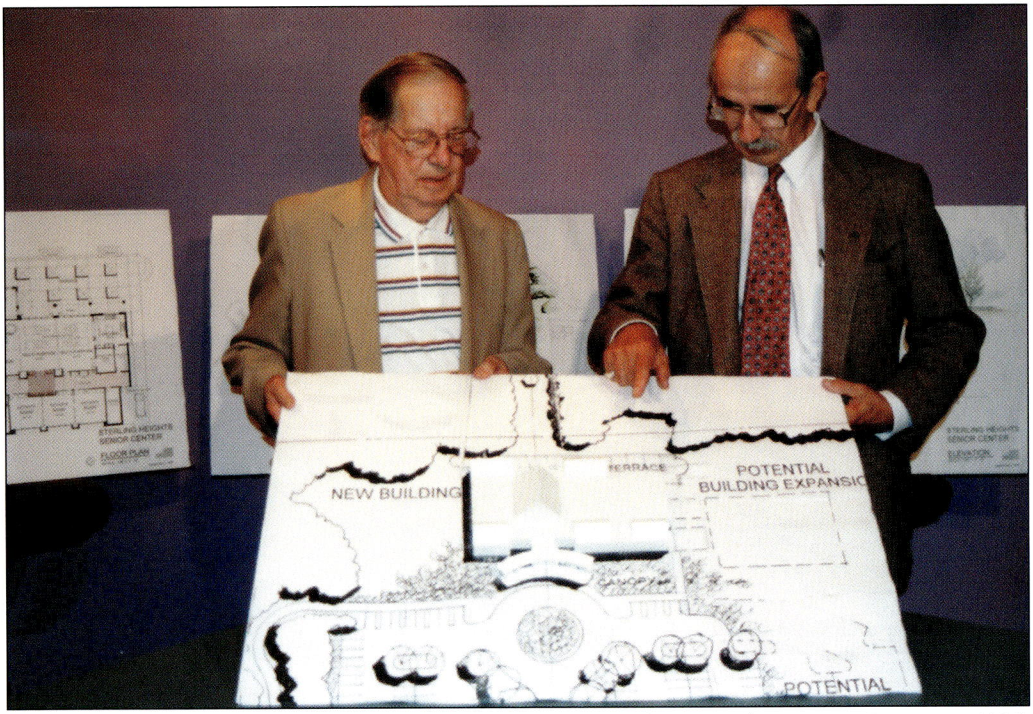

Ed Kopek and Rudy Erdody look over plans for the new Sterling Heights Senior Center in 1996. It was built on Utica Road, just east of Dodge Park Road, and was created for anyone 50 years old and up who wants to maintain an active and healthy lifestyle.

Three

COMMUNITY LEADERS

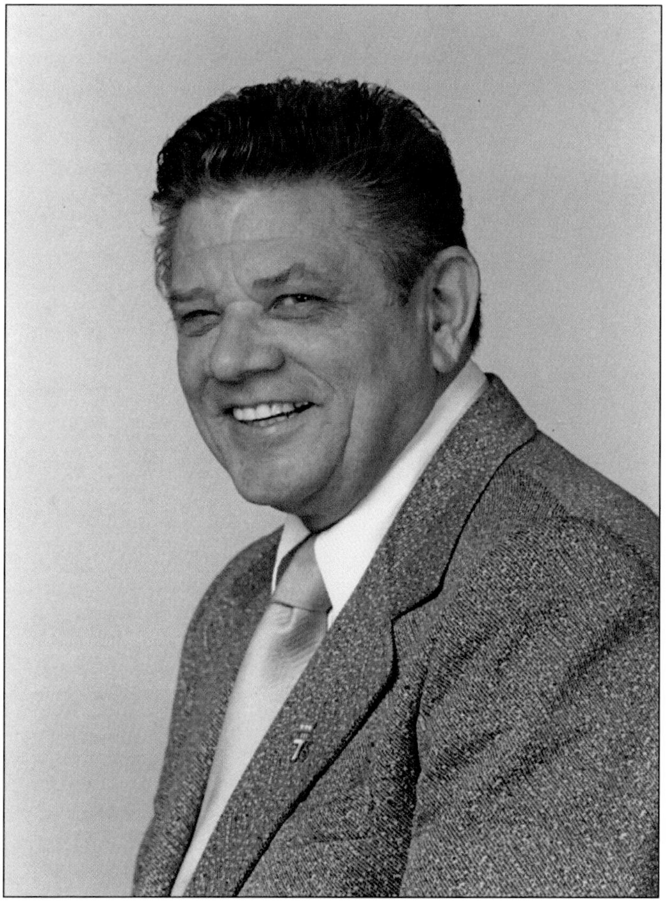

Anthony Dobry had a long political career in Sterling Heights, unique in that he had roles in both the township days and in city days. He moved to the township in 1950 to work in the Chrysler stamping plant and was first president of the Burr School District. He was also a township trustee, township supervisor, charter commission member, city councilman in 1968, and mayor in 1973. If the name sounds familiar, it may be because of the M-59 service drive through the city named for him.

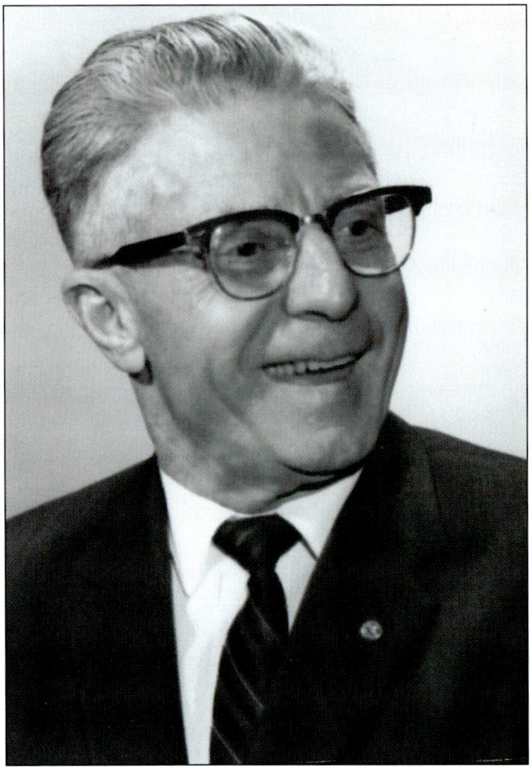

Jack Harvey was born on the family farm in Sterling Township in 1898. He lived a life of service to the community, serving a record 42 years on the Utica Board of Education. He also served on the Sterling Township Planning Commission, was president of the Michigan Milk Producers Association, and was a first-class dairy farmer. Some of his farm acreage he sold to Dresden Village developers, and Henry Ford II High School was built on another part of his former farm. A school, Jack Harvey Elementary, was named in his honor.

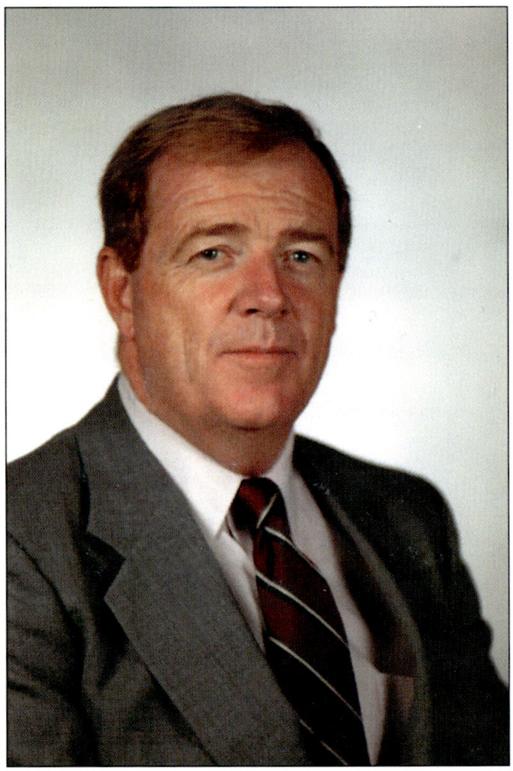

Attorney Paul J. O'Reilly moved into Sterling Township in the 1960s, was part of the charter commission for cityhood, and was chosen by the new city of Sterling Heights as its first city attorney in 1968. O'Reilly served as the city attorney for 35 years until his death in 2003. Senior partner of O'Reilly, Rancilio P.C., which he founded in 1984, he was a highly respected attorney and resident, described as a class act and a gentleman.

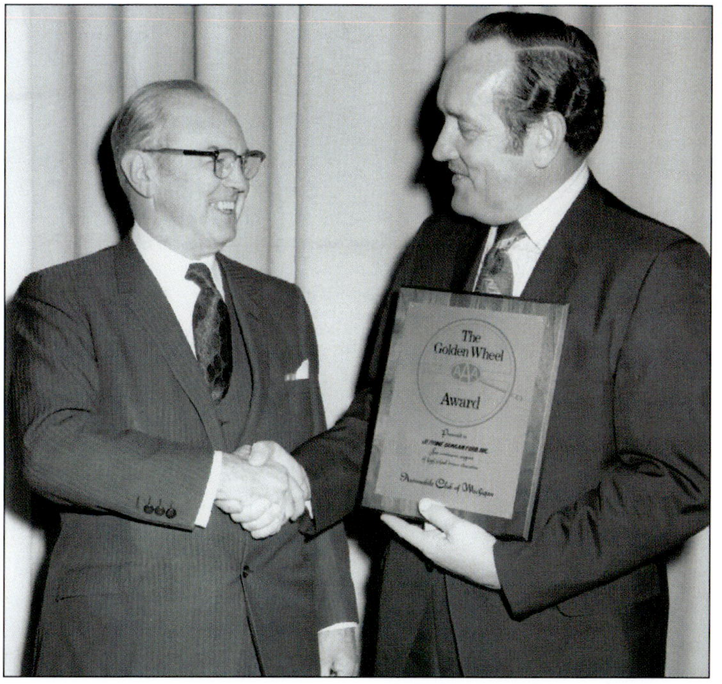

Dick Duncan, cofounder of the Jerome-Duncan Ford dealership with Larry Jerome, receives an award in 1970. The dealership was first located in Utica in 1956, and then moved to Sterling. Dick was a big supporter of Utica Community Schools and has a school, Duncan Elementary in Shelby Township, named after him. He was also past president of the Sterling Heights Chamber of Commerce, president of the Detroit Auto Dealers Association, and had a museum of vintage Ford vehicles behind his dealership on Van Dyke Avenue.

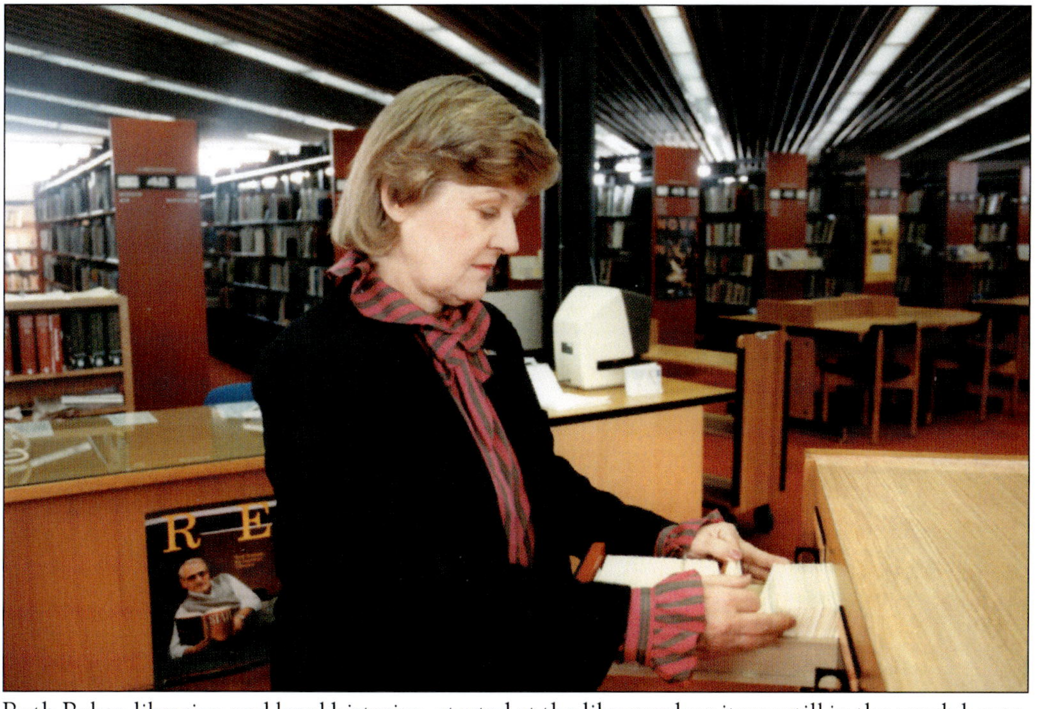

Ruth Baker, librarian and local historian, started at the library when it was still in the ranch house. She developed the reference collection of the growing library and led the staff with professionalism. Her knowledge and interest in the history of the local area created a top-notch local history archive, housed in the library, while her involvement with the Historical Commission and the community allowed her to make even more of a lasting impact on the city.

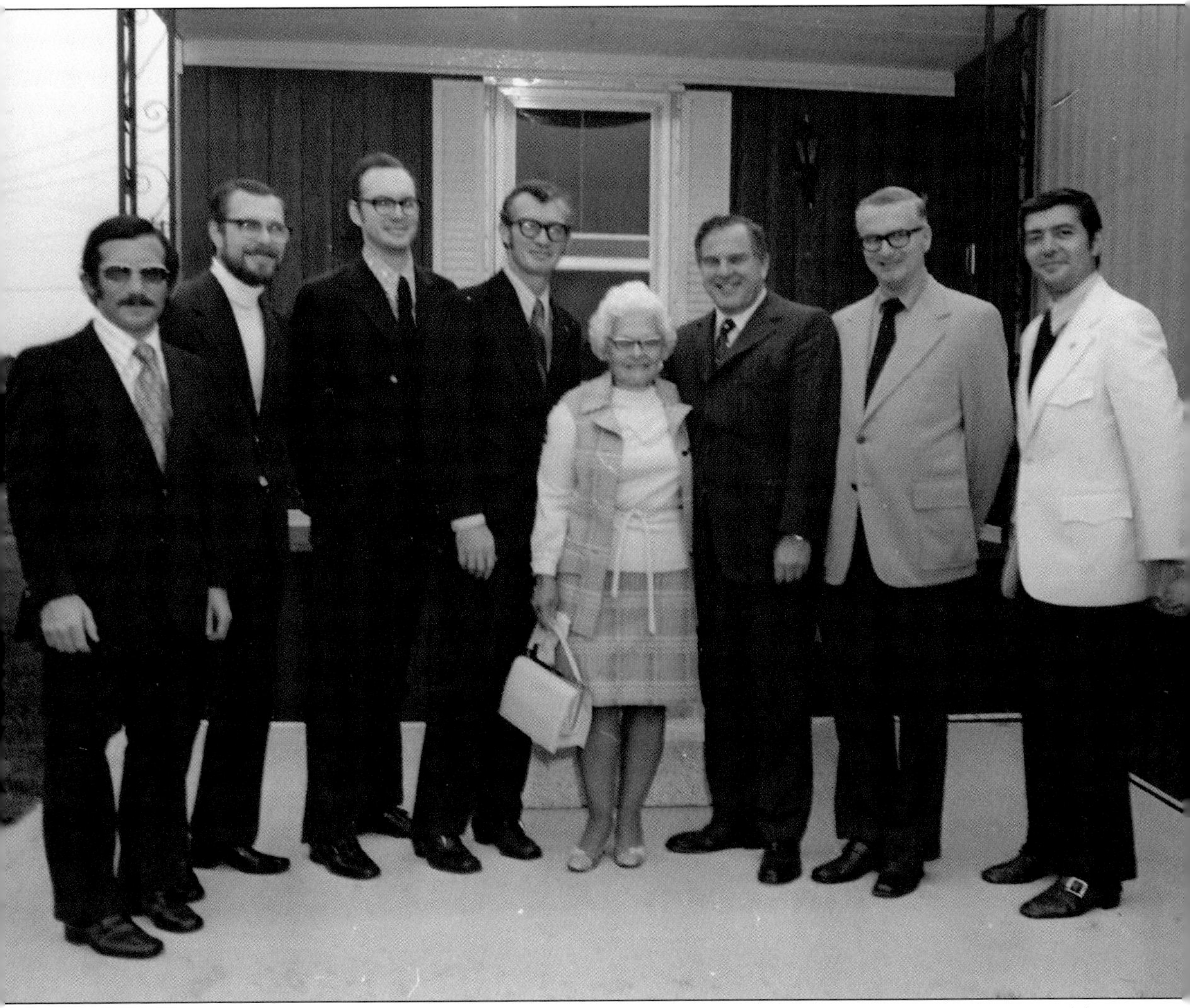

Pictured are, from left to right, unidentified, Charles Kosarek, Dr. Frankfurter, a Mr. Buckley, Nellie Floodquist, Graham Orley, Rudy Pale, and Arthur Kennedy. Graham Orley was a very significant man in the history of the city. A real estate developer and partners with Al Taubman on the Lakeside Project, Orley and Taubman took 18 months to accumulate the land for the Lakeside Mall property from the farmers, which went on to change the future of Sterling Heights and much of Macomb County. He also acquired the land for Delia Park and developed Rudgate Mobile Home Park under his company Elro Corporation. This photograph may show Rudgate. (Courtesy of Charles Kosarek.)

Lillian "Lil" Adams, longtime executive director of the Sterling Heights Regional Chamber of Commerce (now named Sterling Heights Area Chamber of Commerce and Industry), was a woman who could move mountains. She started as director in 1977 with 60 members and grew the chamber to over 1,500 members, the sixth largest in the state. She fought for the expansion of M-59 and the businesses that would grow there and was a tireless business advocate, retiring after 32 years.

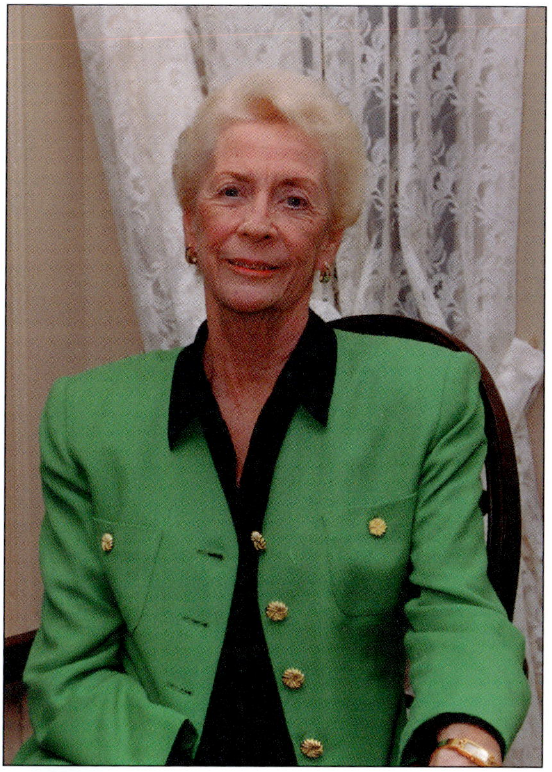

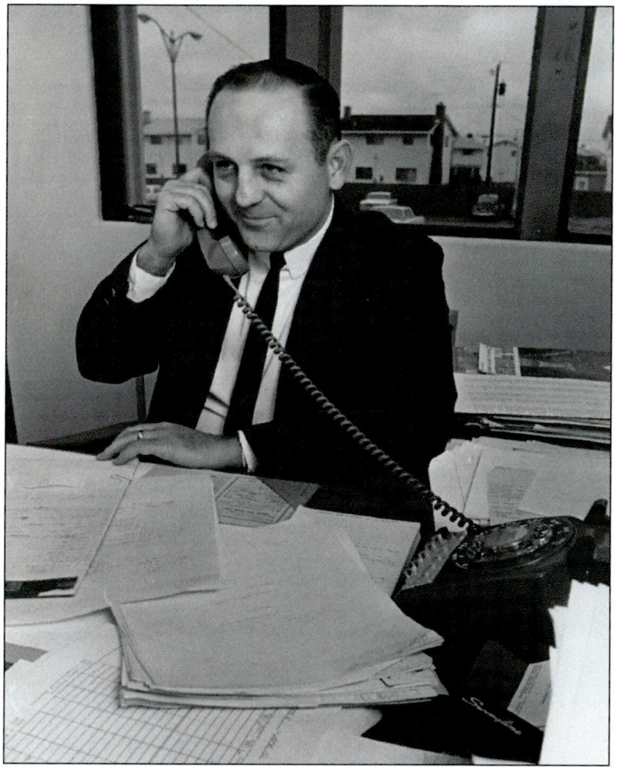

Ray Filipchuck was quoted as knowing more about the community than anyone. Working as the director of Public Services for almost 27 years, being very active in community and professional organizations, helping to develop the city's infrastructure, and acquiring grants to establish the city's park system from 30 to 1000 acres brought the city to name the Department of Public Works building after this well-liked and respected man.

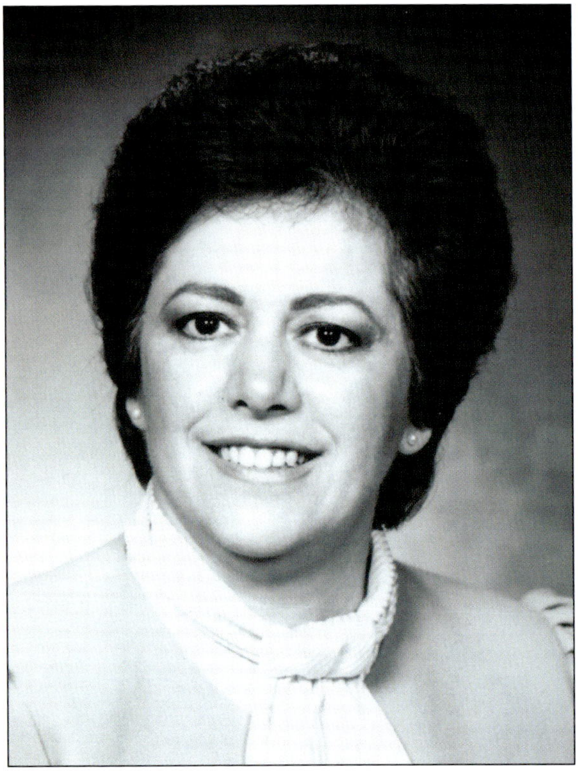

Jean DiRezze Gush has been the city's only female mayor in its first 50 years. She was elected from among the council members in 1985, where she started in 1983. She held the mayoral post until 1991, weathering some contentious times on the city council.

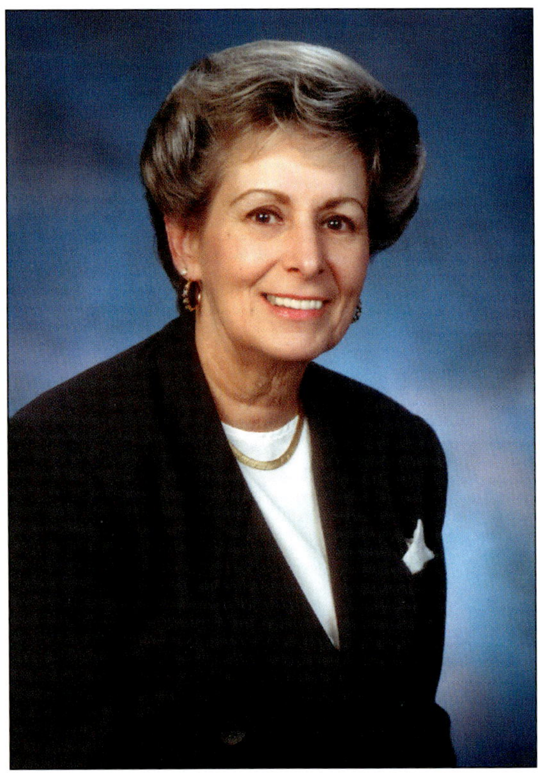

Councilwoman Deanna Koski is the longest-serving council member in Sterling Heights. First elected in 1989, she has navigated the highs and lows of the city climate with professionalism and knowledge of the community. Over the years, she has been very active in professional associations, serving on many committees and earning professional certifications, giving the city of Sterling Heights over 25 years of public service.

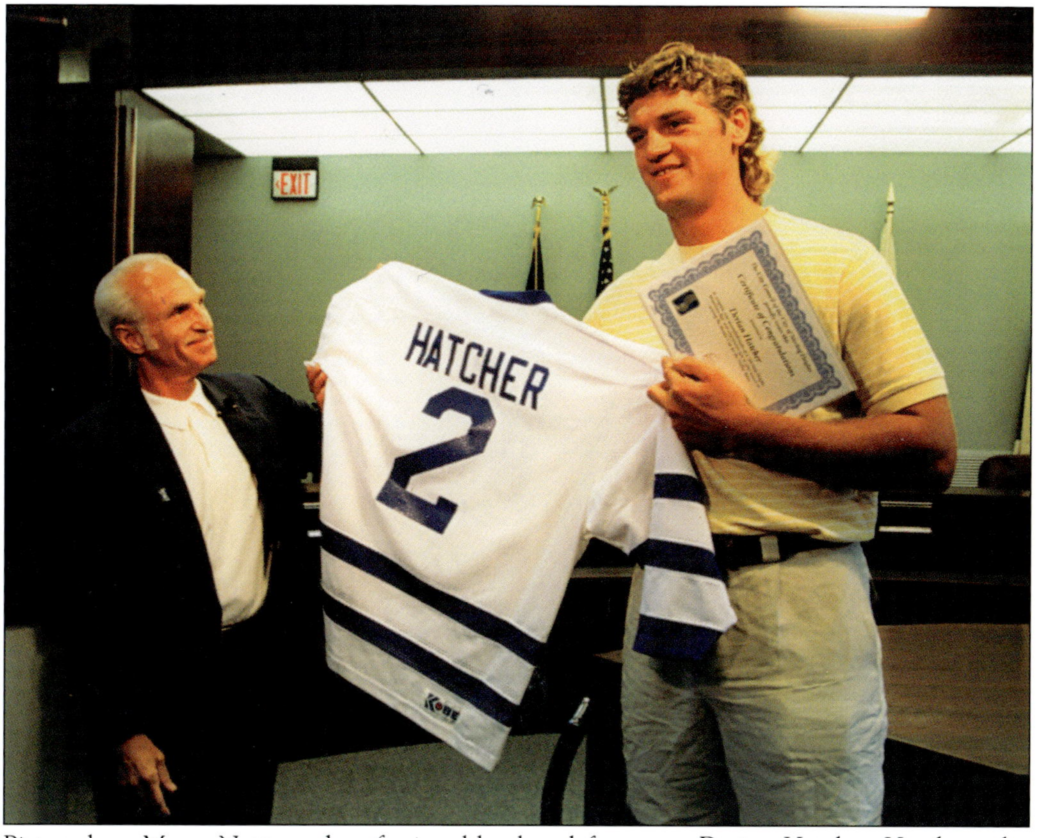

Pictured are Mayor Notte and professional hockey defenseman Derian Hatcher. Hatcher, who was born in Sterling Heights and attended Stevenson High School, played hockey for 16 seasons, beginning in 1990, for Minnesota, Dallas, Detroit, and Philadelphia. He and his brother Kevin were both inducted into the US Hockey Hall of Fame and, together, were former owners of Hatchy's bar and restaurant in nearby Utica.

Wallace "Wally" Doebler has spent most of his life being active in the community: Rotary Club, Community Foundation, Historical Commission, and presiding over the Utica Cemetery. Retirement from General Motors left him time to become an author as well. He wrote a valuable family and community history and genealogy titled *The Wallace H. Doebler Family of Macomb County, Michigan* and another very popular local book, *Summer Along the Clinton*, which featured histories of the local parks.

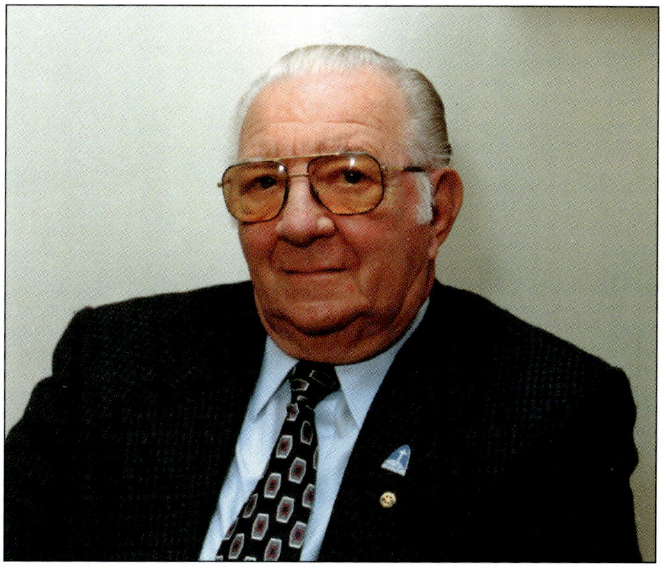

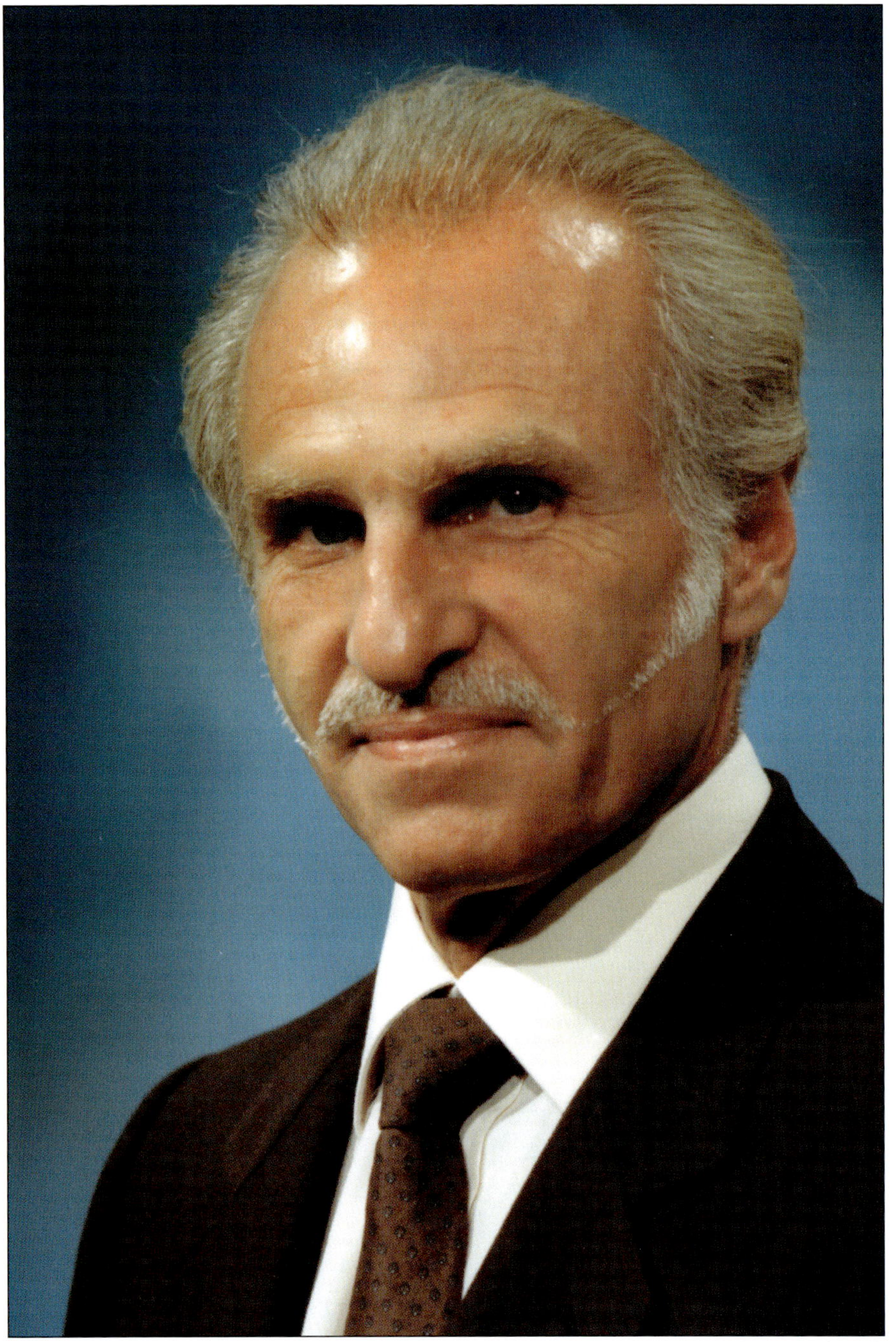

Mayor Richard Notte, beloved by many, was the longest-serving mayor the city has had. He was serving his 11th two-year term when he passed away from cancer in 2014. A Ford Motor Company employee for 40 years and active in the UAW, he was elected to city council in 1983 and became mayor in 1993, being the first directly elected mayor after the rules changed in the city. In later years, he was rarely seen without wearing his signature fedora. He was remembered as an enormous presence and a passionate public servant. The city council voted to rename the City Center complex in his honor. This photograph may have been from the 1980s.

Four

Schools, Churches, and the Library

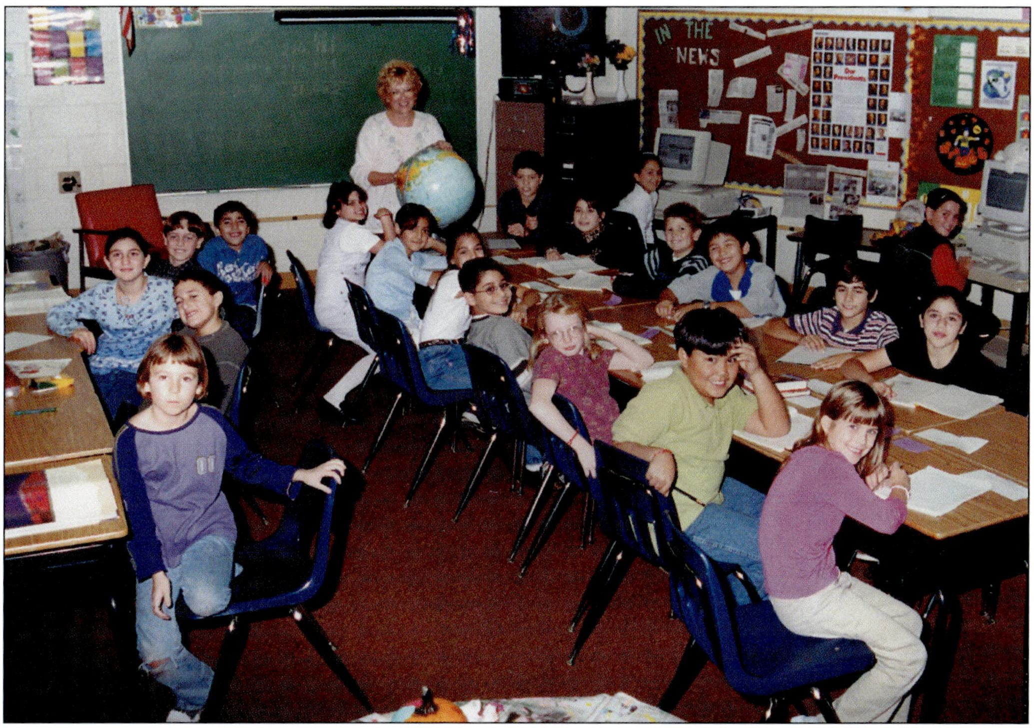

Hatherly Elementary School's fourth grade teacher, Naida Okray, smiles over her classroom of students in 2000. Hatherly, a Warren Consolidated School, is located on Davison Street, west of Mound Road and north of 15 Mile Road. The school opened in 1970, along with two other schools, in the Warren District to meet the growing population. In 2014, it closed as a school due to declining enrollment but continued to be used for other educational programs.

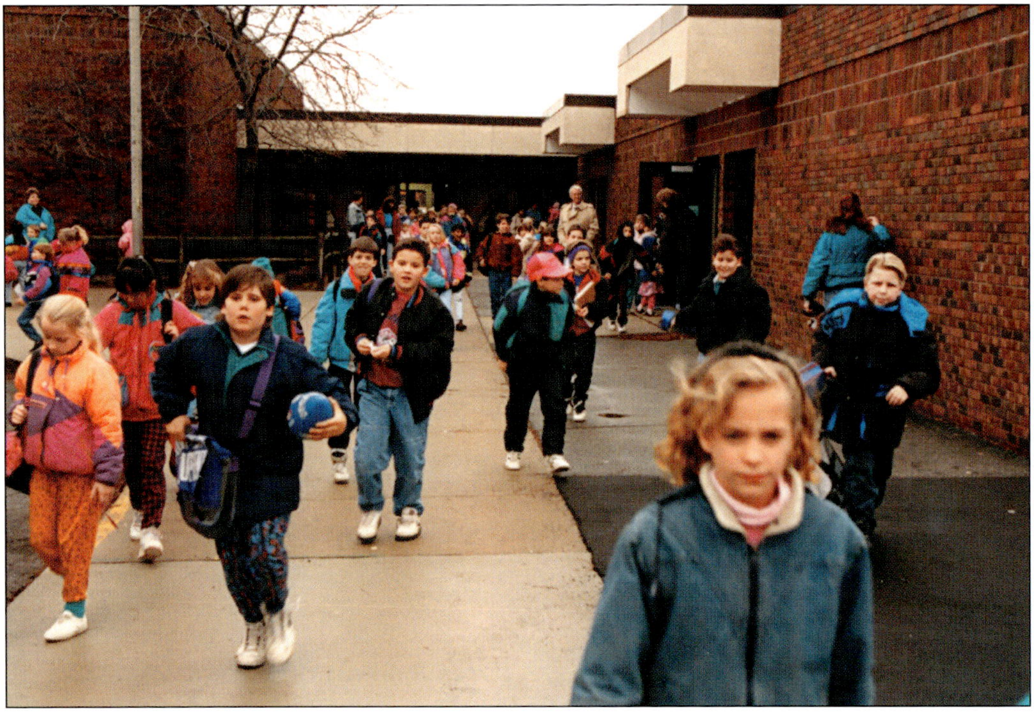

The bell has rung for the end of the day at Walsh Elementary School, located on the corner of 17 Mile Road and Dodge Park Road. The principal, Richard Watterworth, watches from the background in the photograph taken in the early 1980s. The building is no longer an elementary school but is used as the Utica Community Education Center, hosting a preschool and adult education classes.

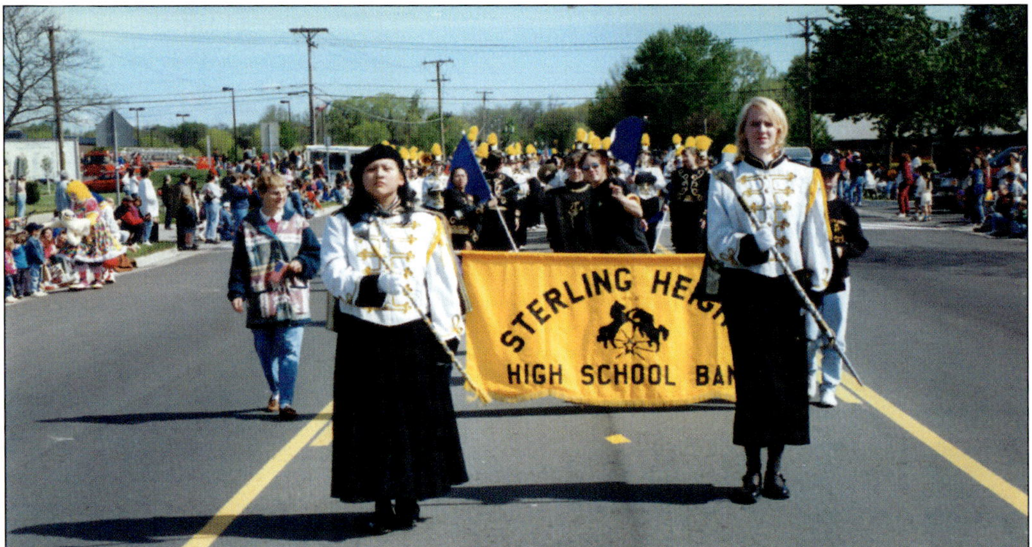

Sterling Heights High School is located on 15 Mile Road, west of Schoenherr Road. Part of the Warren Consolidated School district, the school opened in 1971 and notably had the same principal for the first 20 years, William Gordon. The school also hosts the award-winning Warren Consolidated School of Performing Arts.

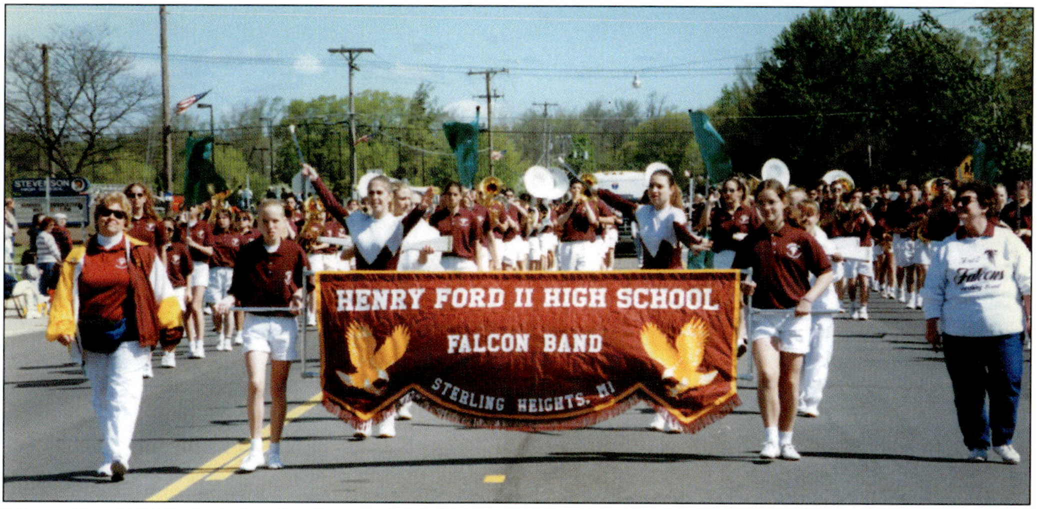

Henry Ford II High School is located on Clinton River Road, south of 19 Mile Road. Built on land that was once part of the old Harvey Farm, the school was dedicated in September 1973 at a ceremony attended by the board chairman of Ford Motor Company, Henry Ford II, himself. The school is part of Utica Community Schools, for which Ford Motor Company is the largest taxpayer.

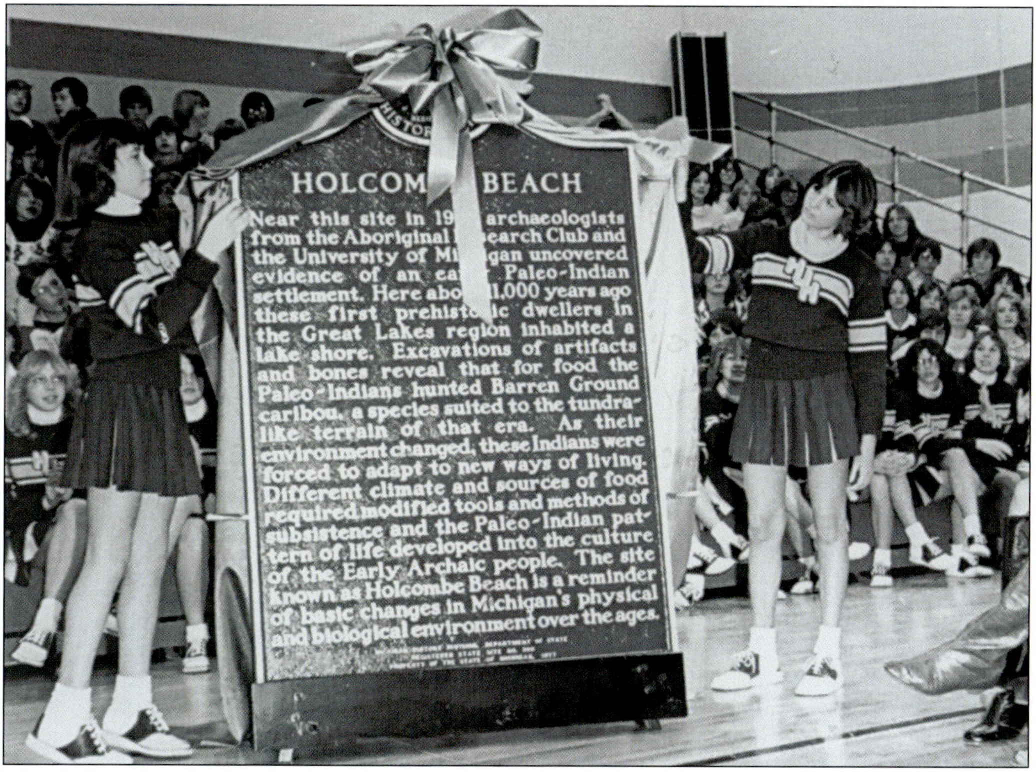

The Holcombe Beach plaque commemorates the Paleo Indian settlement discovered in 1961 by Jerome DeVisscher, a local amateur archaeologist. The Indian settlement, located where Heritage Junior High was later built on Metro Parkway and Dodge Park Road, was home to a prehistoric community 11,000 years ago. Here, the Michigan Historical Marker is displayed by students at its 1977 dedication at the school.

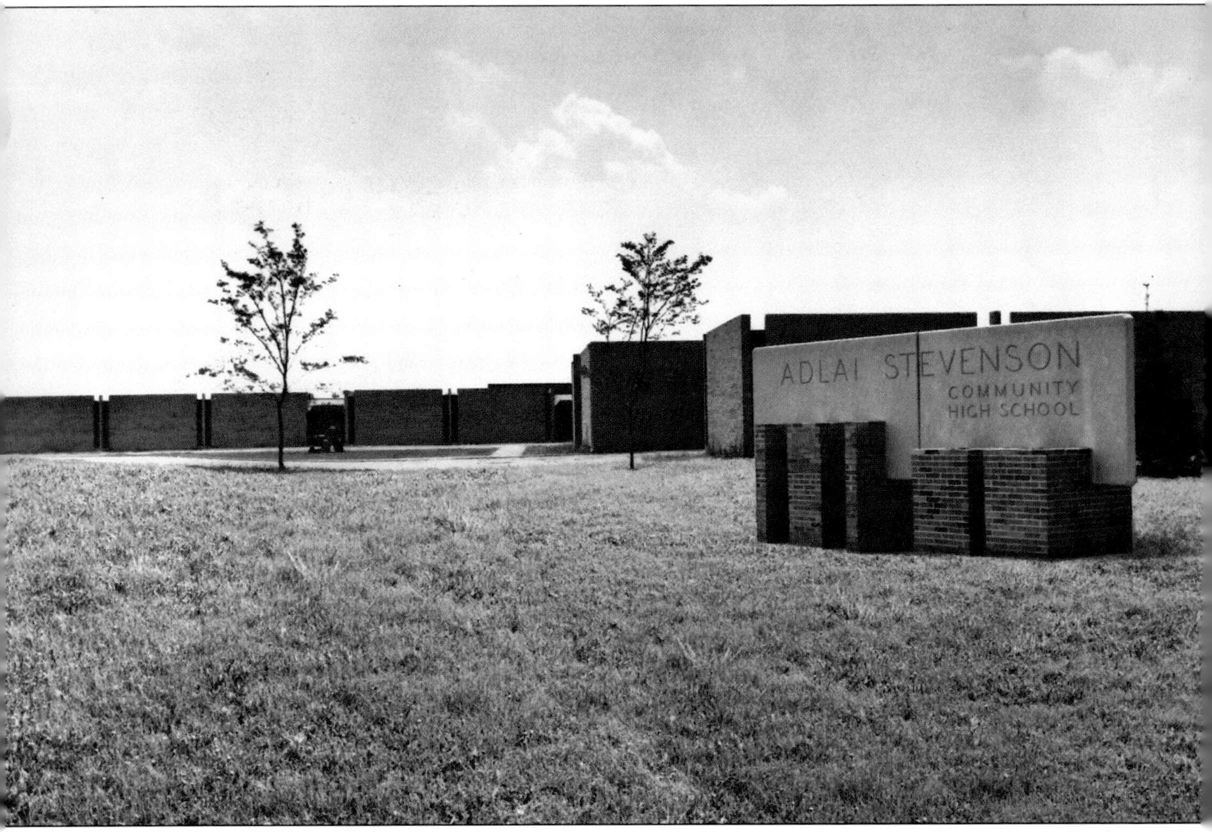

Stevenson High School, the first high school built in Sterling Township, opened in 1968 on Dodge Park Road, south of the city hall at Utica Road. It is part of the Utica Community Schools, and it took many students from the overcrowded Utica High School. The school was named for Adlai E. Stevenson II, former ambassador to the United Nations, former governor of Illinois, and two-time presidential candidate. The land the school sat on had been part of the Upton, Ahrens, Heldt, and Preuhs farms over the years, all prominent farmers. The school is pictured at the start of the 1968–1969 school year. (Courtesy of the *Utica Sentinel*.)

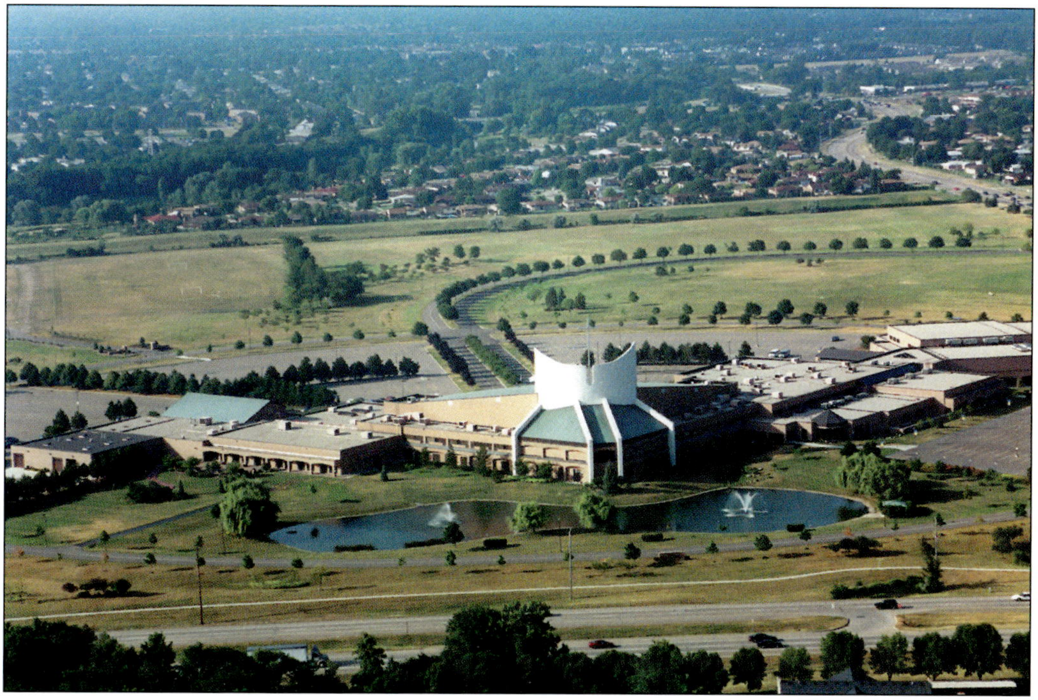

Bethesda Christian Church was created when Bethesda Missionary Temple moved from Detroit to service its many members from the northern suburbs. It opened in 1989 on a 92-acre site on the southeast corner of Metro Parkway and Schoenherr Roads. The largest church in Macomb County at the time, with a capacity for more than 3,500 people, the nondenominational church included a chapel, auditorium, social dining hall, and a school. Its school, Bethesda Christian School, was renamed Parkway Christian School in 2006 when it joined with Zoe Christian Academy.

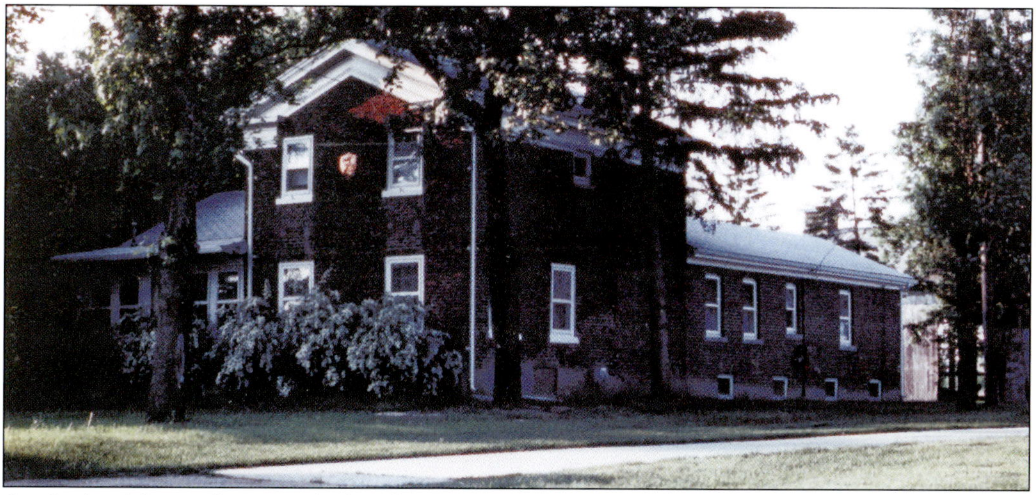

Our Lady of Czestochowa Catholic Church is run by the Society of Christ, a religious society based in Poland. This mission church offers service to Polish immigrants in the Sterling Heights area. This parish was founded in 1979 and is located on 18 Mile Road, between Ryan and Dequindre Roads. The grounds contain the church, provincial house/rectory, the pictured convent, and a bacowka (mountain hut). The convent was a farmhouse on the property before the church moved in.

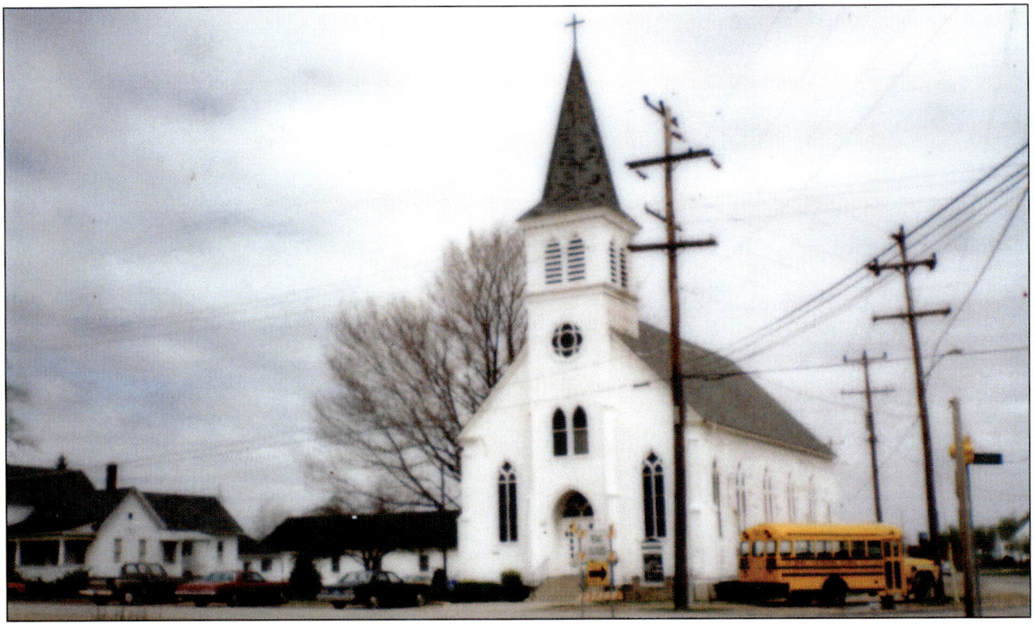

St. Paul Lutheran Church, at Canal and Hayes Roads, had been the heart of the German farm community since it was founded in 1875. In the late 1980s, with the widening of Hayes Road on the horizon, the congregation had hoped the city would move the beloved 1901 white-frame building. Attempts were made by the city to secure funds to move the structure to Dodge Park to be preserved and used as a museum or community center. But by 1990, they found that temporarily moving the utility lines to enable the move down the road doubled the cost of the project, and sadly, the old church was demolished.

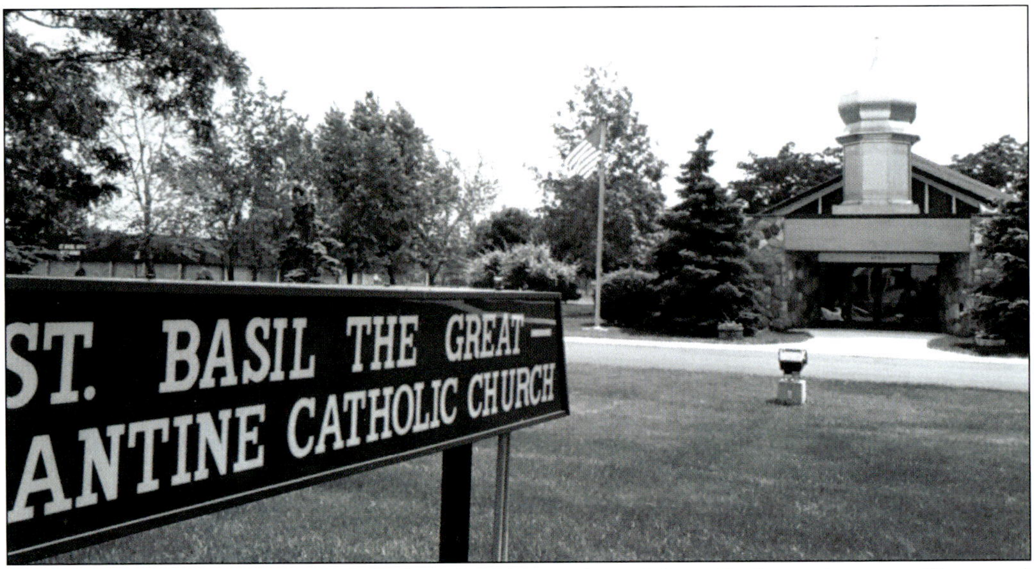

St. Basil the Great Byzantine Catholic Church stands on Metro Parkway, between Ryan and Mound Roads. The parish, for Byzantine rite Catholics, currently has a distinctive gold domed feature, which was not on the building originally. The parish was started in 1962 from a mother parish in Detroit. Masses were held in North Elementary until the current church building opened in 1968.

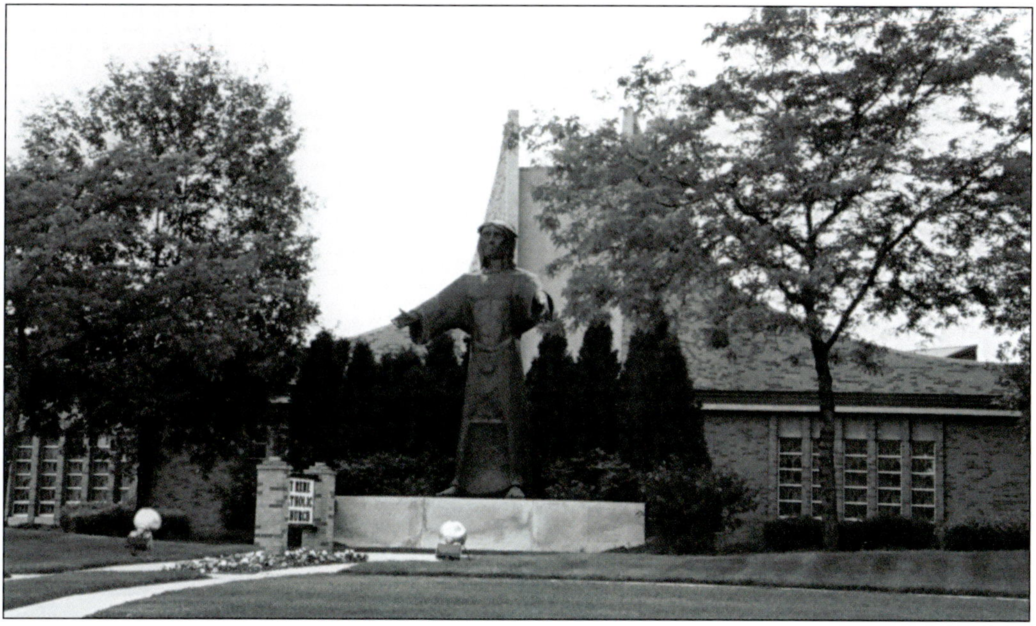

St. Rene Goupil Catholic Church, located on Ryan Road north of 15 Mile Road, was first established in 1970 by Rev. Gerald Martin. Reverend Martin, a highly respected and active member of the community, first celebrated masses at Grissom Junior High until the church building was ready in 1973. The landmark 24-foot bronze statue of Christ was installed in 1985. Monsignor Bernard Harrington followed Martin as pastor in 1984.

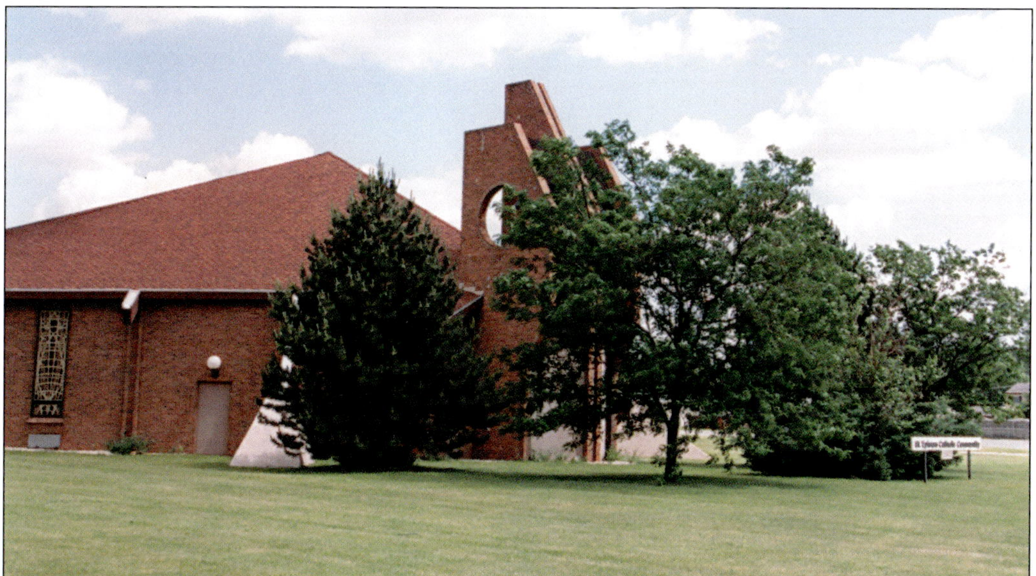

St. Ephrem Catholic Church, on the southeast corner of Dodge Park and 17 Mile Roads, was founded by Monsignor John Gordon in 1964. A temporary church was built at that time, and a permanent church was in use by 1977. Fr. Bob Blondell followed Gordon as pastor of the parish.

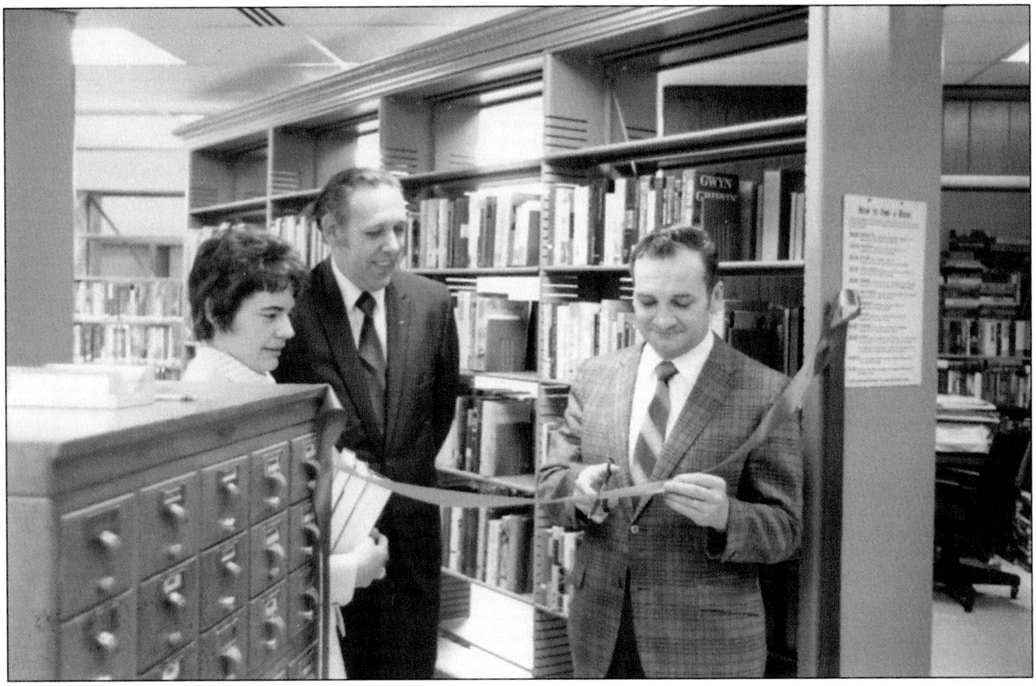

Library director Shelagh Klein and Charles Payne watch as Councilman F. James Dunlop cuts a ribbon celebrating the opening of the first Sterling Heights Public Library on October 27, 1971. The library was housed in 1,000 square feet of city hall's basement on Utica Road at Dodge Park Road. About 12,000 books, three full-time employees, and an eagerness to grow got things rolling.

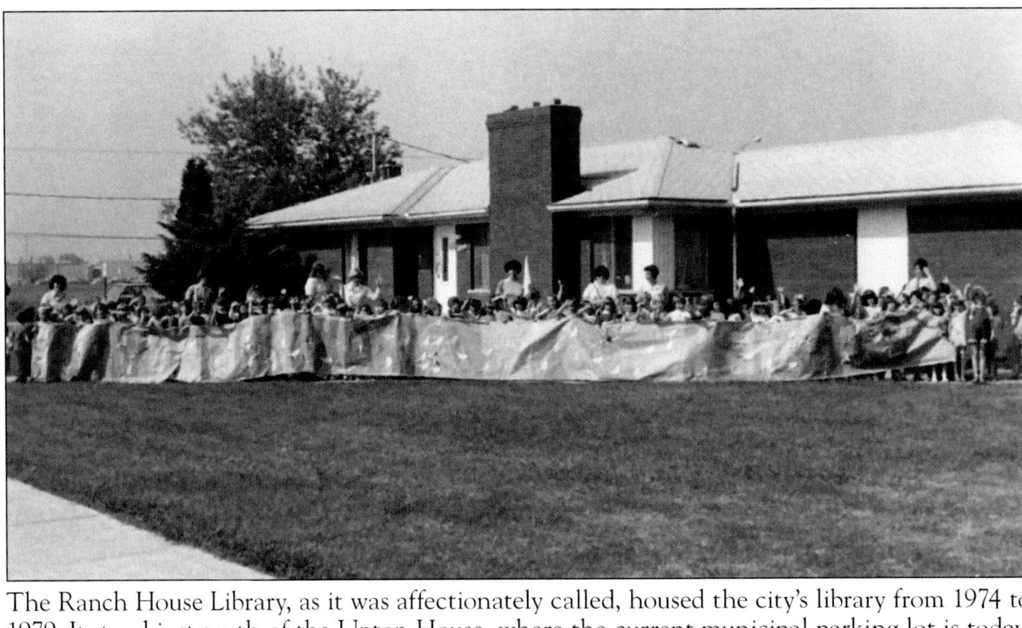

The Ranch House Library, as it was affectionately called, housed the city's library from 1974 to 1979. It stood just south of the Upton House, where the current municipal parking lot is today. In the distance on the left is Stevenson High School. The Ranch House Library added modular units in 1977 to alleviate the lack of space. The deputy director's office was in a bathroom.

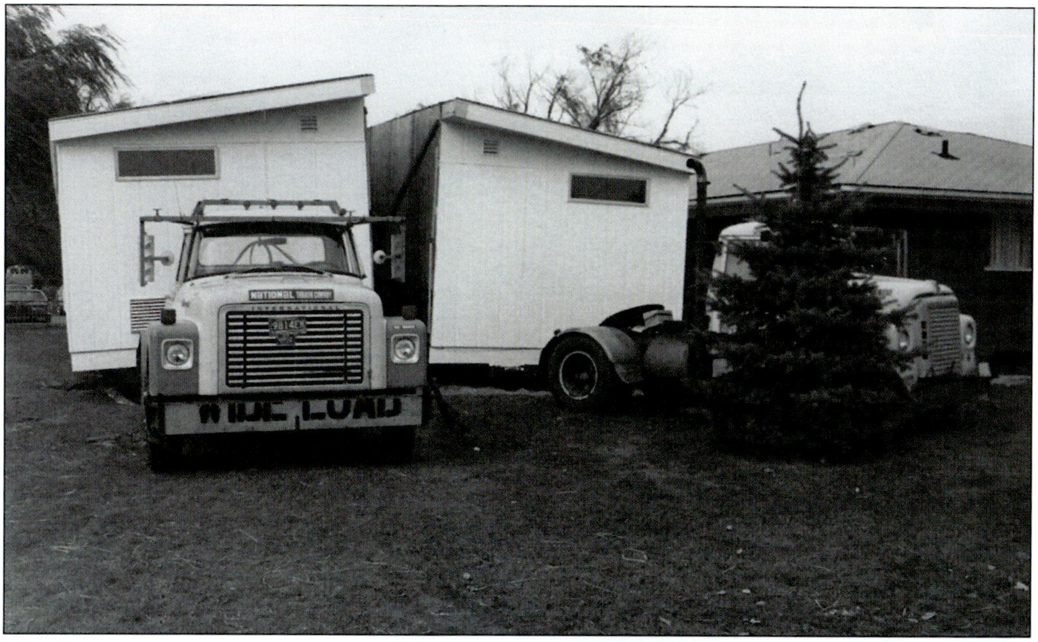

The floor space of the Sterling Heights Public Library grew by 33 percent when these modular units were installed as an addition to the ranch house–style library, seen at right around 1976. The library housed a collection of 30,000 books and 2,000 LP recordings, which helped serve the needs of the burgeoning population during this time.

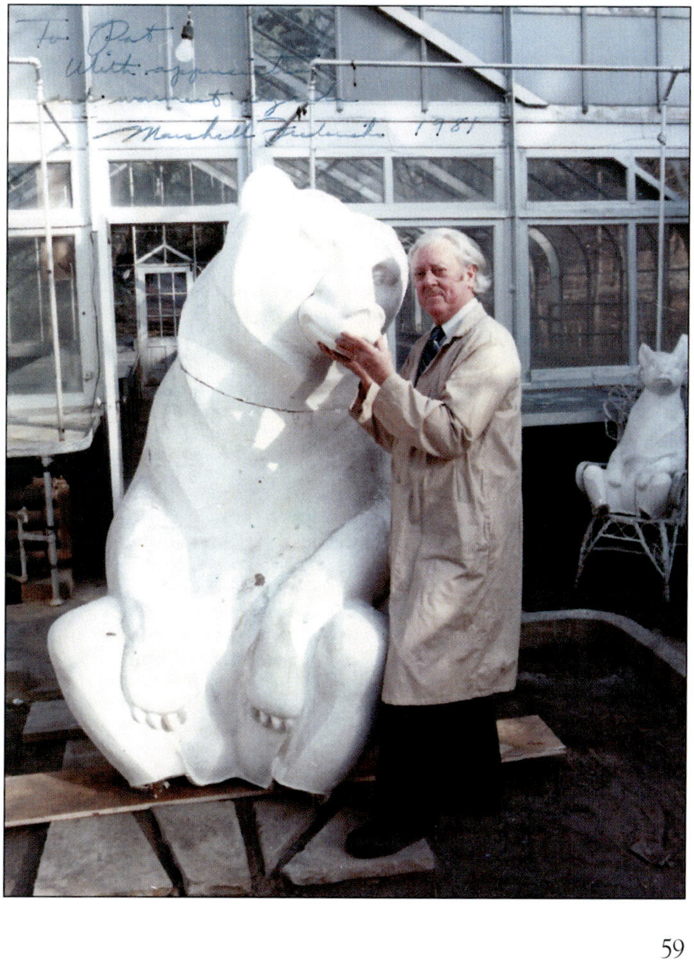

Renowned sculptor Marshall Fredericks poses with the plaster mold for his *Two Bears* in his studio as it is prepared to be sent to a New York foundry to be cast in bronze. Fredericks is also known for his *Spirit of Detroit* sculpture in downtown Detroit and other works in the Midwest. The Sterling Heights casting of *Two Bears* is one of a few installed around the country.

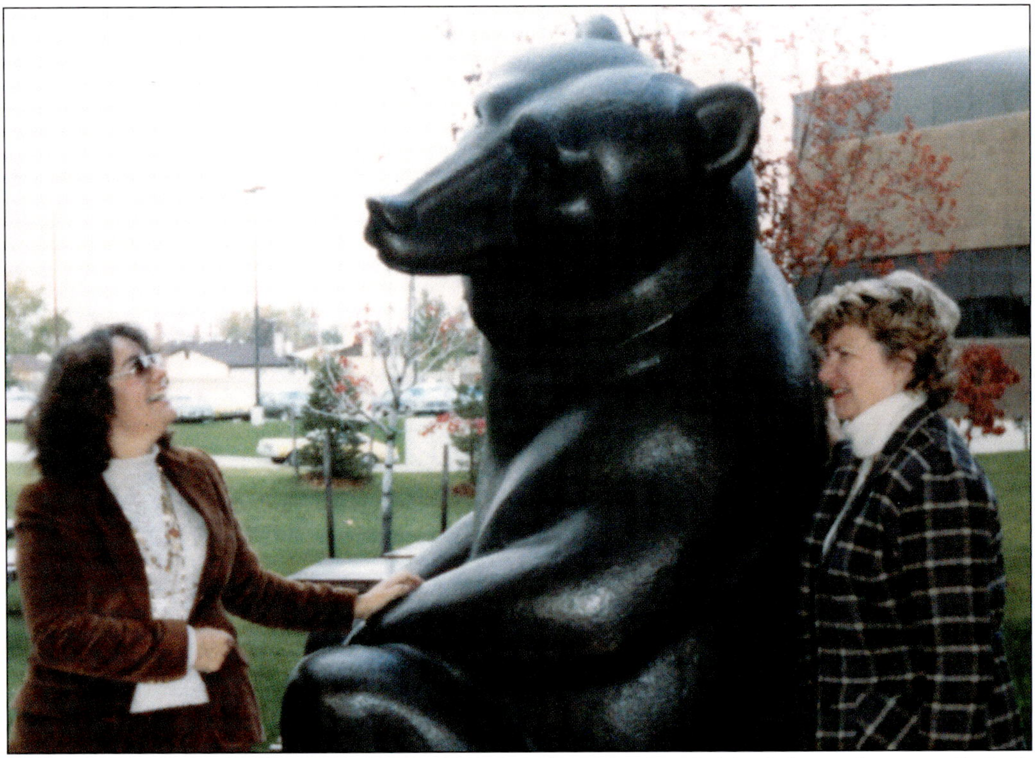

The *Two Bears* sculpture is celebrated by the Sterling Heights Public Library director Shelagh Klein and deputy director Patricia DeForest at its 1981 dedication. The six-foot bronze sculpture by Marshall Fredericks, chosen for its appeal to children, was installed in front of the library and dedicated with fanfare. The $30,000 cost was mainly achieved by robust community donations.

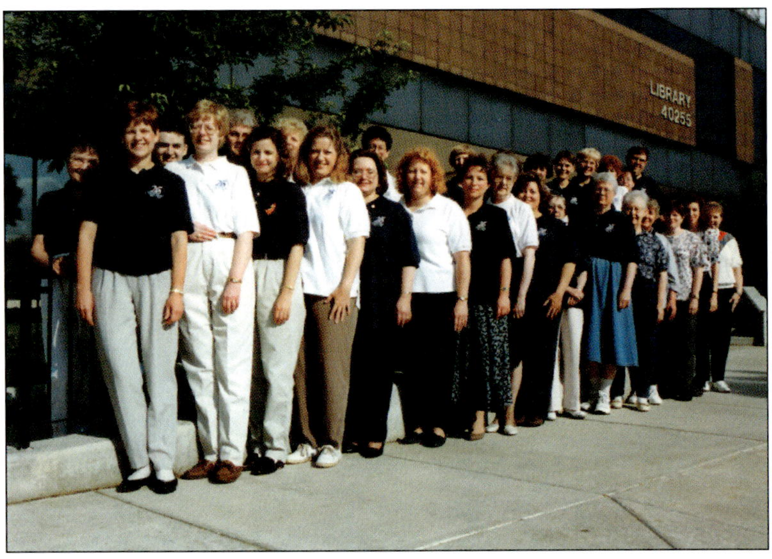

The Sterling Heights Public Library staff poses in front of the library in the 1990s. Library director Carol Lingeman is seen at far left in front, with librarians, clerks, and library pages also included in the group. The occasion may have been celebrating the 25th anniversary of the library, as seen in the logos on the polo shirts.

The beginning of computer usage in the library started in the early 1990s when a bank of computers was installed, allowing users to search for magazine articles and to use the online catalog. The traditional card catalog can be seen in the background and was kept for a time before book searching went entirely into the digital age.

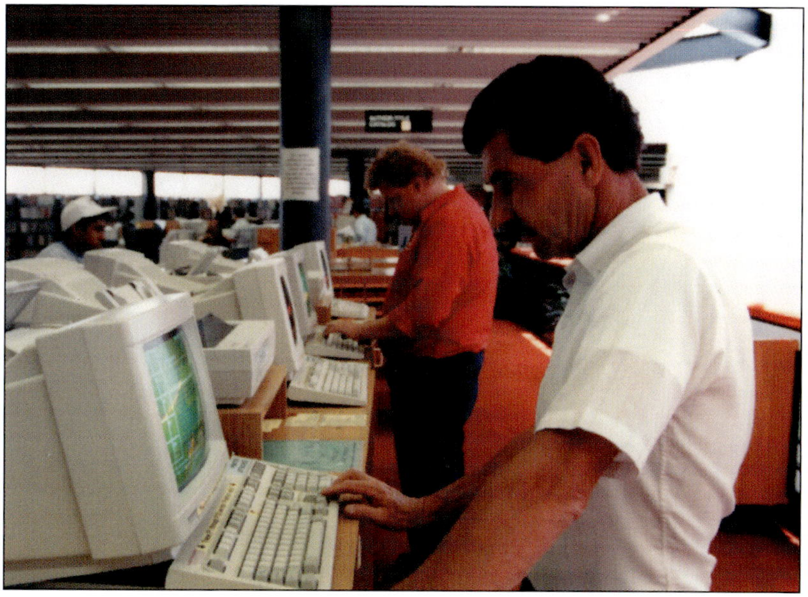

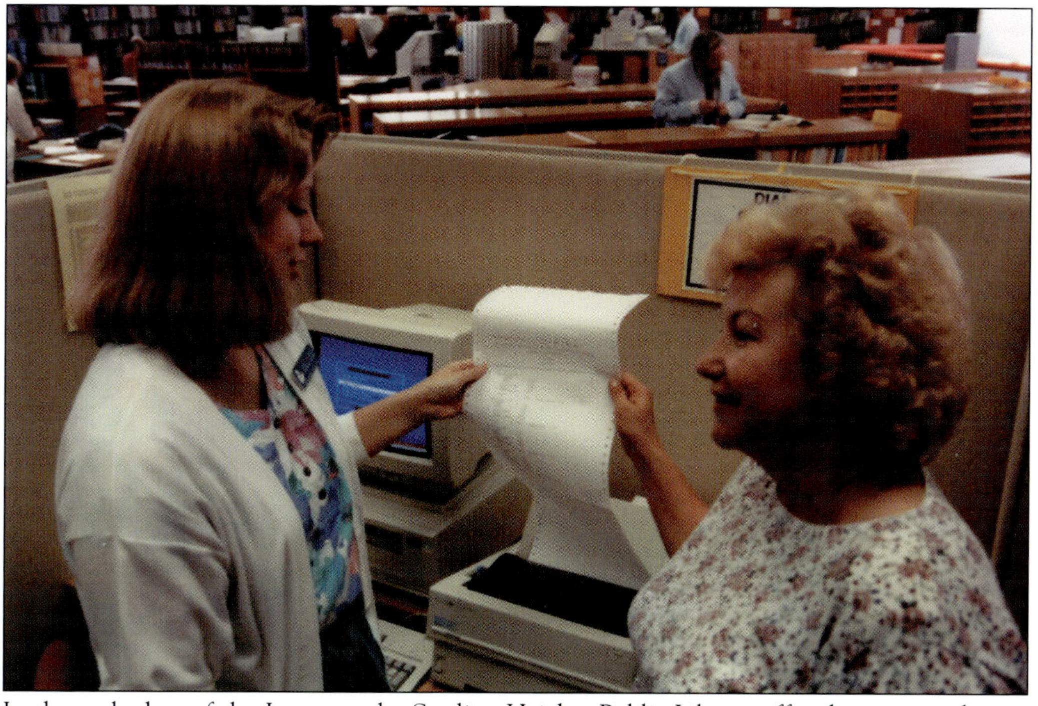

In the early days of the Internet, the Sterling Heights Public Library offered a service where a librarian would access a special subscription collection of online databases to find information to meet the patron's needs. There were special fees for this hard-to-access information. Reference librarian Debbie Vercellone shows a user her results from the pin-fed printer in this photograph from the 1990s.

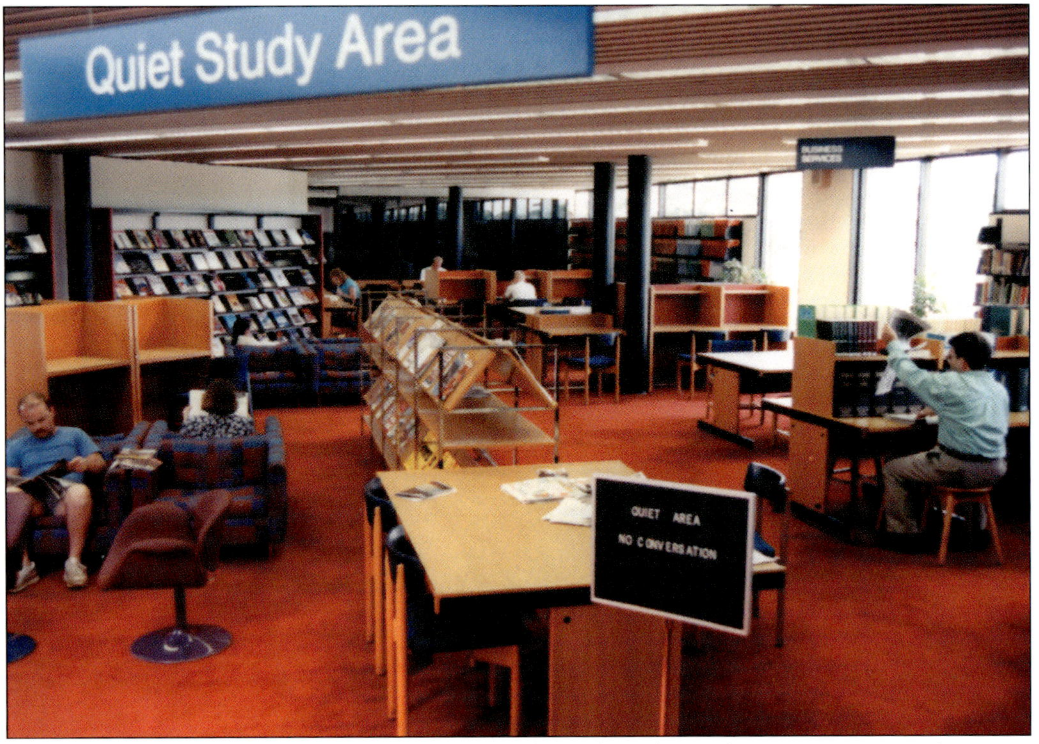

The arrangement of the collections within the library has changed many times over the years. This view shows the Quiet Study Area on the second floor, which at that time housed the magazines and newspapers. This second-floor area now is filled with book stacks and two private study rooms. After the expansion in 2000, Youth Services moved out of the first-floor front area, where the magazines are now.

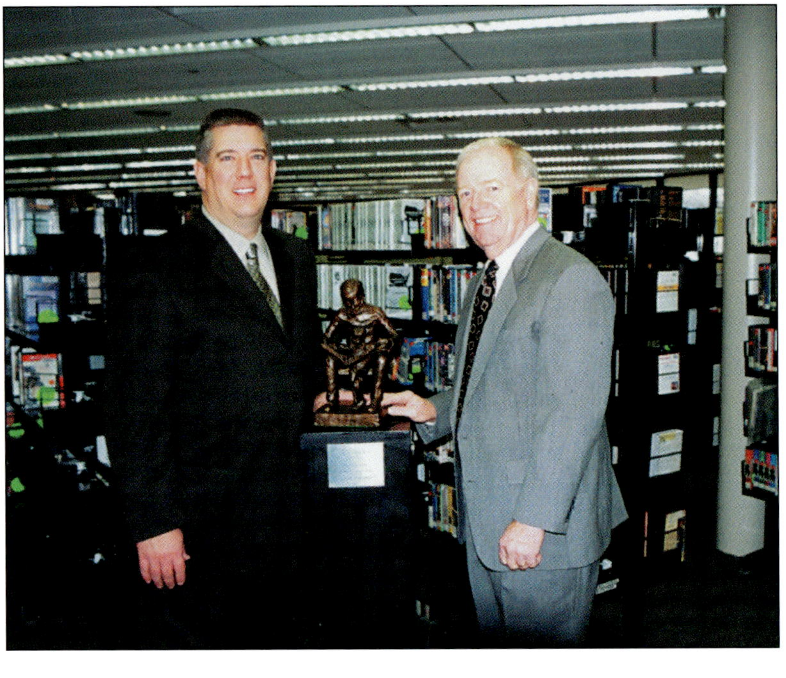

City Manager Steve Duchane (left) and City Attorney Paul O'Reilly (right) pose in the public library with a sculpture named *Discovering New Worlds* by artist Kay Worden. The piece was donated to the library by the law firm of O'Reilly, Rancilio, Nitz, Andrews, and Turnbull, P.C., in honor of the City of Sterling Heights 25th silver anniversary in 1993.

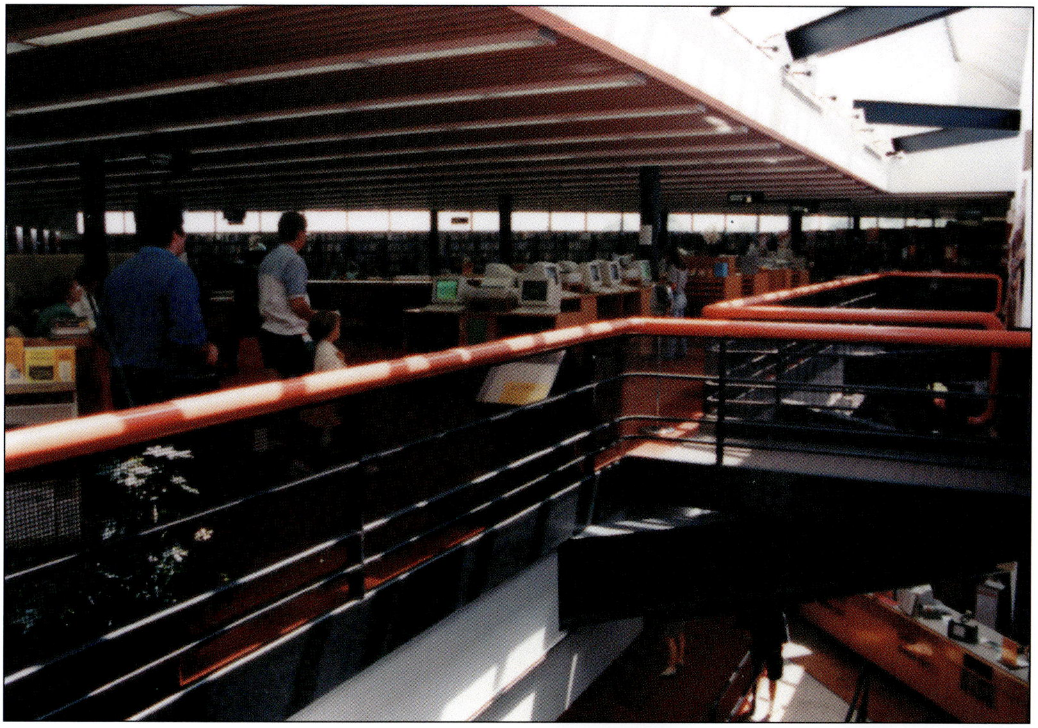

Another view of the second floor of the library shows the online computers, the reference desk at left staffed by librarians Margaret Hanes and Ed Piet, and the circulation desk below on the first floor. This photograph is from the 1990s before the library expansion.

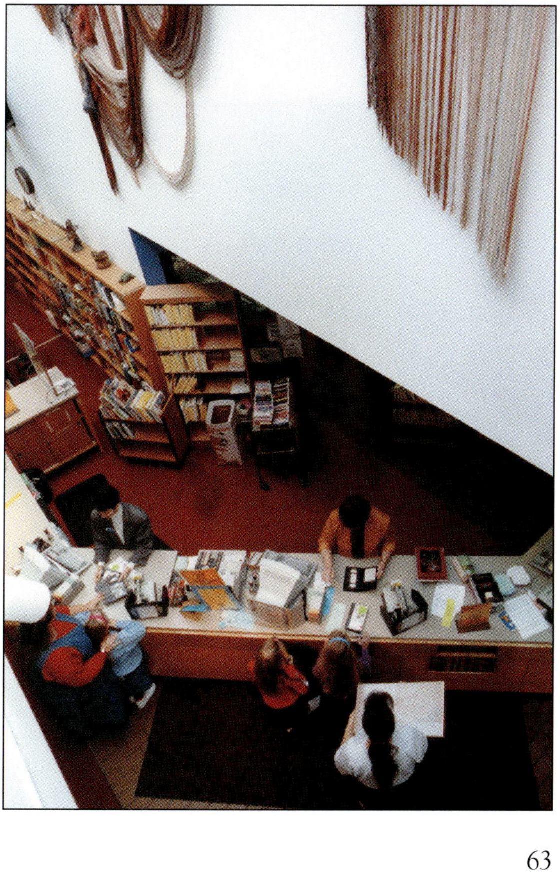

This image is looking from the second floor down to the circulation desk in the 1990s before the desk was moved to the new part of the building. This also shows the original tapestry wall hanging in the large space above the desk. That space was later enhanced with a metalwork sculpture after the hanging was removed because of deterioration.

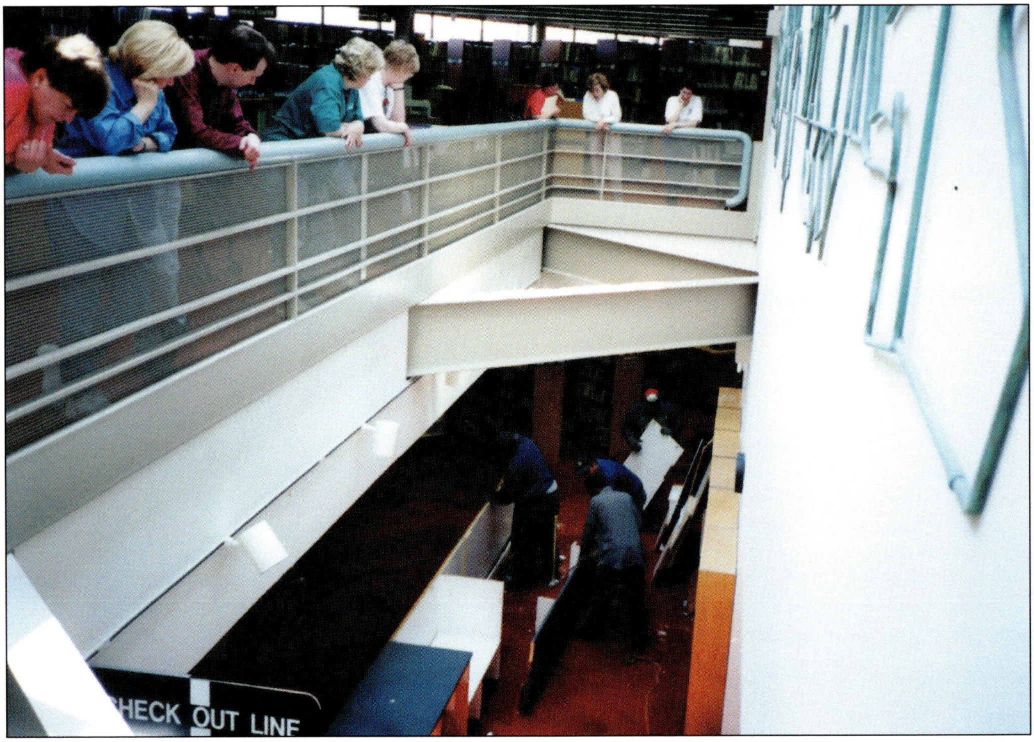

The library was closed to the public for a number of months during the construction of the addition in 2000. Some staff members were there during this time to continue certain functions. It was worth watching construction workers demolish the former circulation counter (the heart and soul of the library) during break time.

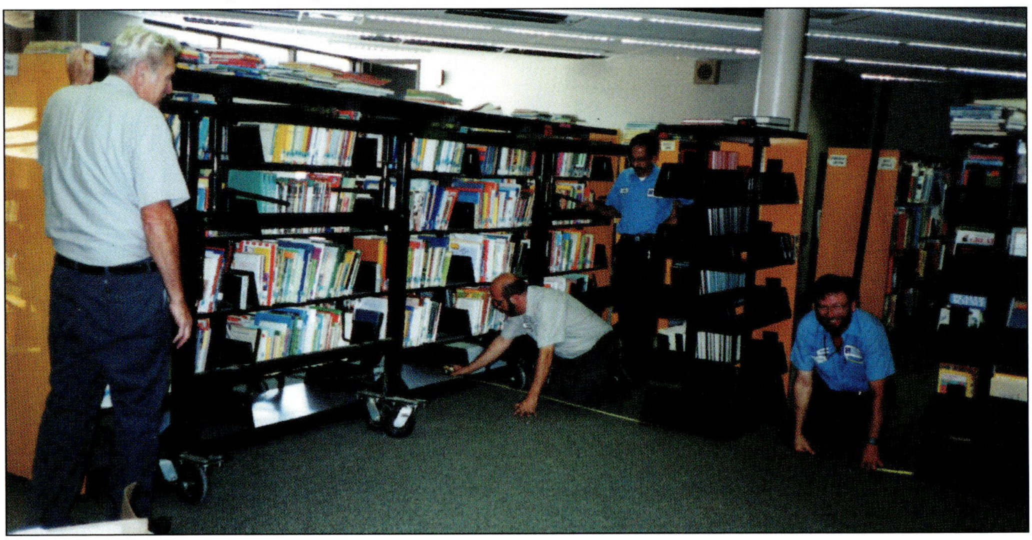

In 2000, when the library had its large addition constructed, all the book stacks in the entire building had to be moved while they still had the books on their shelves. Employees from the city's Facilities Maintenance Department used a borrowed stack mover, which jacked up the units a few inches and allowed wheels to do the work. From left to right are John Zaziski, Dennis Meyer, unidentified, and Frank Debinski. (Courtesy of Gloria Pierce.)

The library was expanded in 2000 as part of the large renovation of the City Center complex. Space for a new Youth Services Department, Circulation Department, Programming Center meeting room, and a new entrance and lobby were all added. Here, from left to right, Joan Freehan of the library board, Denise Shepherd of the Friends of the Library, and library director Carol Lingeman look over the construction plans.

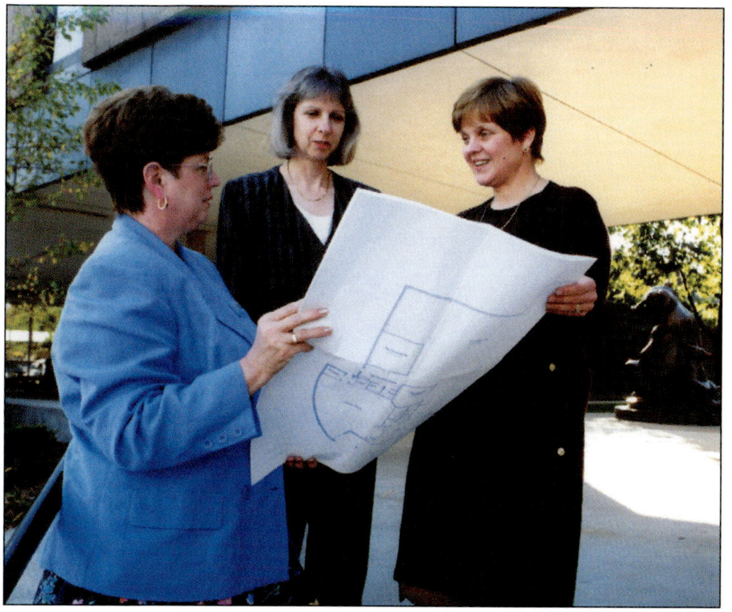

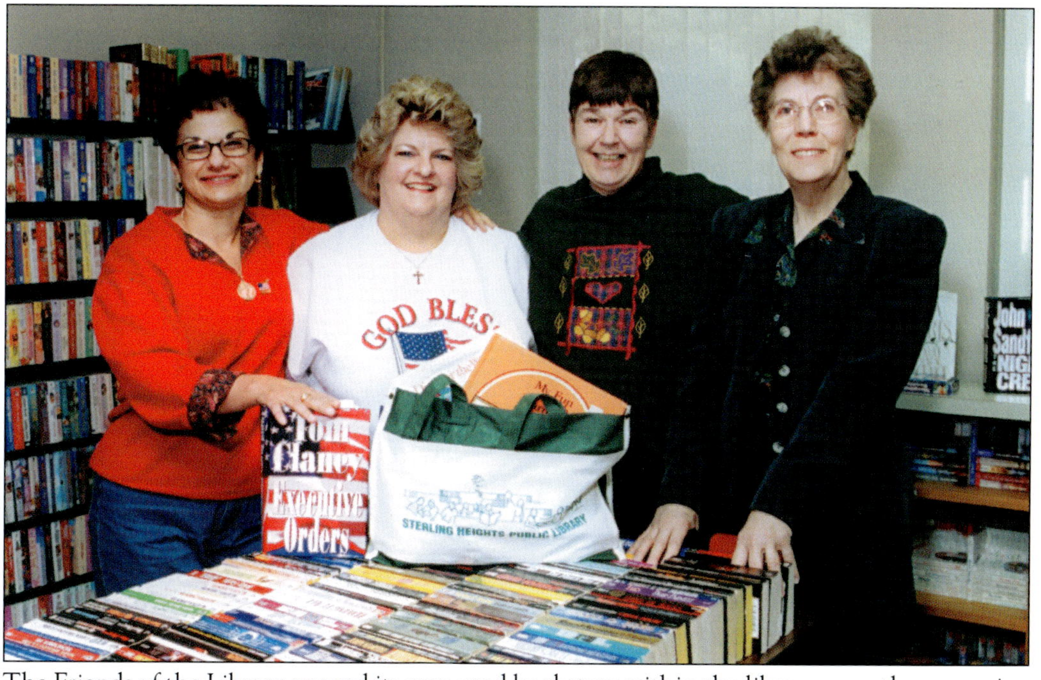

The Friends of the Library opened its own used bookstore within the library upon the reopening of the library after the addition in 2000. Volunteer Pat White, far right, ran the bookstore very successfully, passing the earnings on to the library. James and Joan Waldrop ran it from 2002 to 2014, and John Quainton took over in 2014. Also pictured with White are Friends of the Library volunteers Alice Abraham, Mary Pawlowski, and Sue Brisson.

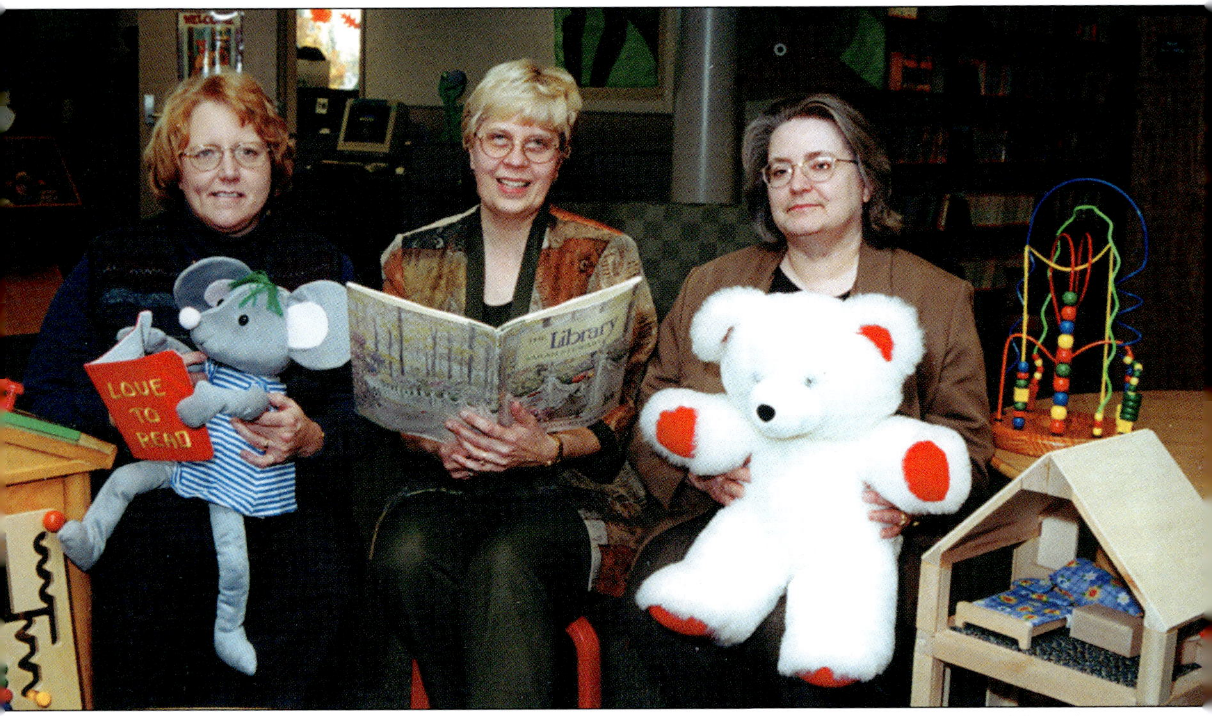

Judy Kotulis, supervisor of the Youth Services Department of the Sterling Heights Public Library, is seated flanked by fellow librarians Linda Markle (left) and Krystyna Kobersy (right). Miss Judy, as she was known, was an award-winning librarian who worked for the city's library for over 30 years, beginning in the old ranch house building. She loved her job and loved exposing the community's children to books. Most residents probably fondly remember a Miss Judy story time. She was honored upon her retirement with a statue in the library lobby of a boy and girl on a bench reading.

Five

Residential Living

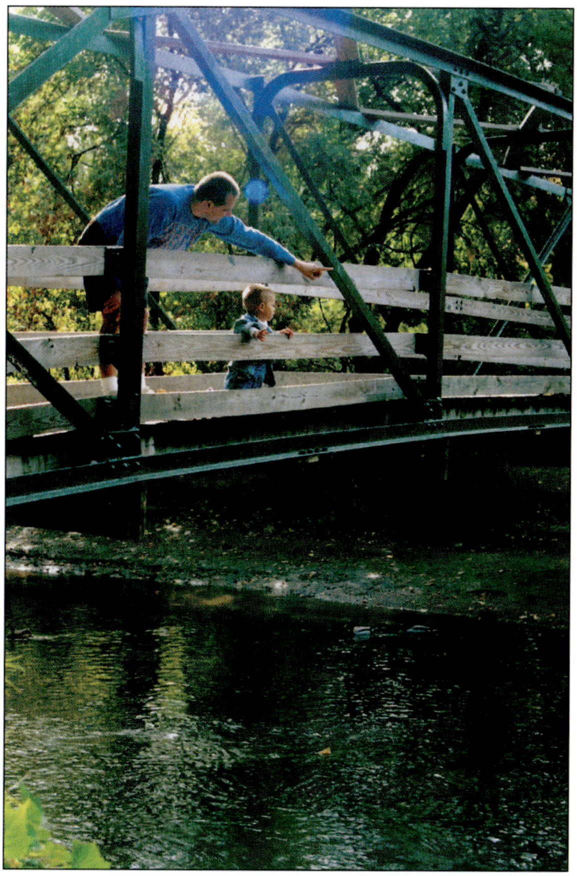

The pedestrian bridge crossing the Clinton River in Dodge Park has been a sentimental favorite for years. The park itself opened for business in 1924. This metal bridge with a wood deck was constructed around 1952 and had its deck replaced in 1992. Still, its lifespan came to an end in 2017 when it was removed and sold to a private buyer in mid-Michigan to be used over their creek. A new bridge was built over the Clinton River, wide enough to accommodate emergency vehicles access to the park and high enough to avoid log jams. (Photograph by Steve Guitar.)

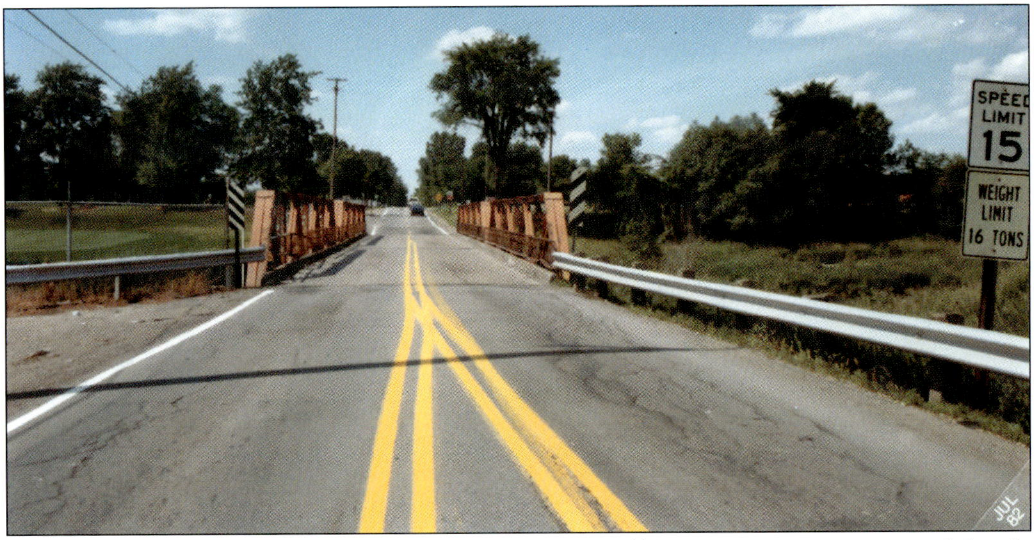

The Maple Lane Bridge that ran alongside Maple Lane Golf Course was very narrow with barely two lanes in 1982. The city had been plagued with many of these narrow bridges, some only one lane, that crossed the many creeks and rivers in the area. The Kleino Bridge, for which an image could not be found, was legendary for being narrow, as most of these old bridges were not built for modern cars. Most were eventually replaced and widened.

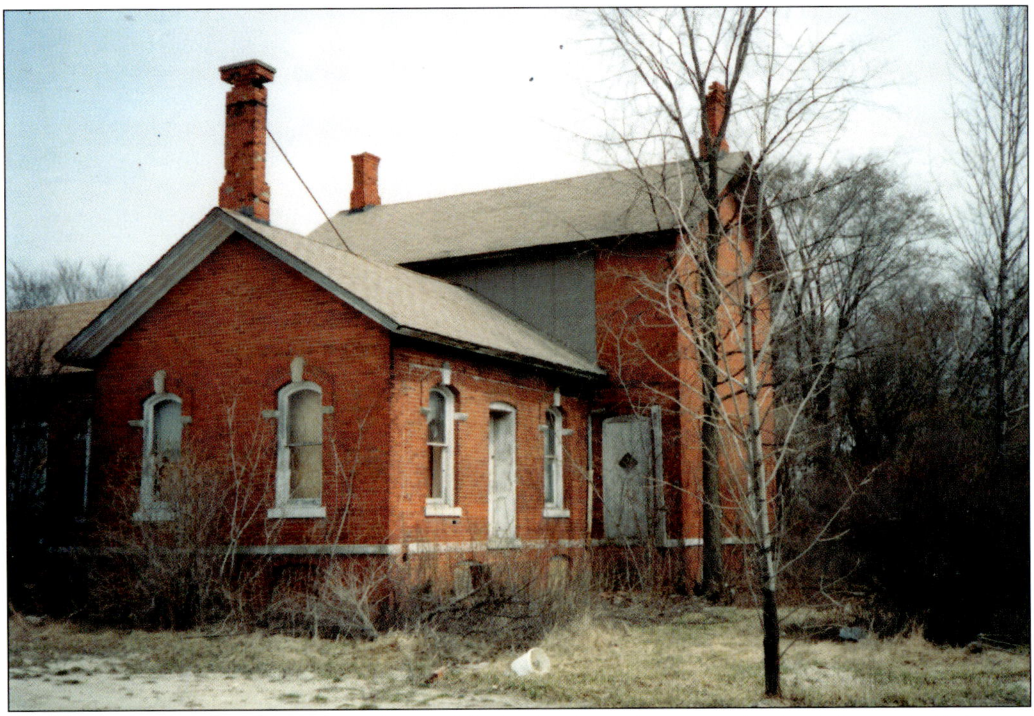

The northeast corner of Ryan Road and 18 Mile Road was home to this brick house built by the Burr family in the 1800s. The Burrs owned a brick and tile yard and donated bricks to be used in the construction of Burr School, which was named for them. The Beemer family lived in this house in more modern times. After the Beemer family passed on, the house stood vacant for many years and was later demolished.

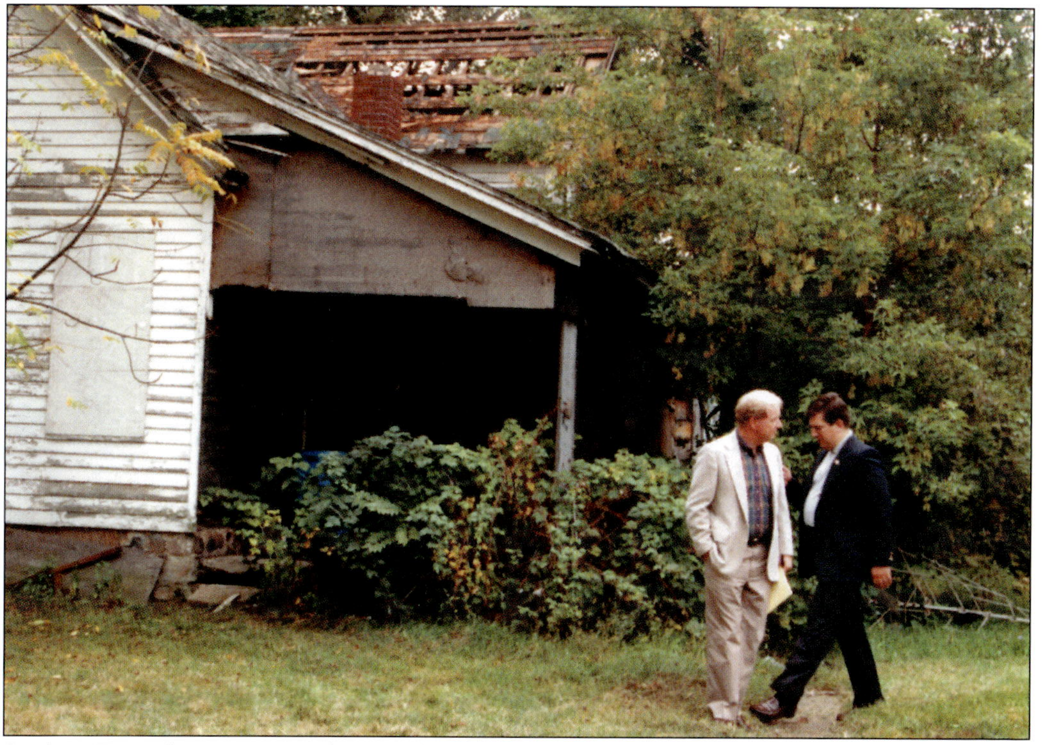

Sterling Township's main roads were dotted with old wood farmhouses still being used. But by the 1980s, subdivisions were being built, and most farmers had moved north. Some houses were purchased by new residents and repurposed as suburban homes, but not all. Many were in severe and dangerous disrepair. Here, attorney Paul O'Reilly and City Manager Steve Duchane check out the situation.

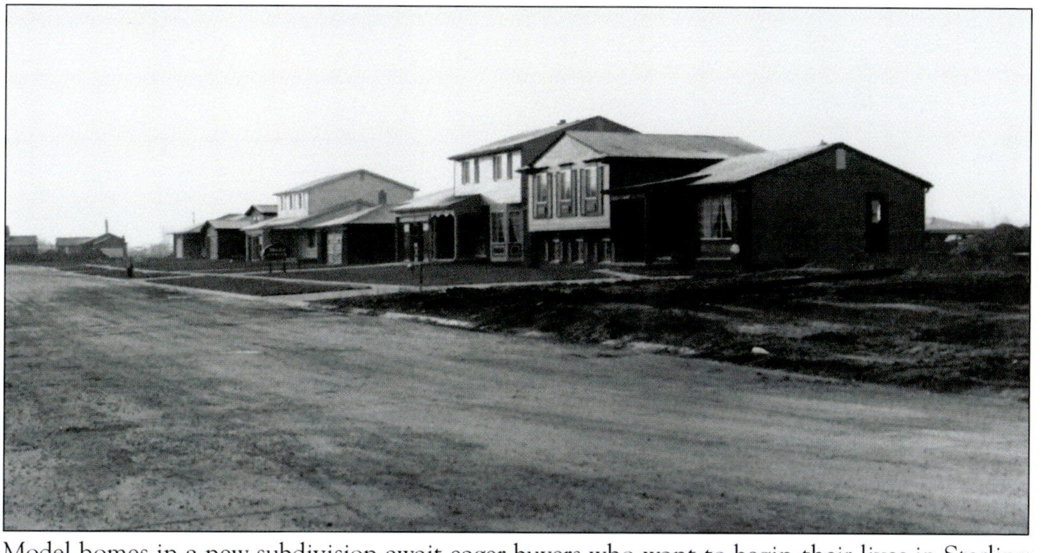

Model homes in a new subdivision await eager buyers who want to begin their lives in Sterling Heights. The photograph may have been taken in the 1970s. Sterling Heights was full of former farm fields, flat land already cleared and ready for builders such as Roncelli, Mosconi, the Palazzolo Brothers, Karams, Thunderbird Homes, and Crescendo Homes to fill them up.

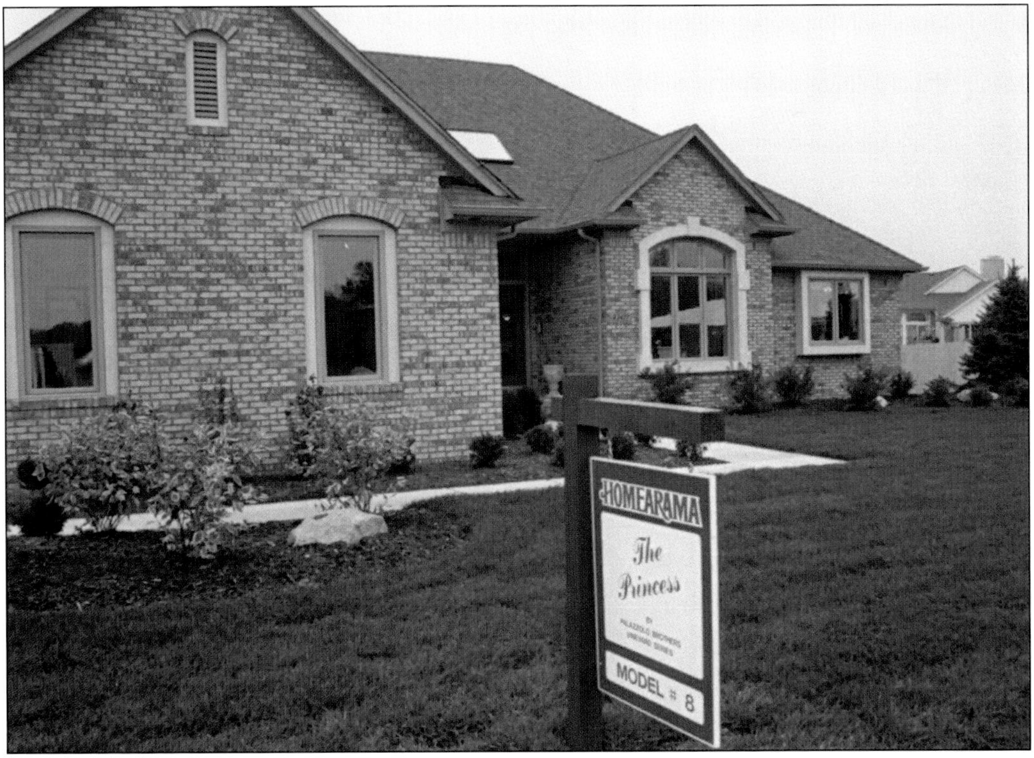

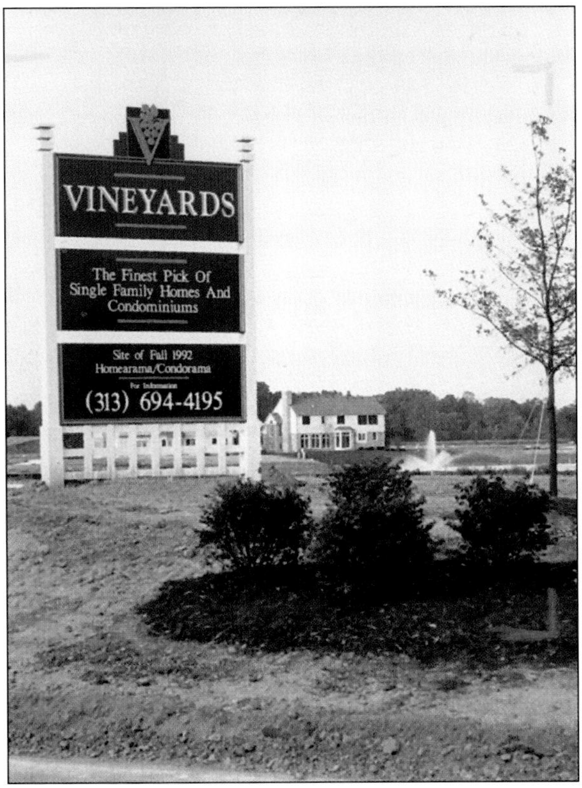

The Home Builders Association of Southeastern Michigan chose Sterling Heights as the site for the 1992 Homearama. A 250-acre site along Ryan Road, south of Hall Road, incorporated a stream and protected nature areas to host this new upscale residential development showcasing 14 to 16 new homes by as many developers.

The Vineyards residential development began construction in 1992 as part of the Homearama event. Developed by Dominic Moceri and John Carlo, it was the first major subdivision in the largely undeveloped northwest quadrant and consisted of 350 upscale single-family homes and 172 condominiums. This was the city's first use of the new cluster housing option, incorporating preserved wooded areas.

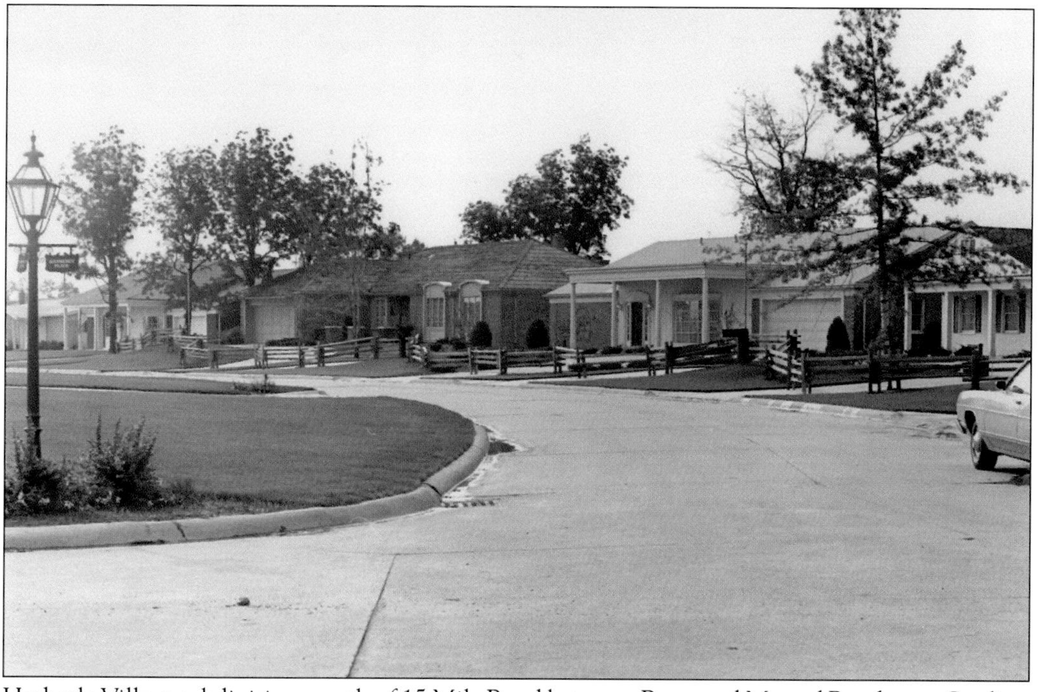

Hatherly Village subdivision, north of 15 Mile Road between Ryan and Mound Roads, was Sterling Heights's original upscale neighborhood. Winding streets with houses in a wide variety of designs made it the place to be for upper-income residents. Homes in the original development were built in the late 1960s, with more land added to the neighborhood later. This photograph shows some homes on Hatherly Place set up as sales models.

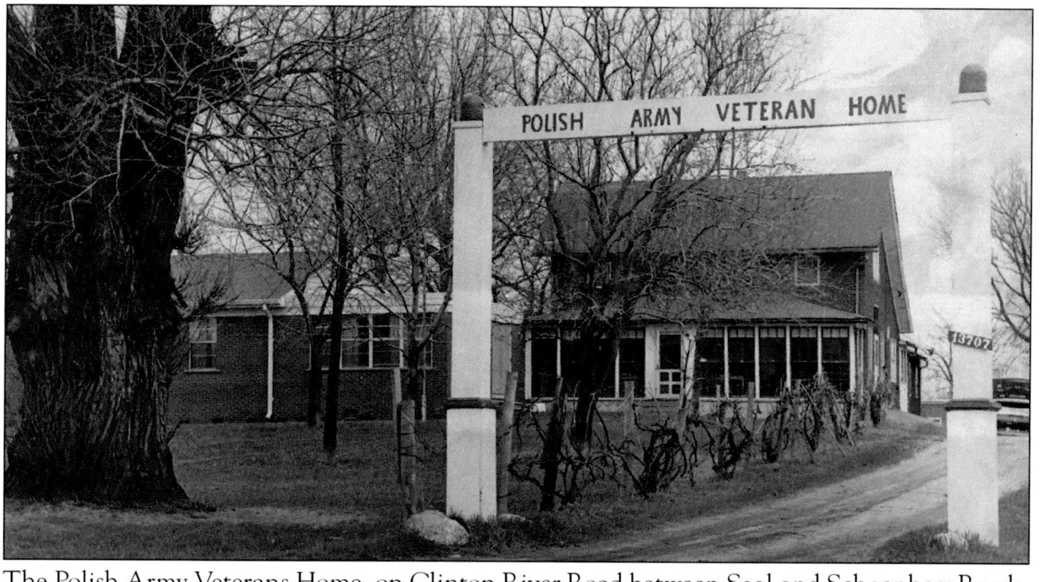

The Polish Army Veterans Home, on Clinton River Road between Saal and Schoenherr Roads, was home to many elderly and disabled seniors over the years. The 34-acre property was first purchased in 1927 from an old Polish farmer. The farmhouse, pictured, was used as the senior home. The more modern portion to the left was built in the 1950s. The farmhouse was later demolished, and eventually the nonprofit home shut down entirely.

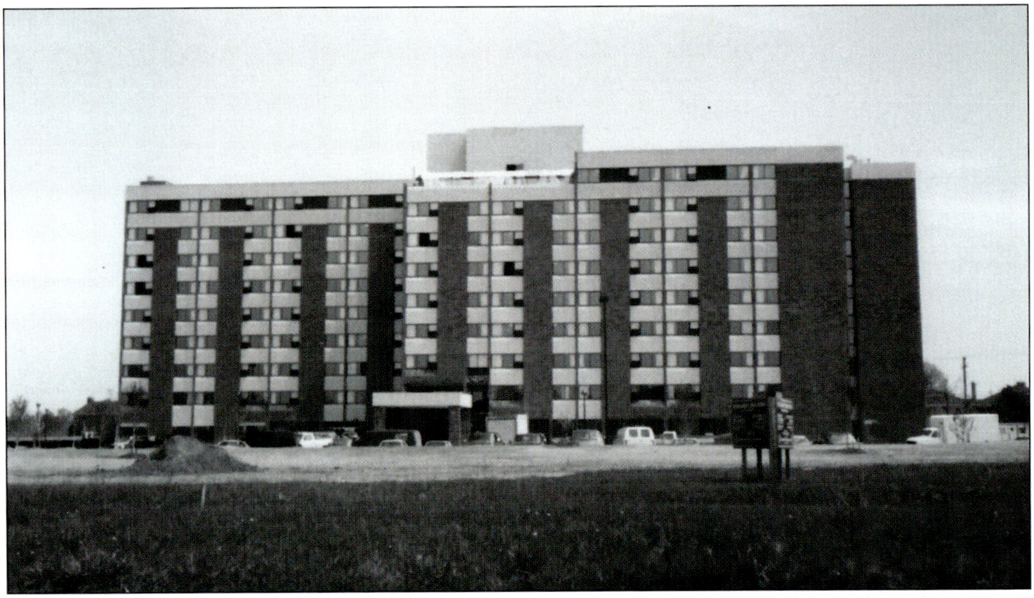

Schoenherr Towers, a city-owned residential facility built in 1985, is located on Schoenherr Road, south of Plumbrook Road. The facility rents to low-income or disabled residents. This photograph shows the building under construction.

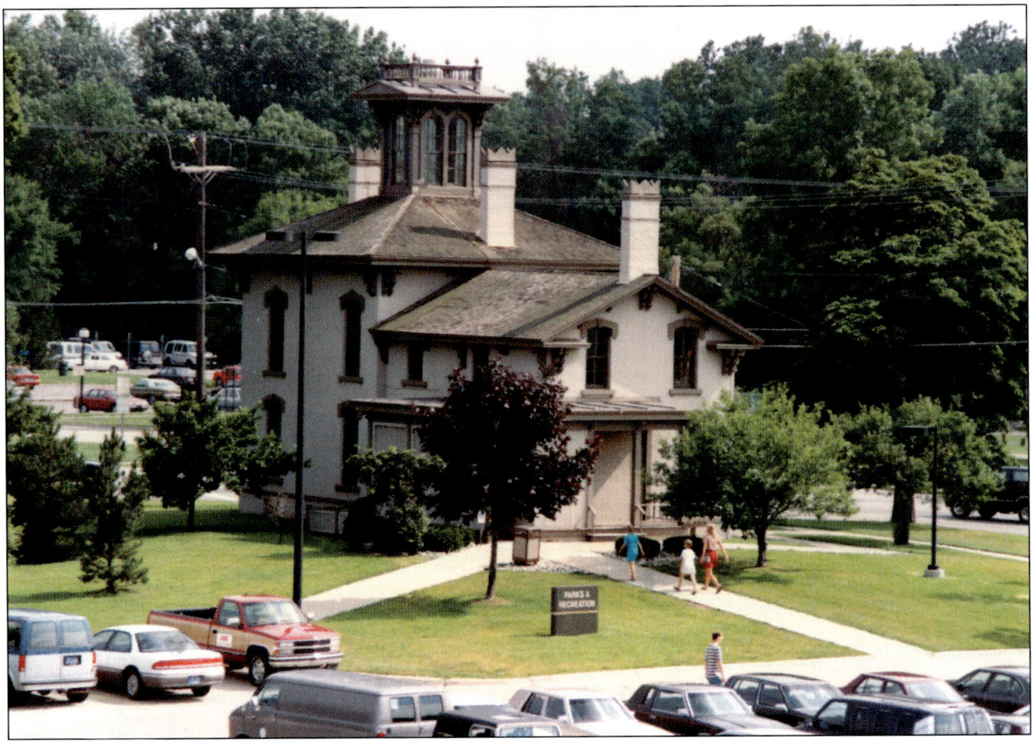

The Parks and Recreation Department offices were located in the Upton House beginning in 1978, until it got its new building. After the original restoration of the 1867 Italianate home built by prosperous farmers William and Sarah Upton, residents came to this building to register for classes and buy their discount tickets.

This rare photograph from the late 1960s of the Upton House, on the corner of Utica and Dodge Park Roads, shows the original barns that were part of the property when it was a working farm. The barn area is now part of the city hall parking lot. The house was built in 1867 and, at the time of this photograph, was being used as the Macomb Child Guidance Center. The Shell service station can also be seen in the distance at right. (Courtesy of Teresa Taylor.)

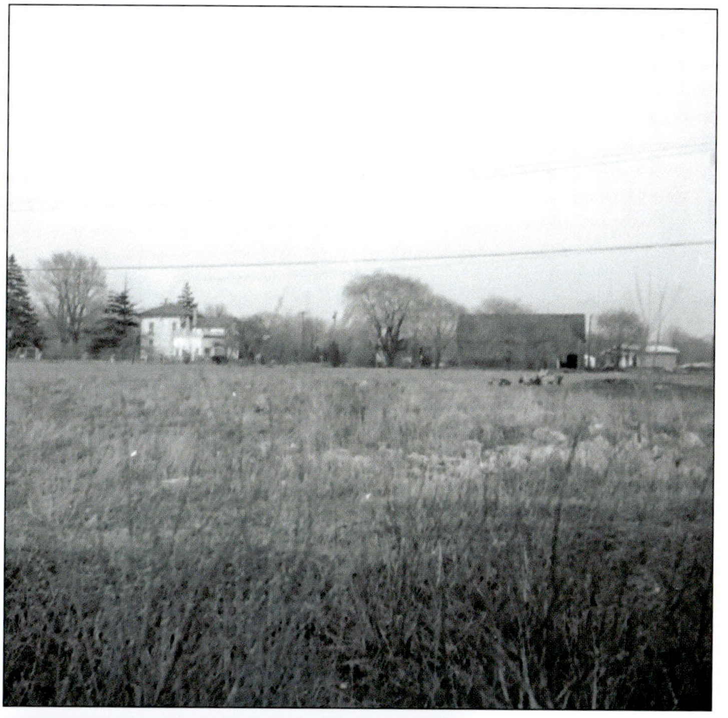

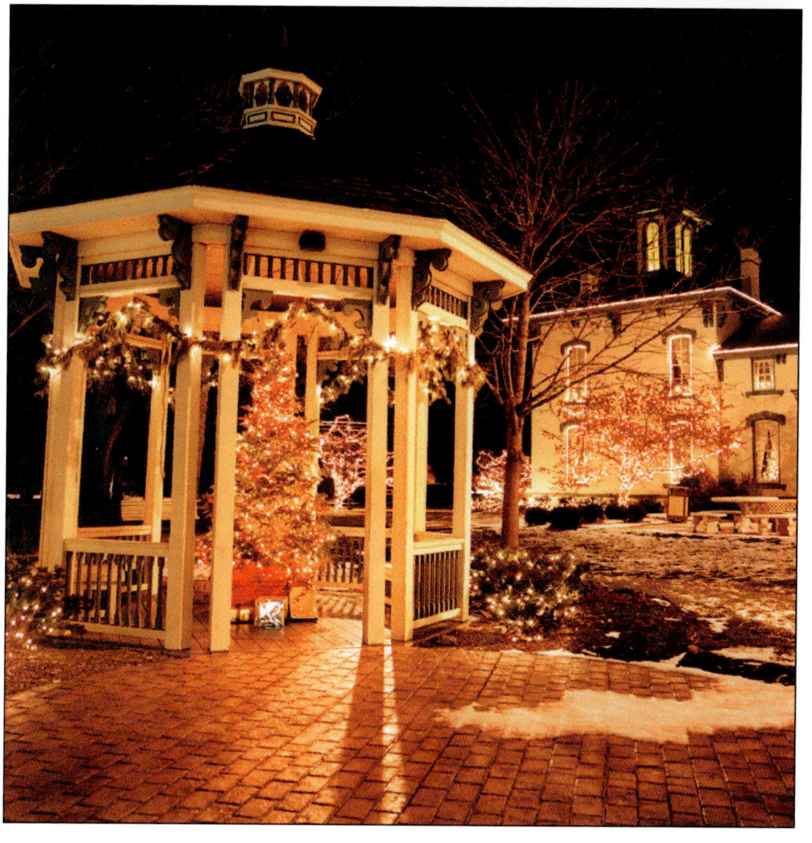

This photograph, taken during the 2003 Christmas holidays, showcases the gazebo on the grounds of the historic Upton House. The gazebo's construction was coordinated by the Sterling Heights Garden Club, using donations, and was dedicated in 1987. In spite of the controversy over it at that time (as historical renderings of the Upton House never featured a gazebo), the structure has been popular for weddings and prom pictures and a focal point for the grounds.

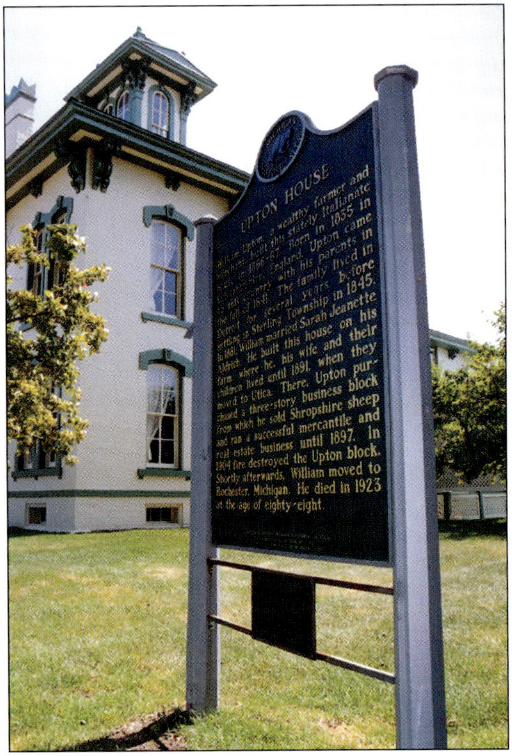

After applying to the Michigan History Division of the Michigan Department of State, the Upton House was found to qualify for this large outdoor marker signifying its status as a Michigan Historic Site in 1985. The brick home was built by William and Sarah Upton in 1867 on the corner of Utica and Dodge Park Roads. The site is also listed in the National Register of Historic Places.

Upton descendants gather at the Upton House. From left to right are Lois Ullrich, Jeanette Ullrich, Marjorie Upton DeFrancis, James Upton DeFrancis, and James's three sons William, Marcus, and James. Sisters Jeanette and Marjorie are the great-granddaughters of William and Sarah Upton, who built the landmark house. These descendants were very active in enabling the restoration of the landmark home owned by the city.

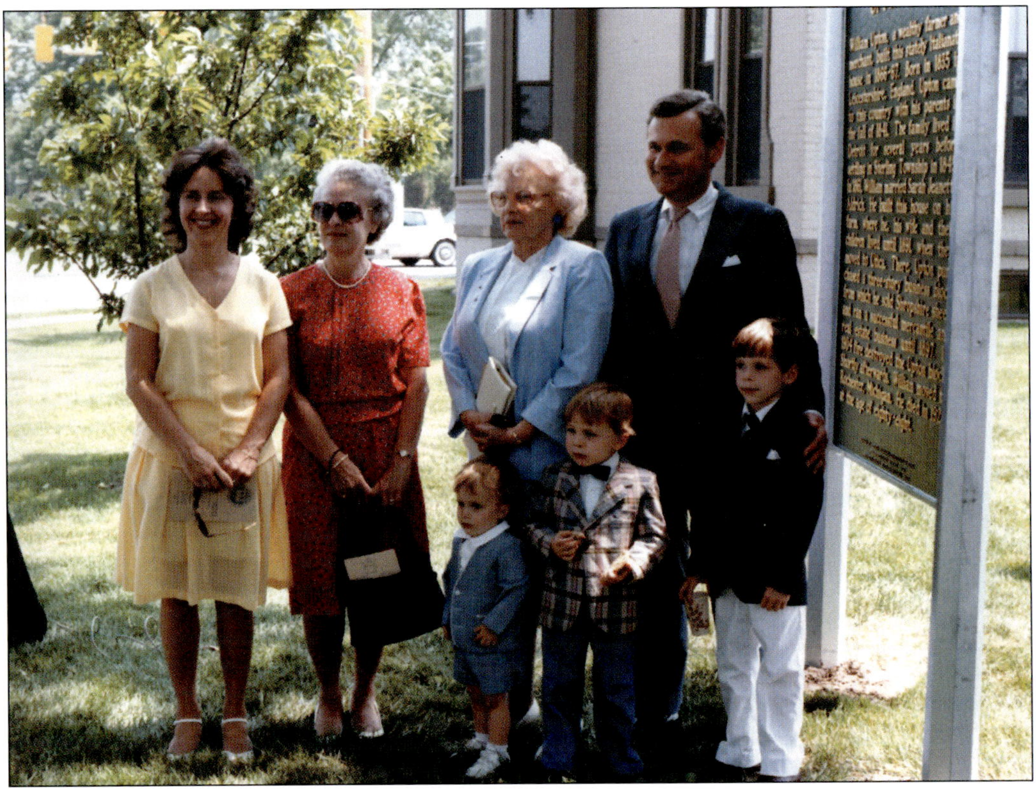

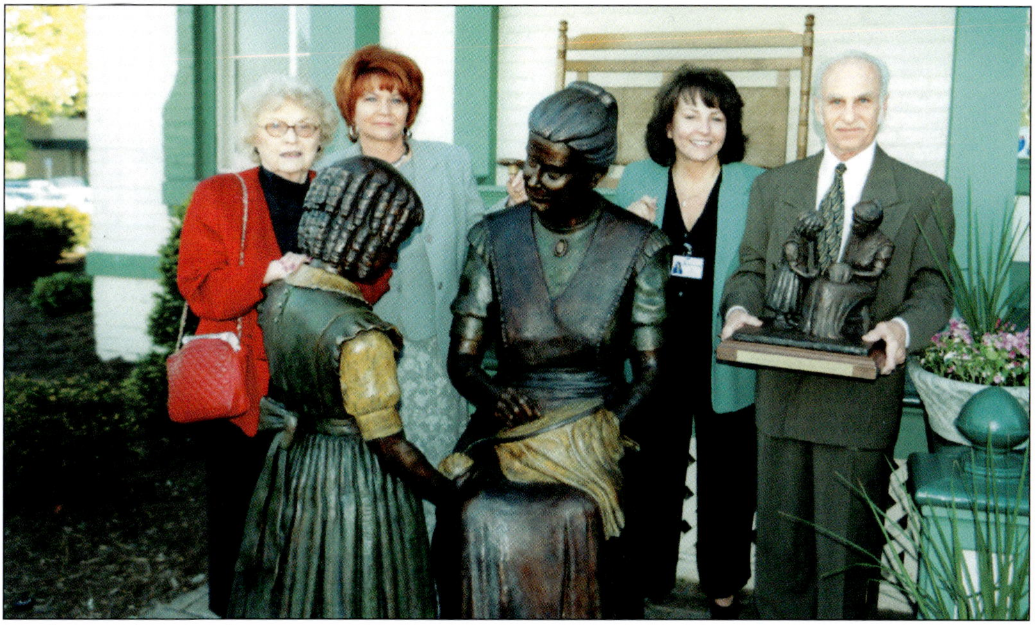

Sarah's Heirloom is the name of the bronze statue that graces the front of the Upton House. Dedicated in 2002 and created by sculptor Janice Trimpe, it portrays Sarah Upton teaching her granddaughter needlework. Pictured from left to right are Marjorie Upton DeFrancis (direct descendant of those portrayed), Janice Trimpe, Community Relations director Pat Lehman, and Mayor Richard Notte holding a miniature replica statue.

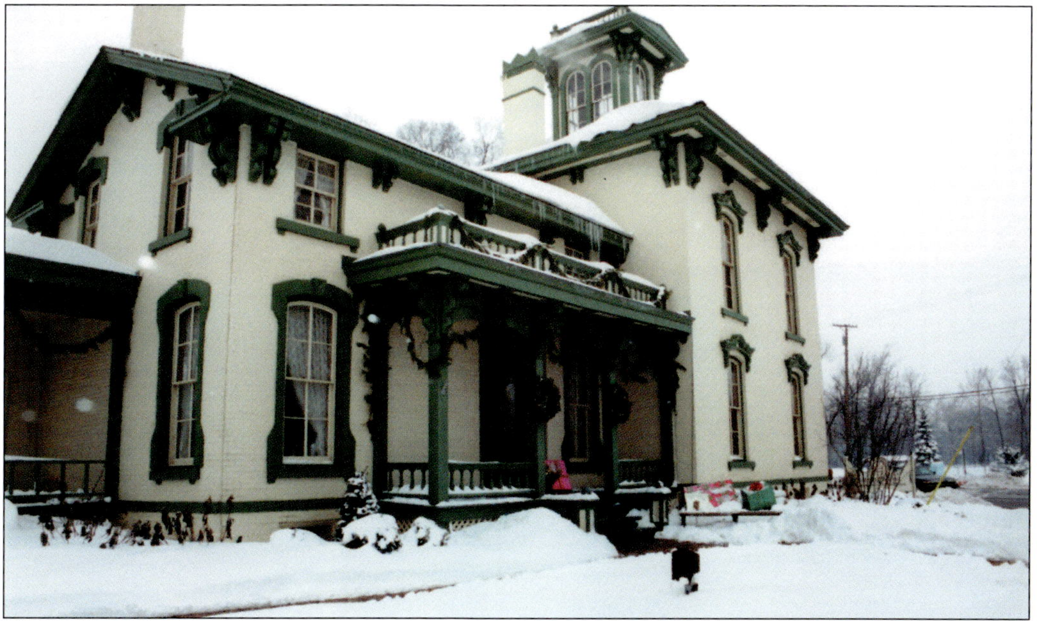

Winter snow surrounds the Upton House on the corner of Dodge Park and Utica Roads. The house always gets decorated for the holidays by the city. Many years there have been beautiful strands of lights around the windows, wreaths, and a decorated Victorian-style Christmas tree peeking out past the lace curtains. All is in preparation for the Sterling Christmas event in December, but it is a warm beacon on the corner all season.

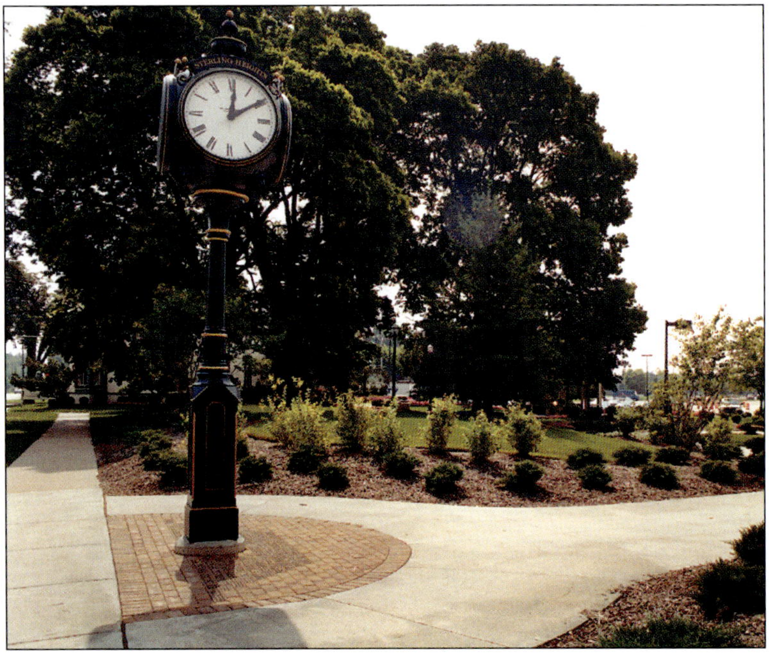

The City Center Commons clock tower is a beautiful focal point near the corner of Utica and Dodge Park Roads. Standing just northwest of the Upton House on Utica Road, the clock was part of a 2000 renovation of the City Center property, which also included the memorial brick pavers surrounding the clock, a sculpture garden, and a new memorial rock fountain in front of the expanded municipal building.

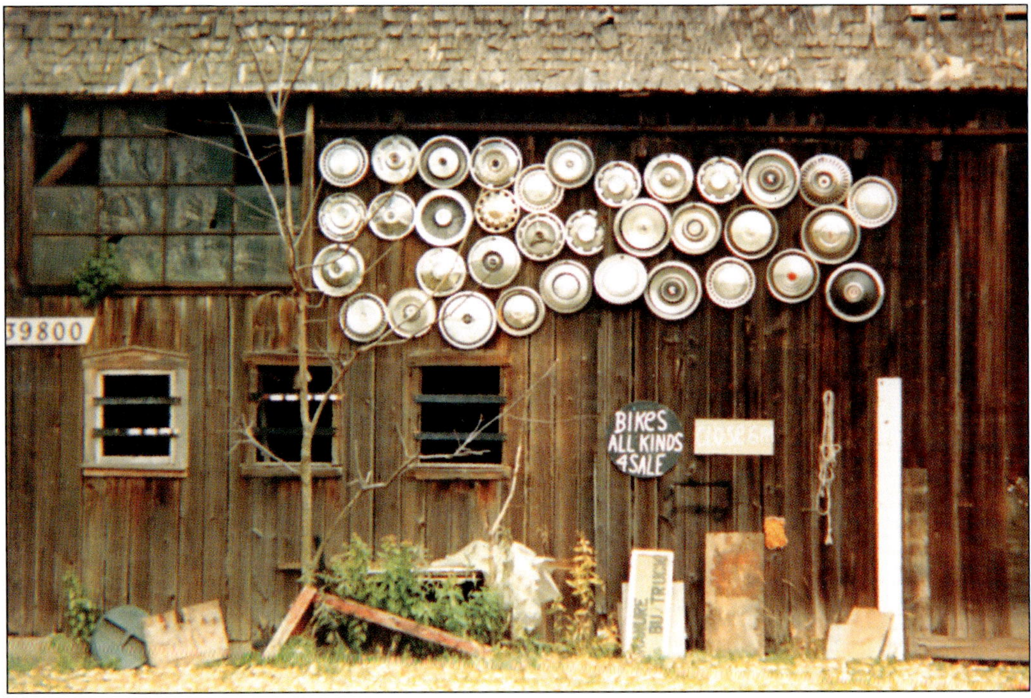

Some may remember this old barn on Utica Road, east of Dodge Park Road. There are not many barns left in the city anymore, and this one had plenty of character at the time and tried to blend the old structure with modern uses. No longer standing, its footprint is now just a grassy field. The barn may once have been part of the Ober farm over 100 years ago.

Six

Recreation

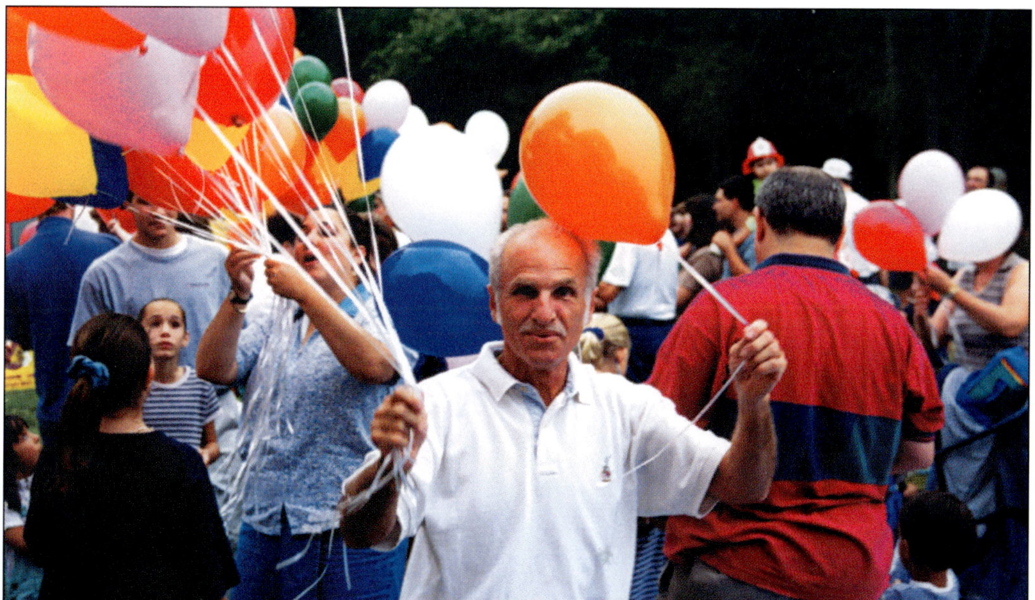

Mayor Richard Notte hands out balloons during the 1998 balloon launch event that for over 30 years was part of the annual Sterlingfest festivities. Recognizing a change in environmental sensibilities, the event began using beach balls instead of the thousands of balloons in 2014.

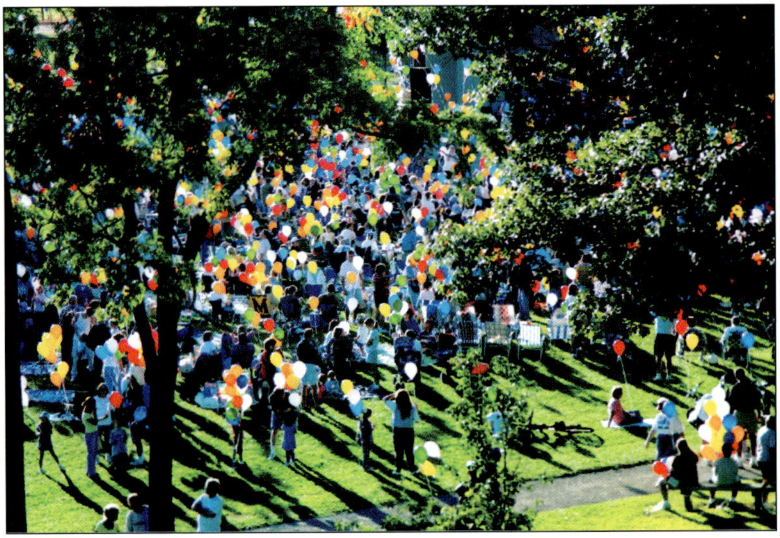

The photograph of the crowd waiting for the Sterlingfest balloon launch in the late afternoon light has the effect of colorful jewels glinting in the sun. The festival no longer does a balloon launch due to environmental concerns but offers a beach ball activity instead.

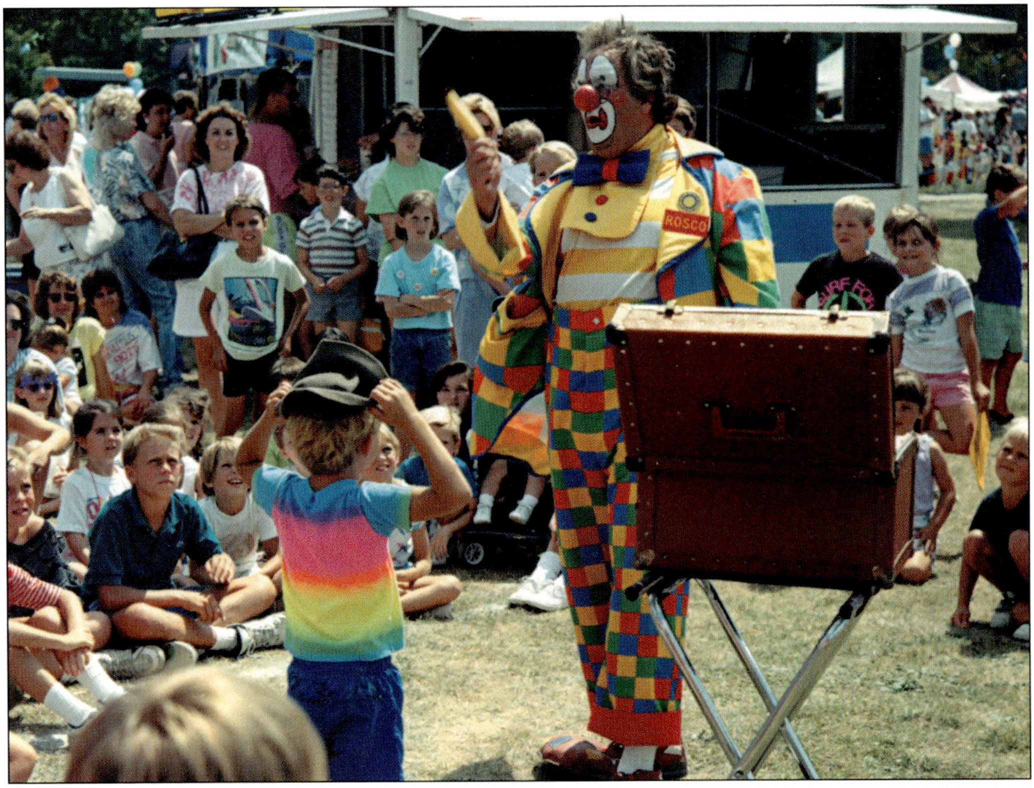

Rosco the Clown entertains both the young, and not so young, at Summerfest/Sterlingfest, probably sometime in the 1990s. Rosco, often known as Ross Champion, has been a fixture at many city events over the years. A native of Mount Clemens, he started his clowning career in 1979, becoming an institution at parties, events, festivals, and libraries, while still finding time to be vital to community service organizations in the area.

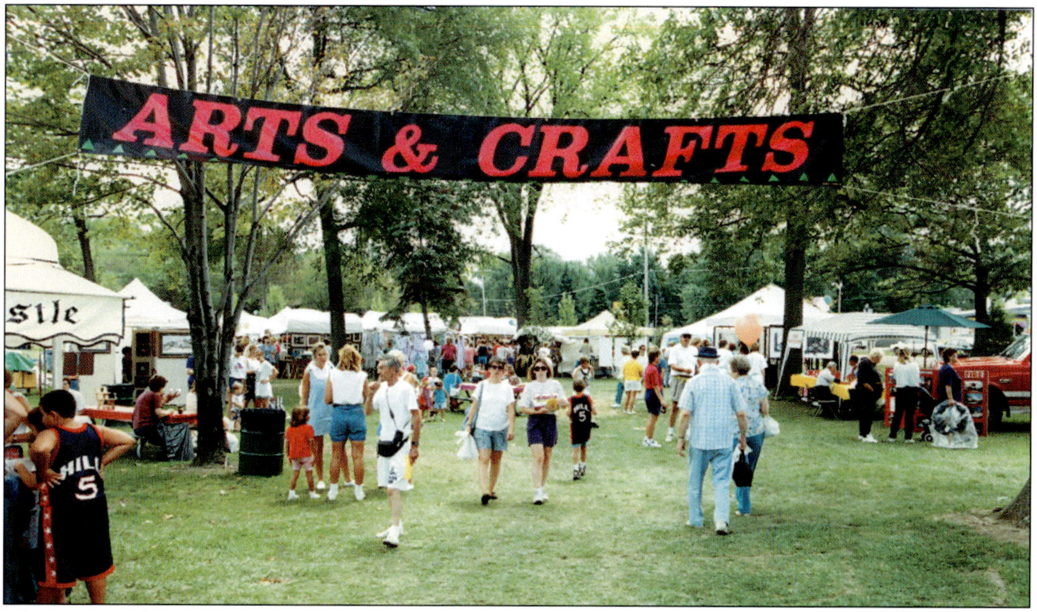

The arts and crafts area of Summerfest/Sterlingfest was originally located under the trees in Dodge Park, just south of where the current music stage is today. In later years, the art fair booths were moved across the street into the parking lot area in front of the municipal buildings. This created room for the amusement rides, additional stages, and an expanded restaurant row. The photograph may have been taken in the 1990s.

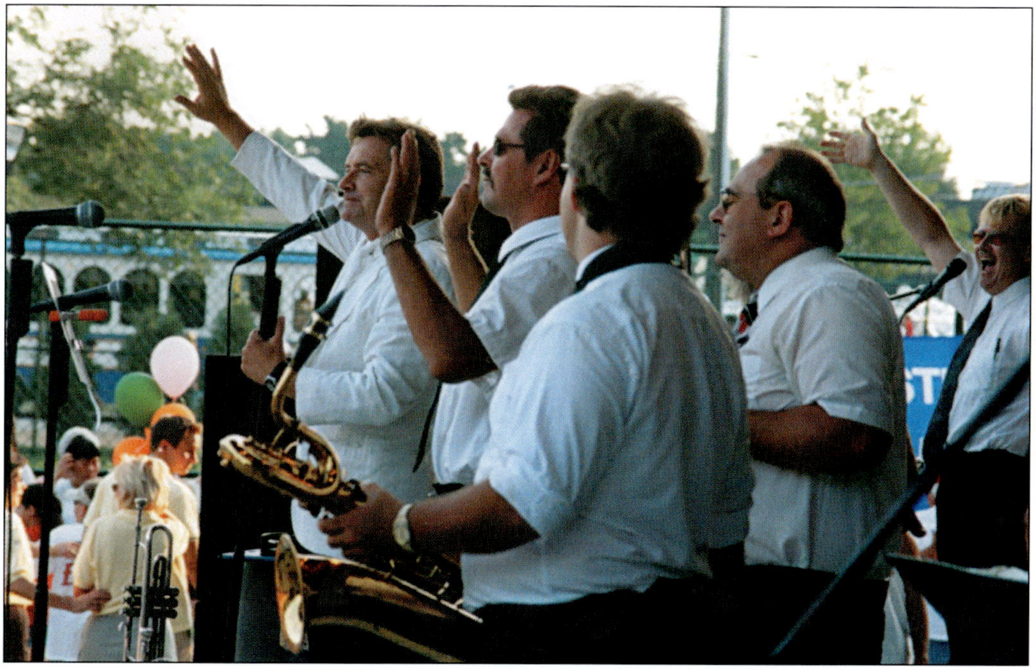
Steve King and the Dittilies began performing their fun and much looked forward to show as part of Summerfest/Sterlingfest in 1984. Featuring hits from the 1950s and 1960s, they were often paired with the popular balloon release/beach ball night. In more recent years, they have appeared as part of the Music in the Park series.

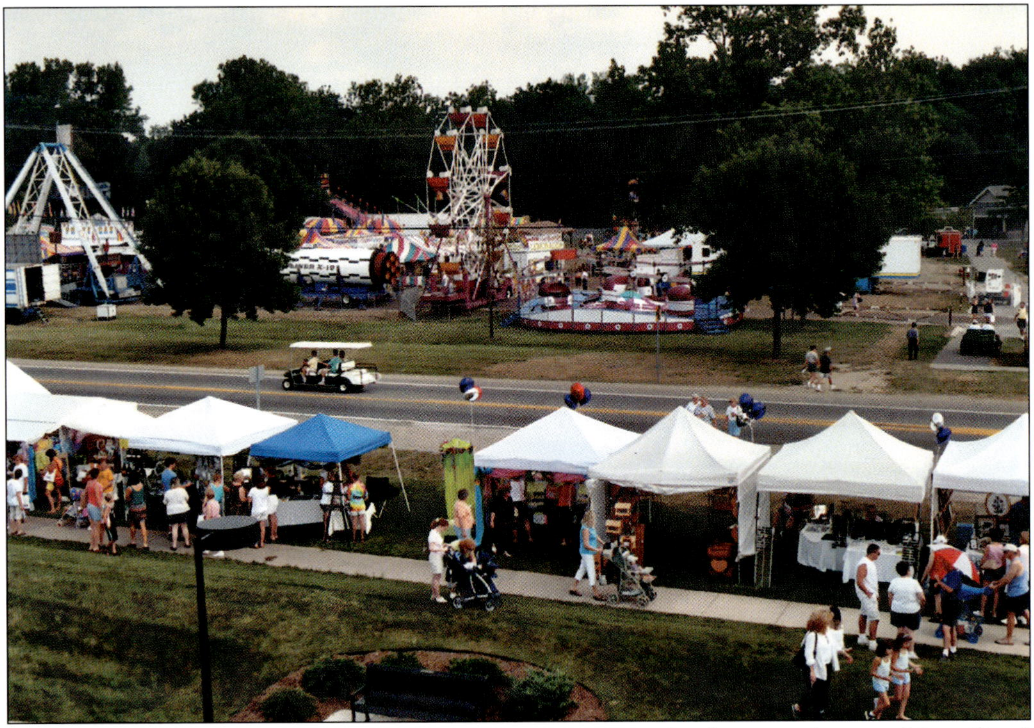

Looking north across Utica Road into Dodge Park at Sterlingfest 2003, a few of the art fair booths and the family midway can be seen. There is something for everyone. The early years of the fair did not have carnival rides.

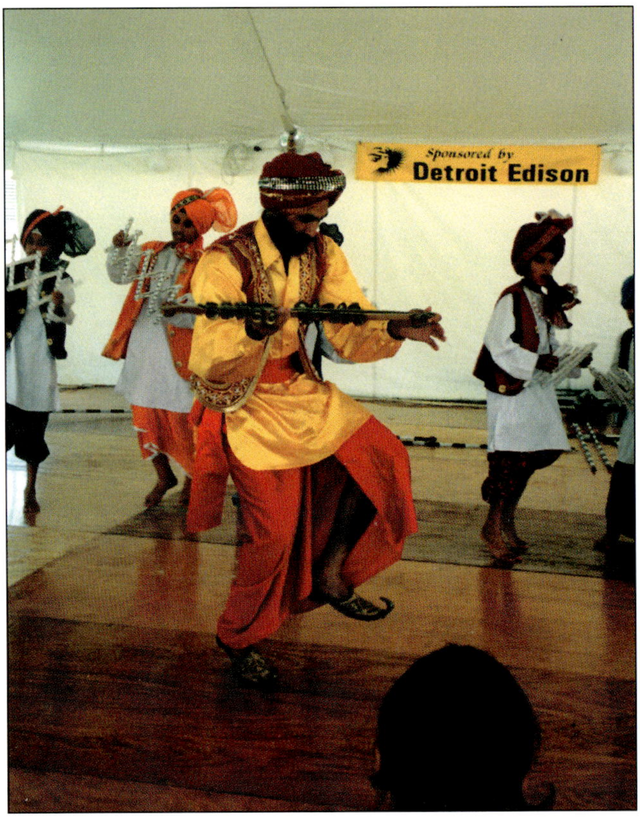

A performance by an Indian dance group colorfully entertains at Sterlingfest. Multicultural awareness has become a central point in the city of Sterling Heights as groups from many parts of the world move here and try to assimilate while maintaining their ethnic heritages and traditions. The annual Cultural Exchange event is another opportunity to educate residents and expose the community to the cultures of others.

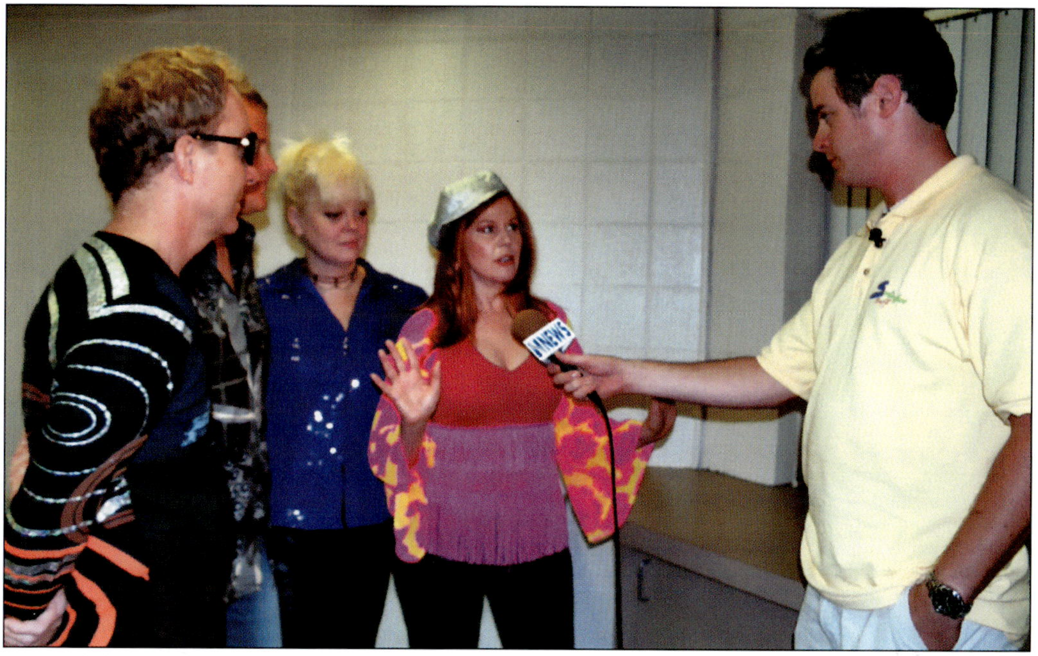

Matt Phillips, SHTV employee and Michigan Emmy nominee, is seen interviewing the B-52s before their performance at Sterlingfest 2003 for a news report to be seen on the city's cable channel. The Community Relations staff is also responsible for meeting the contractual needs of the talent brought in. The band required vegan food, not so easily obtained in 2003 Sterling Heights, creating interesting memories for the staff.

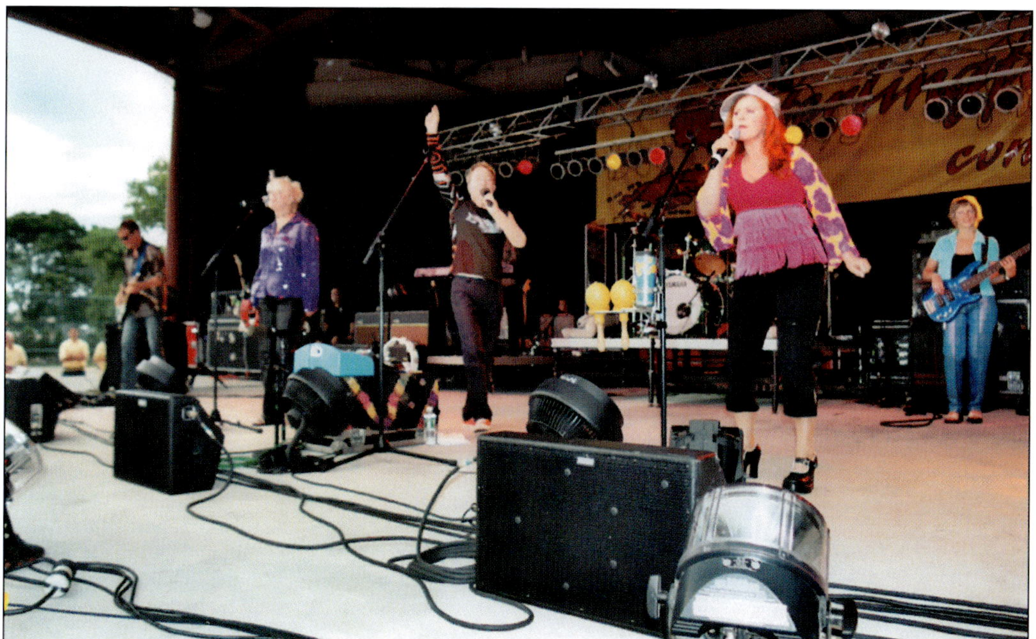

The B-52s perform at the Sterlingfest band shell in 2003. The crowd had a great time, as the music drifted through the summer air in Dodge Park, families picnicked, old friends reunited, children drank their fresh lemonade, and some adults enjoyed the beer tent.

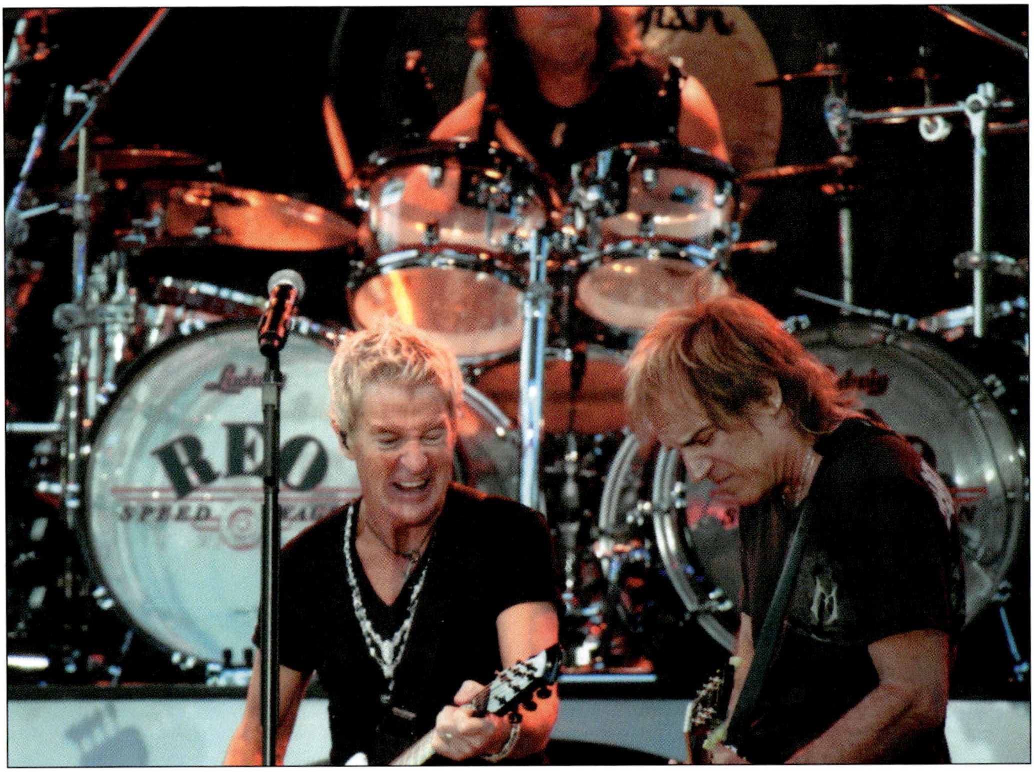

For the city's 40th anniversary in 2008, the city brought in REO Speedwagon for the main Saturday night free concert at Sterlingfest. It is estimated that close to 18,000 people turned out to enjoy the fun and excitement of the performance on a beautiful summer evening at the Dodge Park band shell. The concerts are funded mostly by corporate donations.

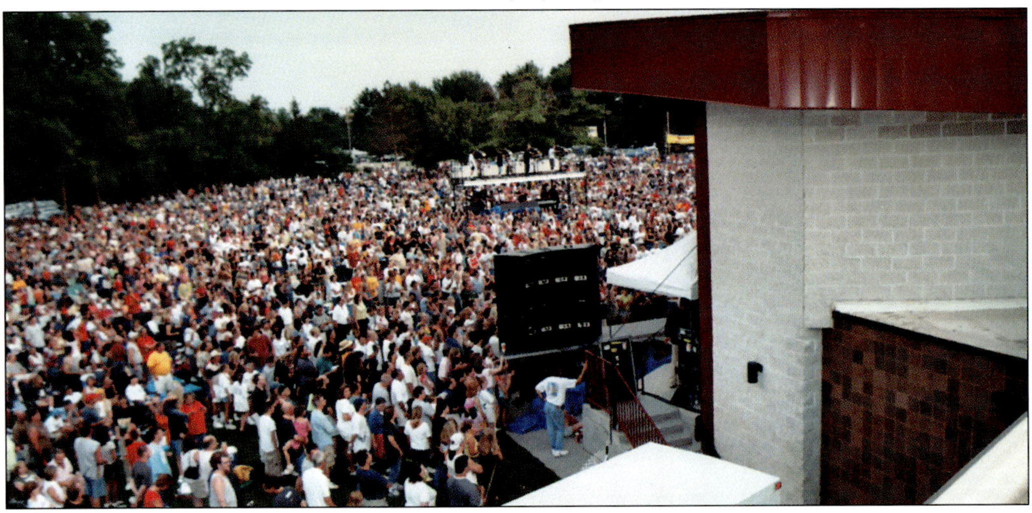

A crowd waits, probably for the main act, at the Sterlingfest band shell. Thousands of people often attend the Saturday night performance of the three-day event. Depending on the year's budget, there could be a big name band, like REO Speedwagon, Rick Springfield, the B-52s, or K.C. and the Sunshine Band. Some years, tribute bands entertain the crowds for an evening of excitement, music, and community. It is always a free event.

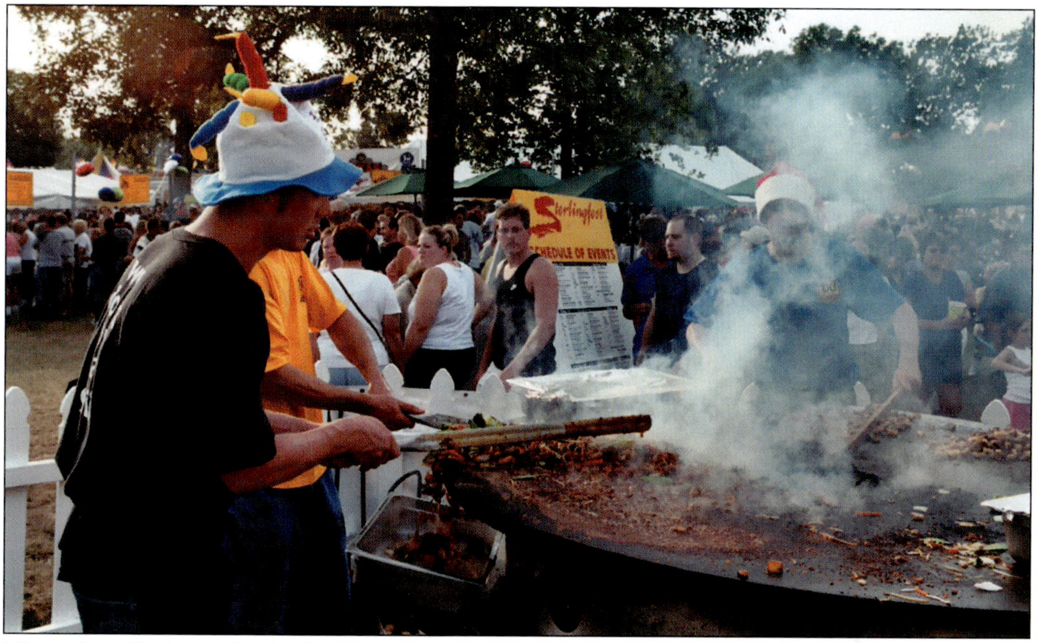

Mongolian Barbecue had a food booth at Sterlingfest Restaurant Row, entertaining diners with their chopping, cooking, and jokes, not to mention the hats. The chain restaurant opened a location on Hall and Schoenherr Roads in 2000 in the former Montgomery Ward tire store building.

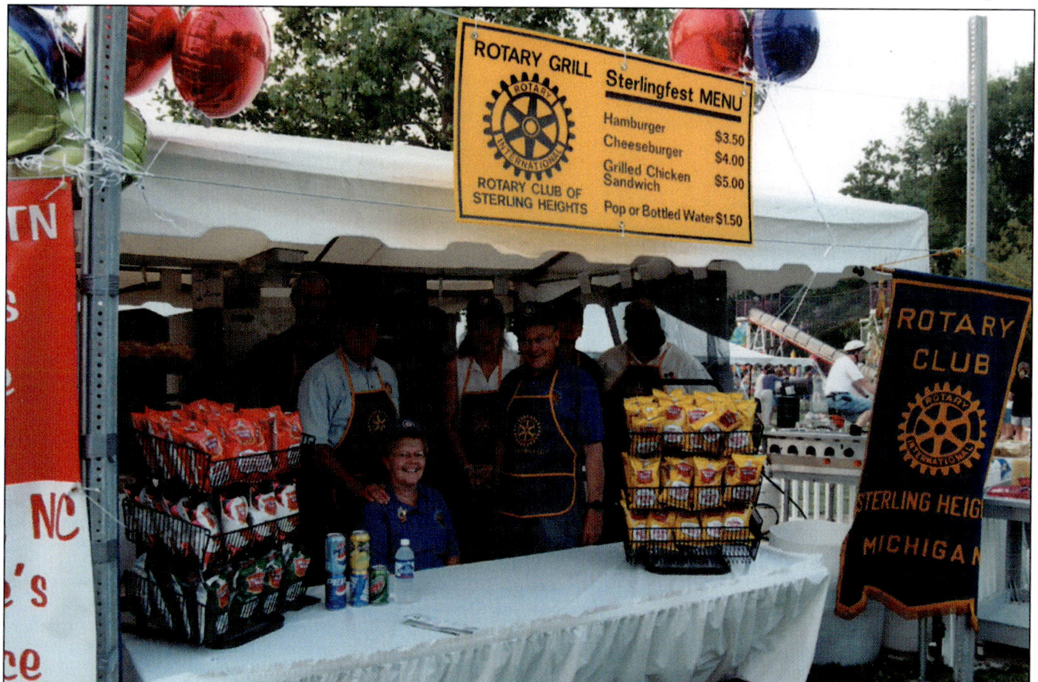

The Sterling Heights Rotary Club mans its booth at Sterlingfest Restaurant Row. Restaurant Row has been a popular area for families to grab a bite during their time spent at the fair, with many options to choose from. A number of popular area eateries, as well as community service groups, have booths every year. It is a nice opportunity for the community to try out some fare at the fair!

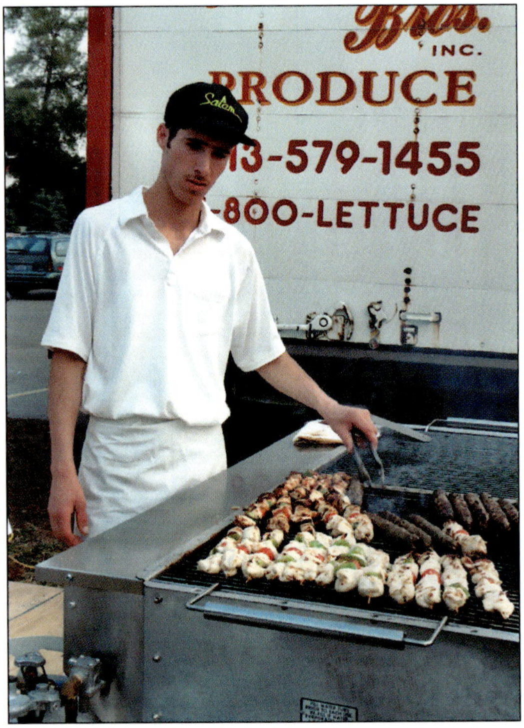

The shish kebabs on the grill at Sterlingfest Restaurant Row must have smelled delicious. Middle Eastern food has become very popular and common in the city as the influx of new residents emigrating from those areas increases. The restaurant hosting this booth is unidentified.

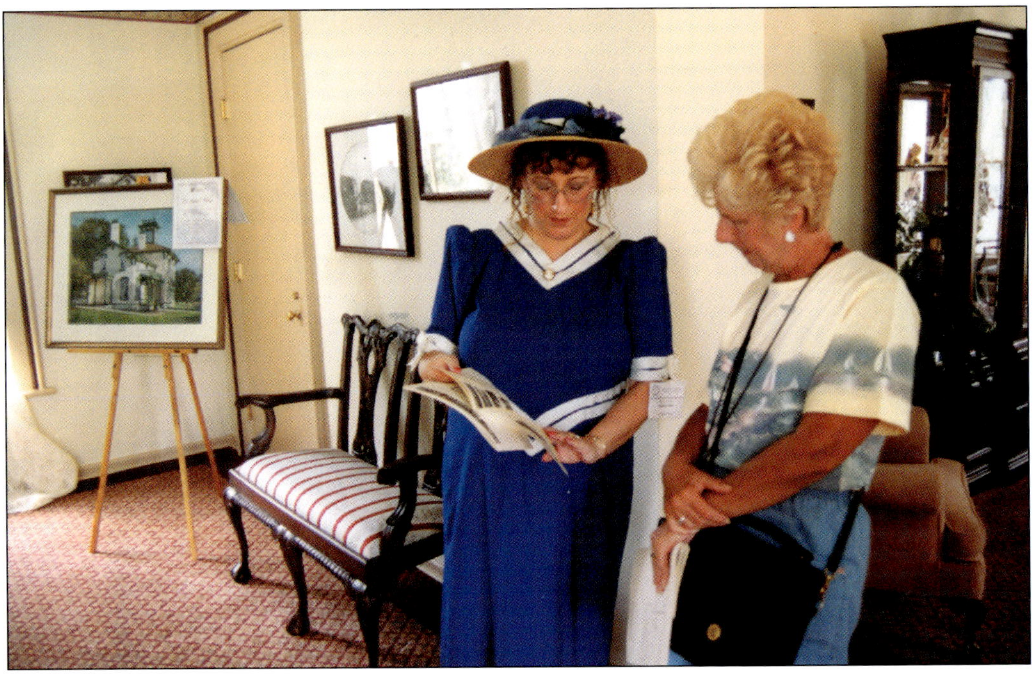

Upon completion of the interior restoration of the Upton House, tours started being offered during special events, such as Sterlingfest, Sterling Christmas, and by special request. In this photograph, probably from the early 1980s, Diana Grabowski Heldt shows a visitor some informational material while dressed in period costume. Heldt's in-laws actually owned and lived in the home during the early 1900s.

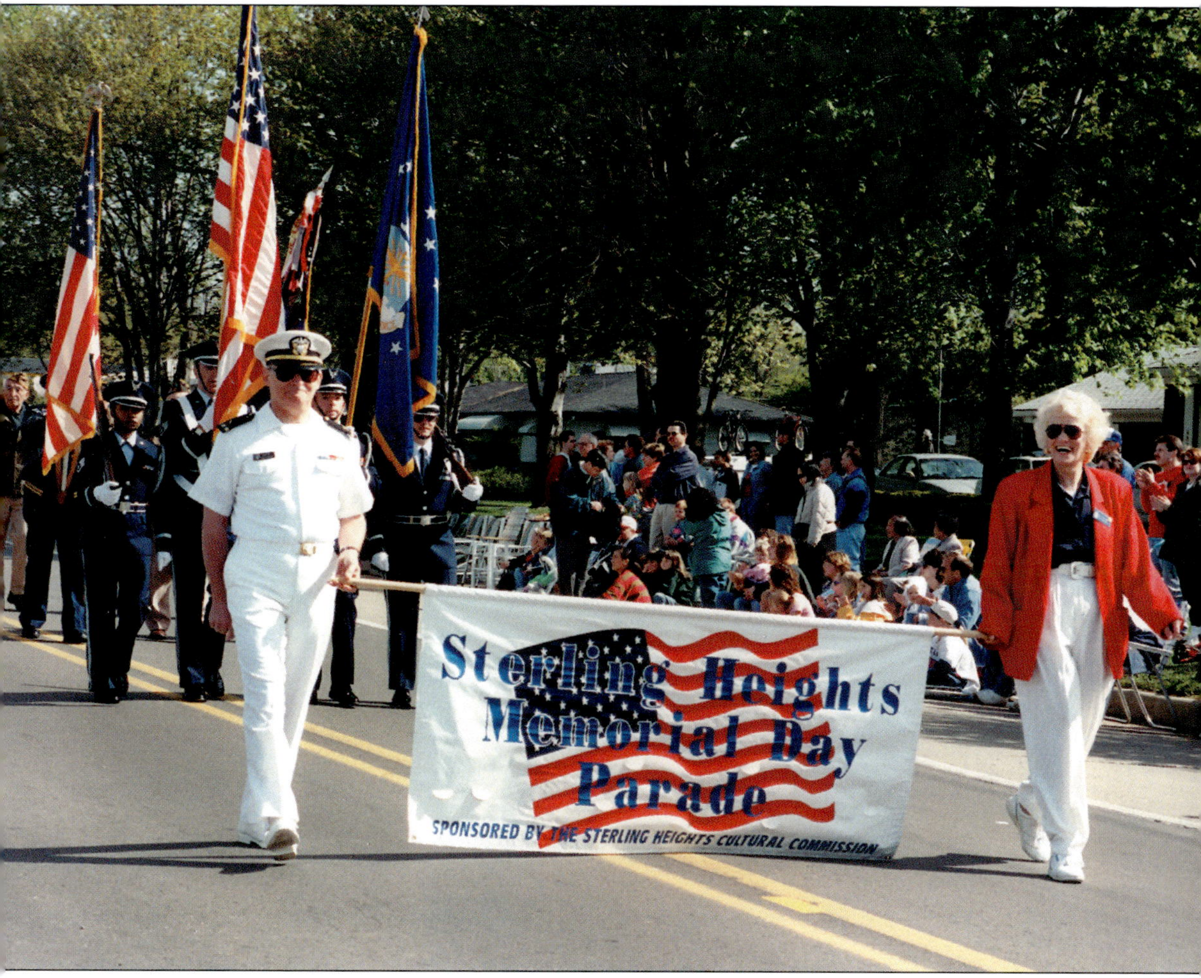

The annual Sterling Heights Memorial Day Parade premiered in 1980, spurred by Councilwoman Nancy Ulrich and run by a committee of four residents. The parades feature marching bands, floats, clowns, city officials, fire trucks, and Scouts. The original route started at Heritage Junior High, at 16 Mile Road, and went north on Dodge Park Road to the city center. The year 1989 brought a reversal in the route, and in 1990, the parade controversially became an official city function. The banner is carried by longtime Sterling Heights Cultural Commission chairperson Sharon Arend.

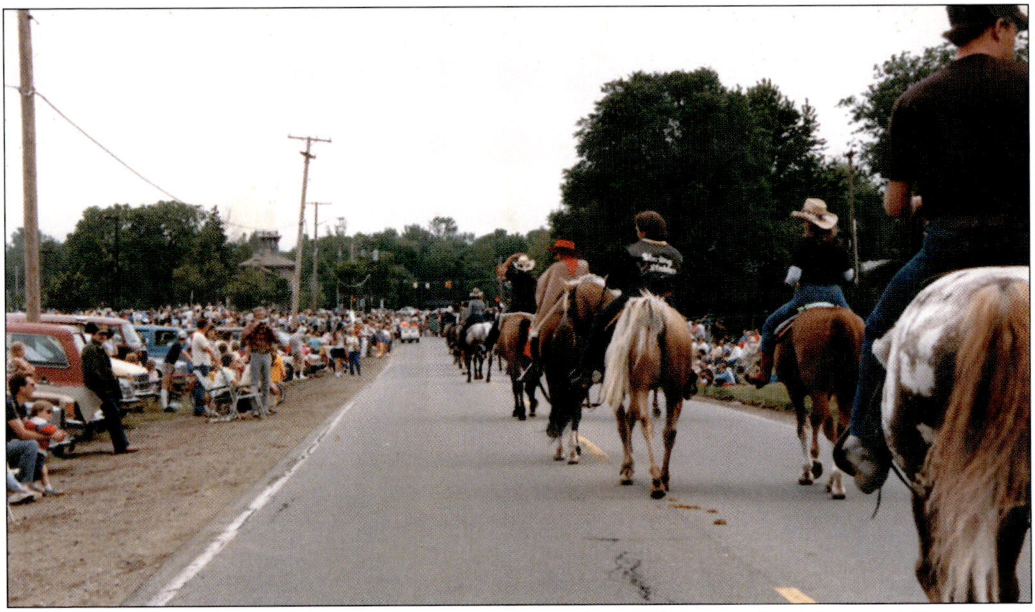

Horses and riders from Sterling Stables participate in the Sterling Heights Memorial Day Parade sometime around the 1980s, making their way north up Dodge Park Road toward Utica Road. Huge crowds line the approximately two-mile route, which features the City Center complex and the stately Upton House at left. (Courtesy of Alan and Linda Haggerty of Sterling Stables.)

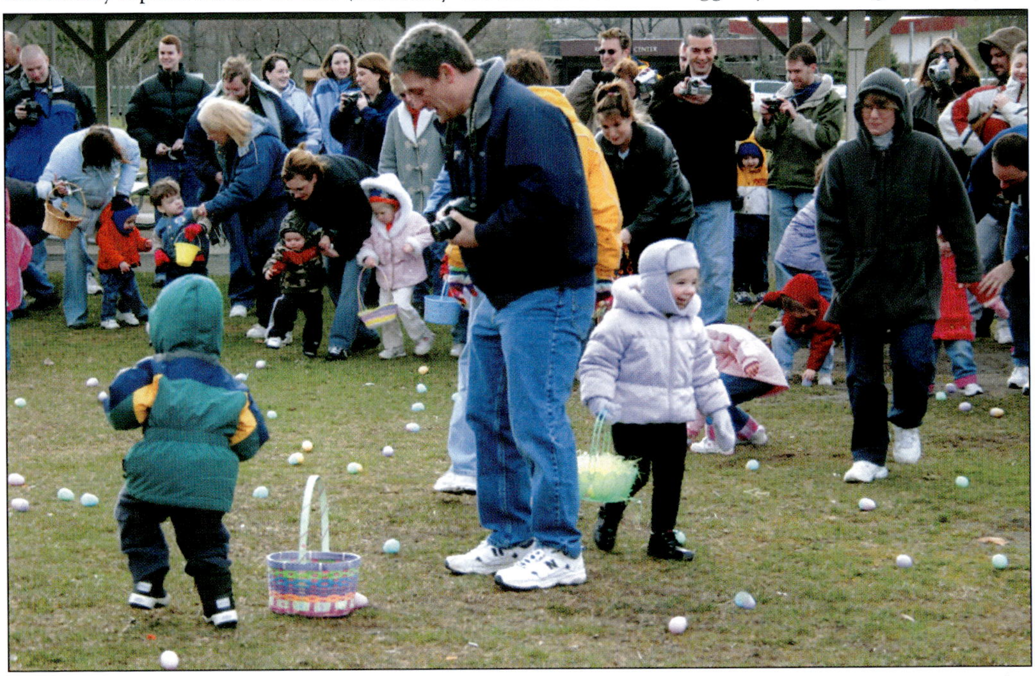

The city's Parks and Recreation Department hosted its first Easter egg hunt in 1974 in Dodge Park. The event has been held every year since then, sometimes drawing as many as 1,200 kids, parents, and grandparents. Around 5,000 candy-filled plastic eggs, and even some hard-boiled eggs in the early years, are the treasured prizes. A visit with the Easter Bunny often topped off this fun, but often chilly, day for area families.

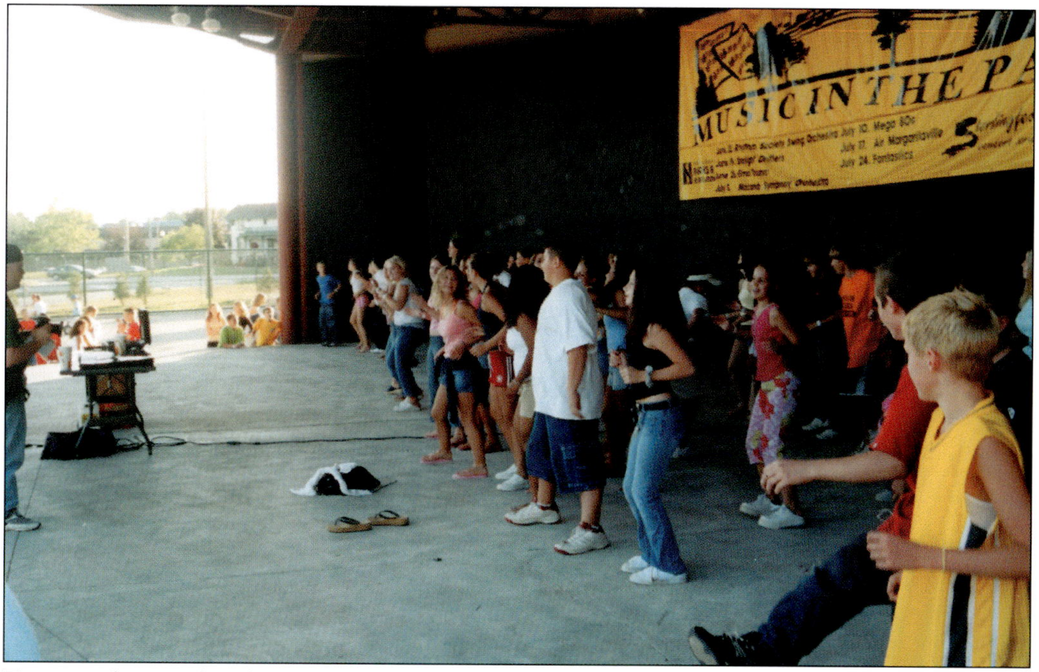

Teens are having fun dancing on the stage of the Dodge Park band shell, probably sometime in the early 2000s. The Parks and Recreation Department has offered events for teens, and this may have been part of Teenfest, which also included many other activities, such as a rock climbing wall and other games.

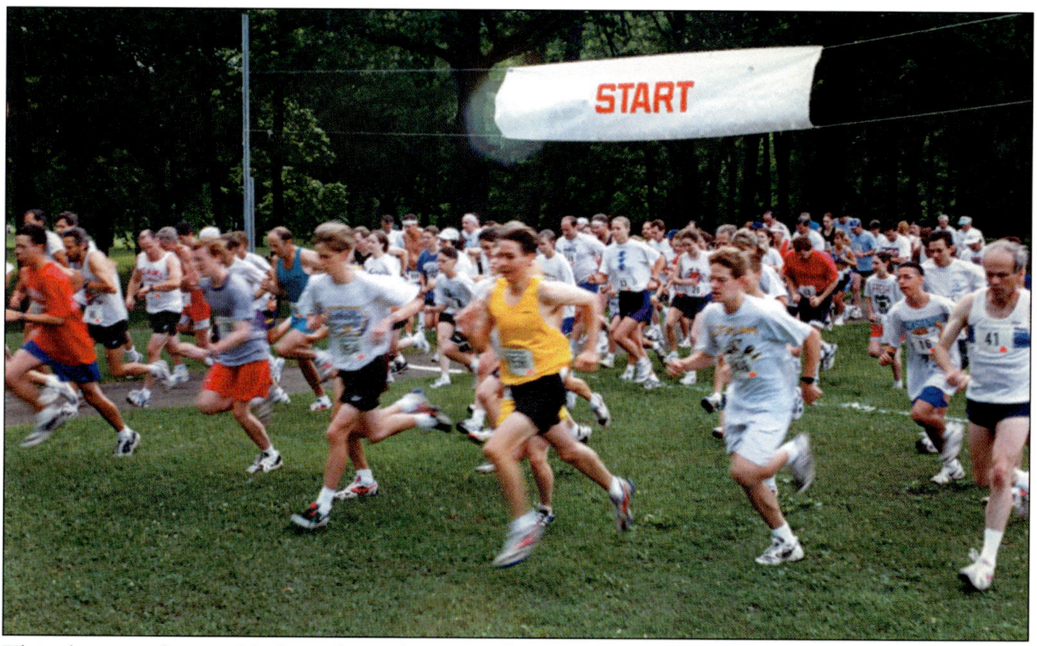

This photograph, possibly from the early 2000s, shows the Dodge Park Three Mile Run. The annual race, organized by the Parks and Recreation Department, was first held in 1977 and consisted of two laps around Dodge Park. Hundreds of runners from all over the state competed and were in divisions based on age and gender.

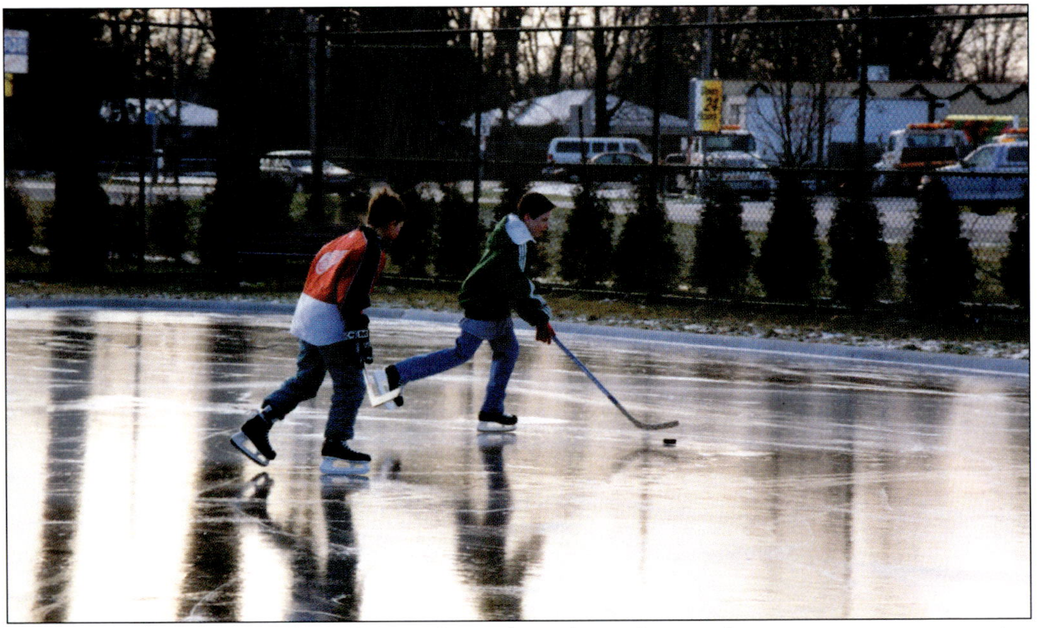

Wintertime ice skating on the rink in Dodge Park can be a relaxing afternoon activity, or a rousing pickup game of hockey might be more someone's taste. The Parks and Recreation Department has offered a groomed ice rink for years, and soon there will a new covered area for skating outdoors when the new facility is built in the park. This photograph also shows a longtime party store in the background, for which there are plans for demolition.

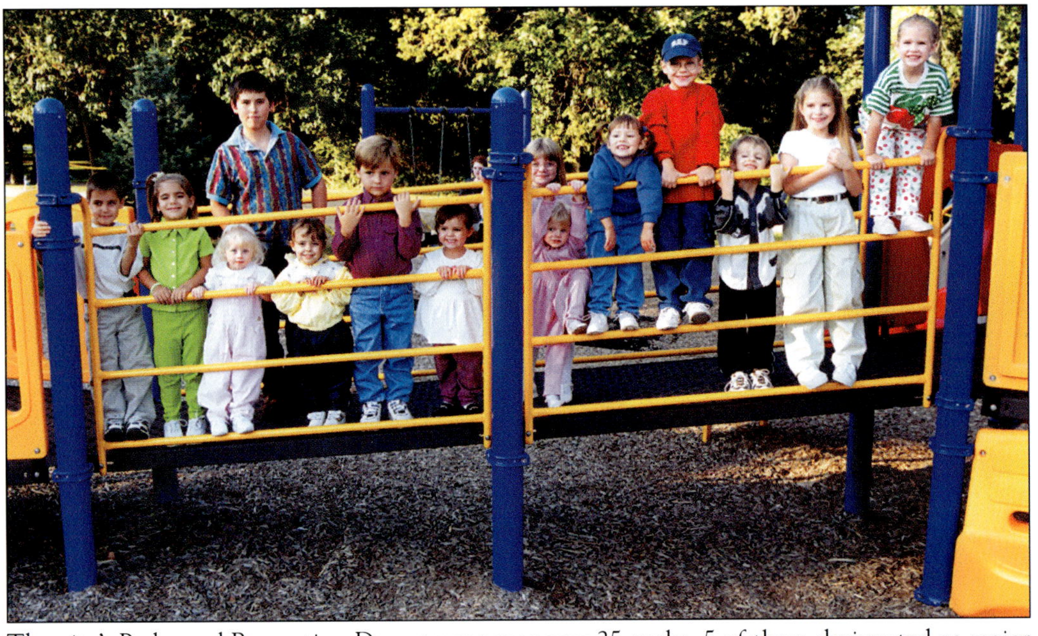

The city's Parks and Recreation Department manages 25 parks, 5 of them designated as major parks. Neighborhood parks and their proximity to everyone has always been one of the shining characteristics of the city, well thought out and provided by a partnership of city officials and subdivision developers from the early days. Almost all have play structures. This 2001 photograph may have been taken in Nelson Park.

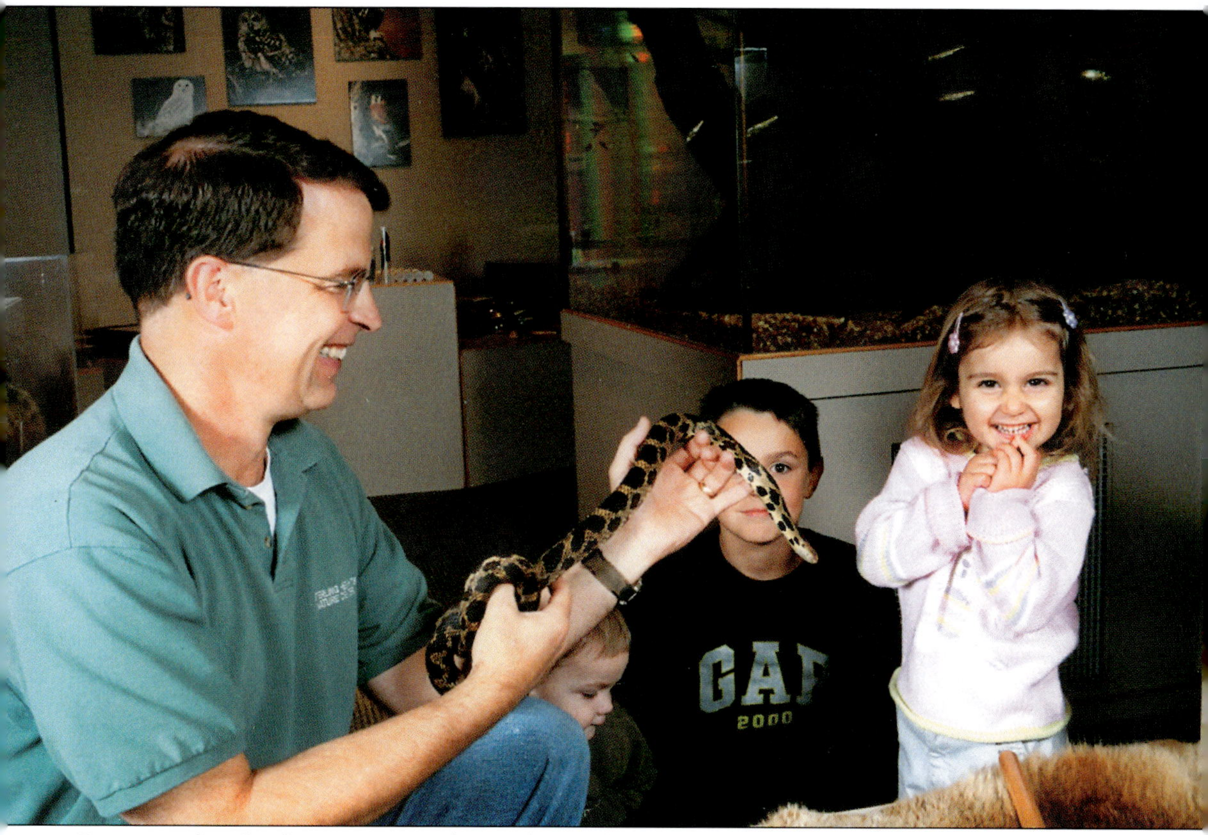

City naturalist Gordon Lonie introduces a live snake to some young visitors at the Nature Center. Lonie was director of the center from 1982, when it opened, until his retirement in 2009. Lonie's knowledge, dedication, and sense of humor made him a favorite of visitors. The center was enlarged in 2002 and now features a small auditorium for nature movie showings, an aquarium, taxidermy displays, and a glass atrium. Located on Utica Road, just east of Van Dyke Avenue, the Nature Center focuses on animals native to Michigan, the Clinton River, and this area.

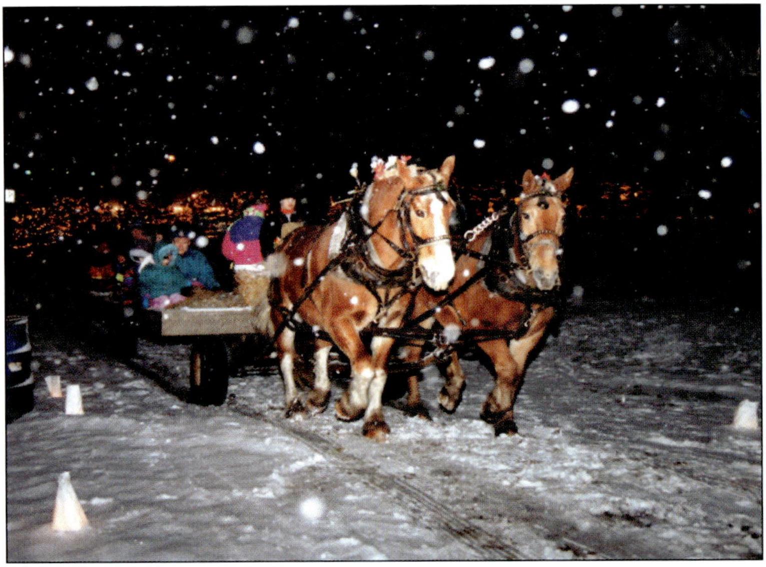

A horse-drawn wagon ride was part of the fun at a Sterling Christmas event, probably in the 1990s. These family favorite annual events hosted by the Parks and Recreation Department began with tree lightings in the township days and have grown to add visits from Santa, caroling, wagon rides, petting farms, hot chocolate, Upton House tours, and more.

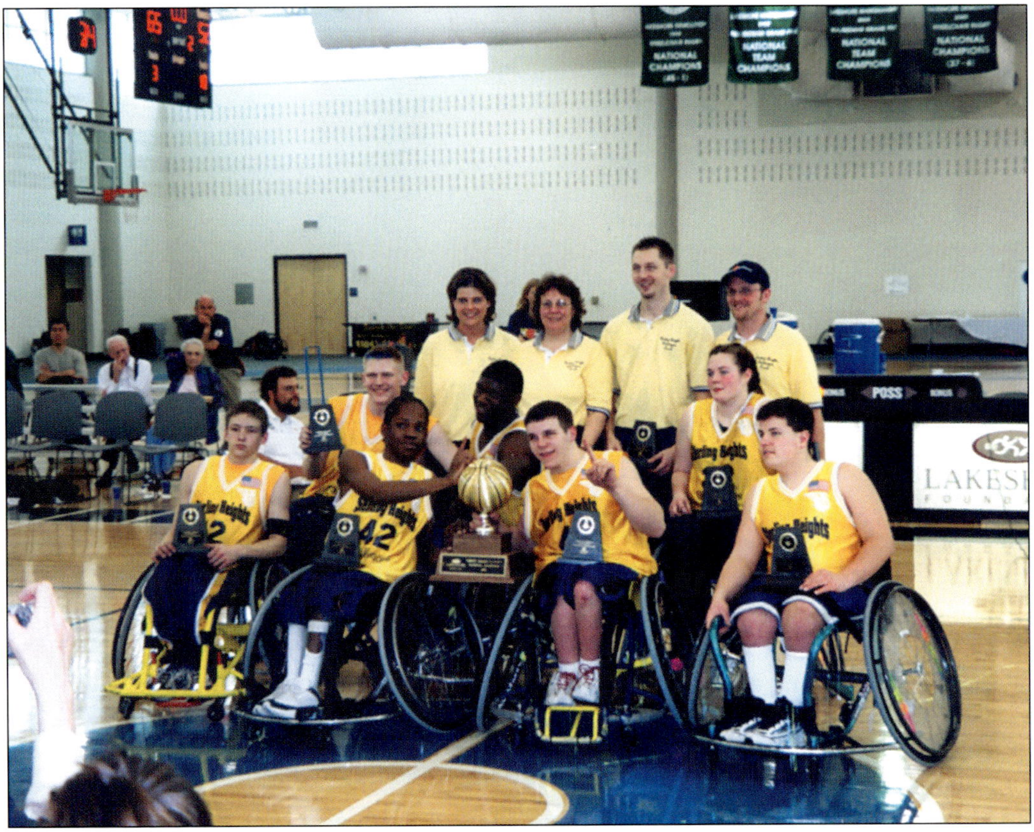

When Sterling Heights began their Special Recreation Program in 1981, it was the first full-scale program for the mentally and physically disabled that existed in Macomb County. The program offered enrichment classes, wheelchair basketball, soccer, gymnastics, social meetings, and other activities for people with special needs. This photograph shows Diane Winterstein, Special Recreation Program supervisor, with her winning wheelchair basketball team.

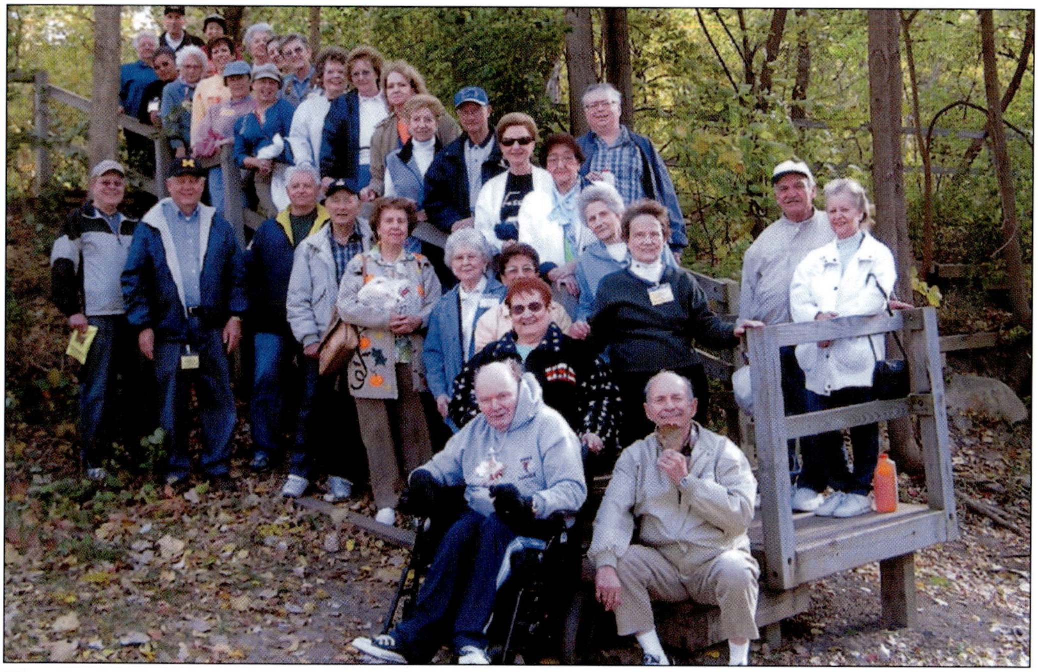

This group of seniors participated in a Walking Club through the Sterling Heights Senior Center. The center has offered senior citizens of the area a myriad of activities to be entertained and to stay active. This outing may have been at one of the city parks, or it may have been a bus outing to somewhere a little farther away on a beautiful autumn day.

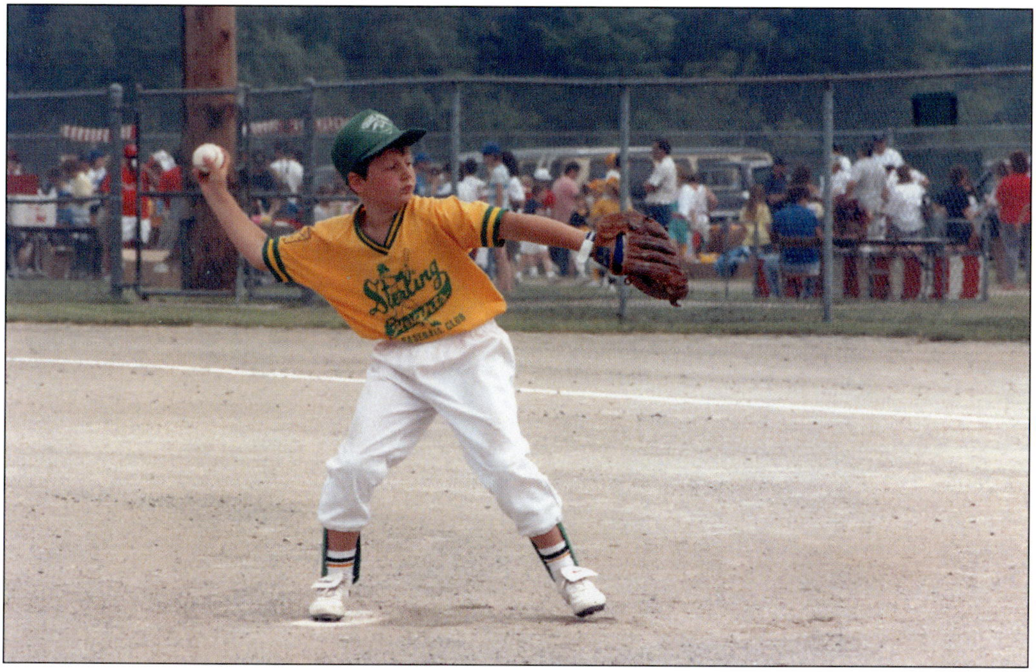

A boy pitches to an unseen batter during a game on an opening day of the Sterling Heights Baseball Club. The club, run by parents and assisted by the Sterling Heights Parks and Recreation Department, has been a mainstay for many years. This game is at Baumgartner Park.

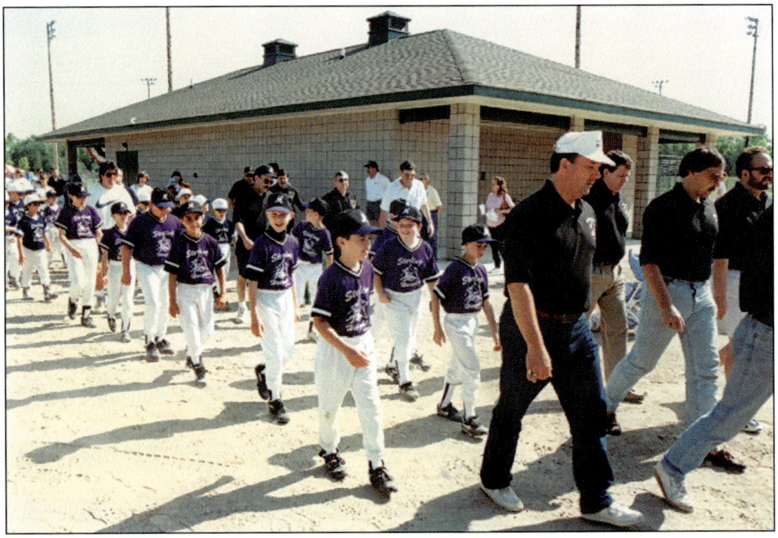

Opening day 1996 was held at Delia Park, and excitement is in the air. The Sterling Heights Baseball Club teams and coaches parade out for the day's festivities. These events usually include members of city council and the mayor in attendance.

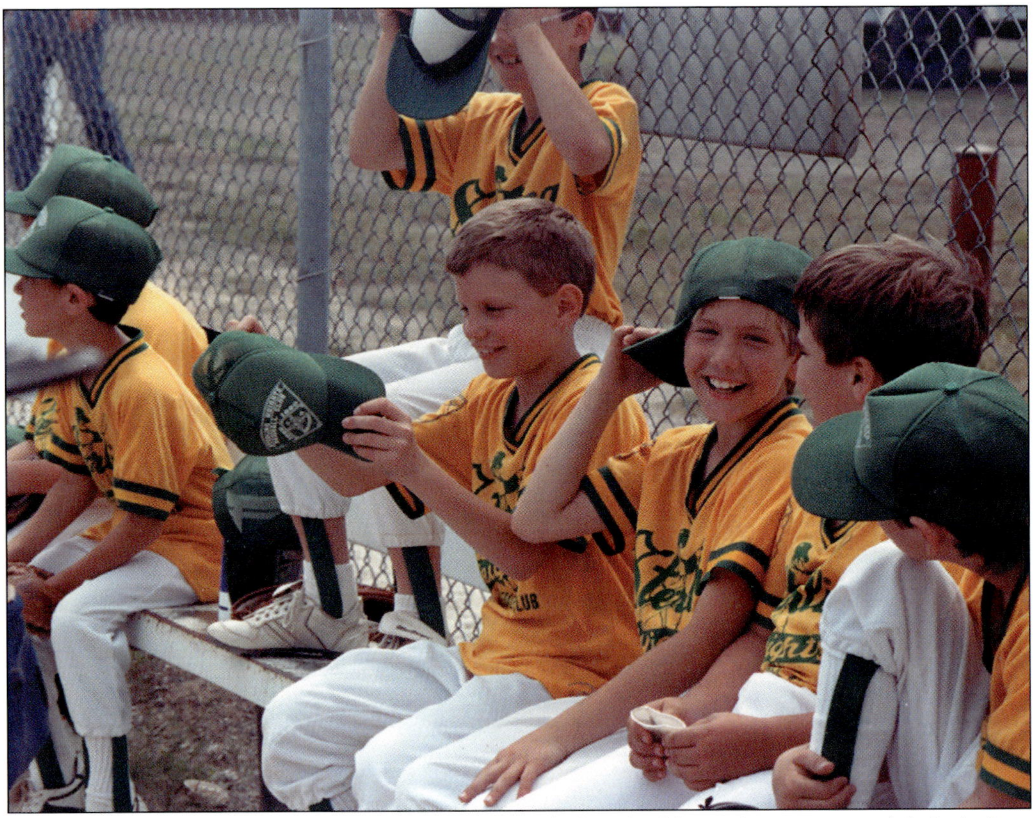

The joy on these boys' faces as they wait to play baseball is the fabric of summertime life for kids in Sterling Heights. Local children have memories of participating in city-sponsored events, playing at parks and in the creeks, exploring fields, riding horses, riding bikes on the fresh concrete of new subdivisions, skateboarding, going to carnivals, and swimming. Life is good.

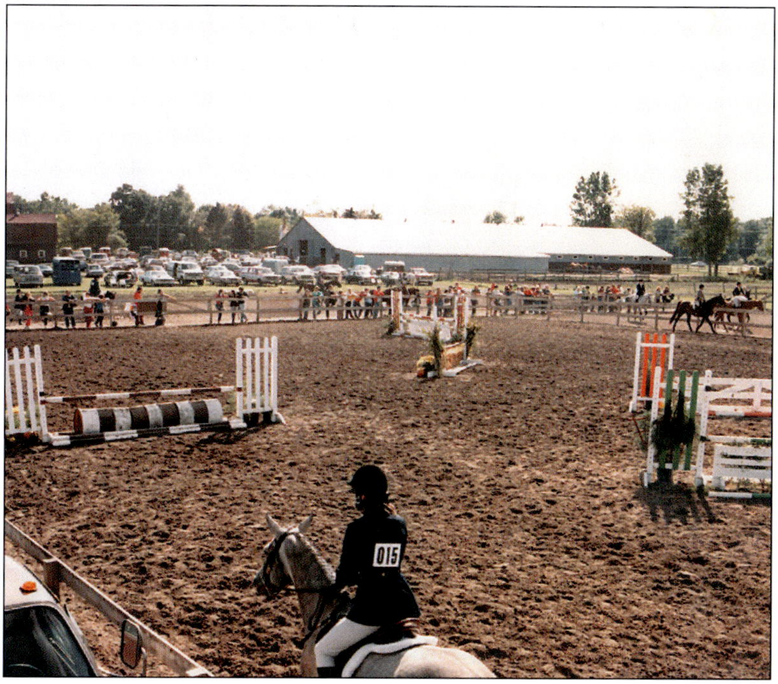

Sterling Stables, owned by Alan and Linda Haggerty and located on the corner of Schoenherr and Clinton River Roads, hosts a horse show around 1985. The site had been used as a stables business for many years, formerly named J & R Stables and Jack's Stables. The Haggertys sold in 1997, and the property was developed into the Saddlebrook residential condominiums. (Courtesy of Alan and Linda Haggerty.)

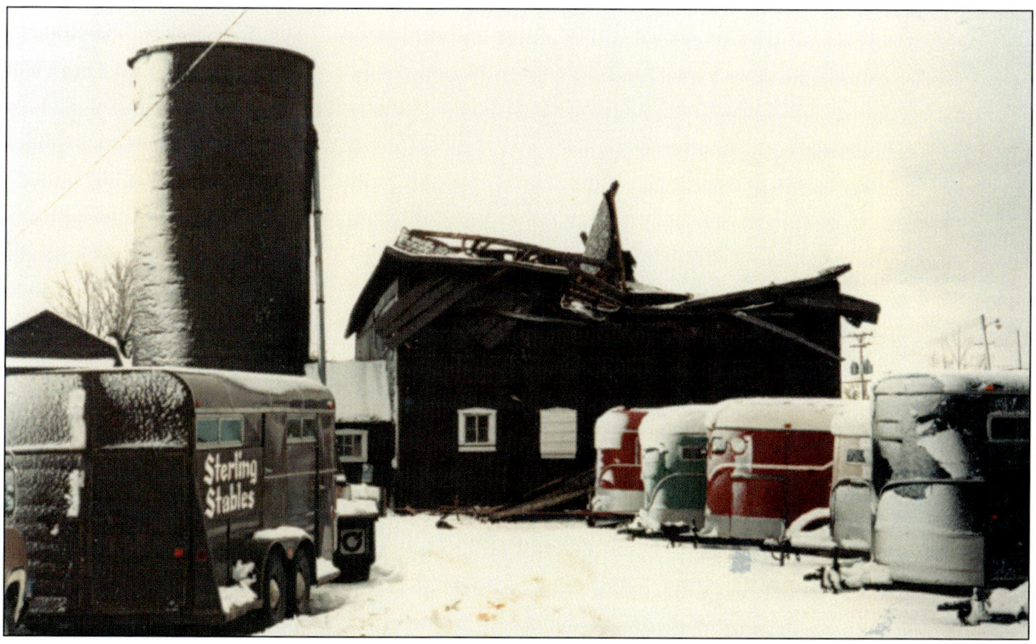

Heavy snow from a February 1985 snowfall brought down the roof of this barn belonging to Sterling Stables, located on the corner of Schoenherr and Clinton River Roads. A few horses sustained minor injuries. The stable property, including this barn, was originally part of a farm owned by John and Elizabeth Upton, early Sterling Township settlers of the 1840s. (Courtesy of Alan and Linda Haggerty of Sterling Stables.)

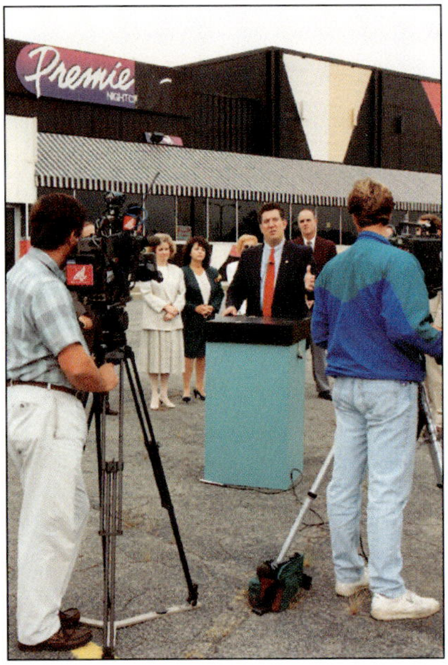

Occupying the former Gateway Theater on Van Dyke Avenue, the Premier Center opened on New Year's Eve 1979 as a local nightclub and bar. By 1982, owners were bringing in major big-name talent. The next 10 years saw new owners, additional events, and financial struggles. It eventually closed as a nightclub in the early 1990s. Pictured is City Manager Steve Duchane, backed by other city officials, announcing its fate. The building has continued to be used by other businesses.

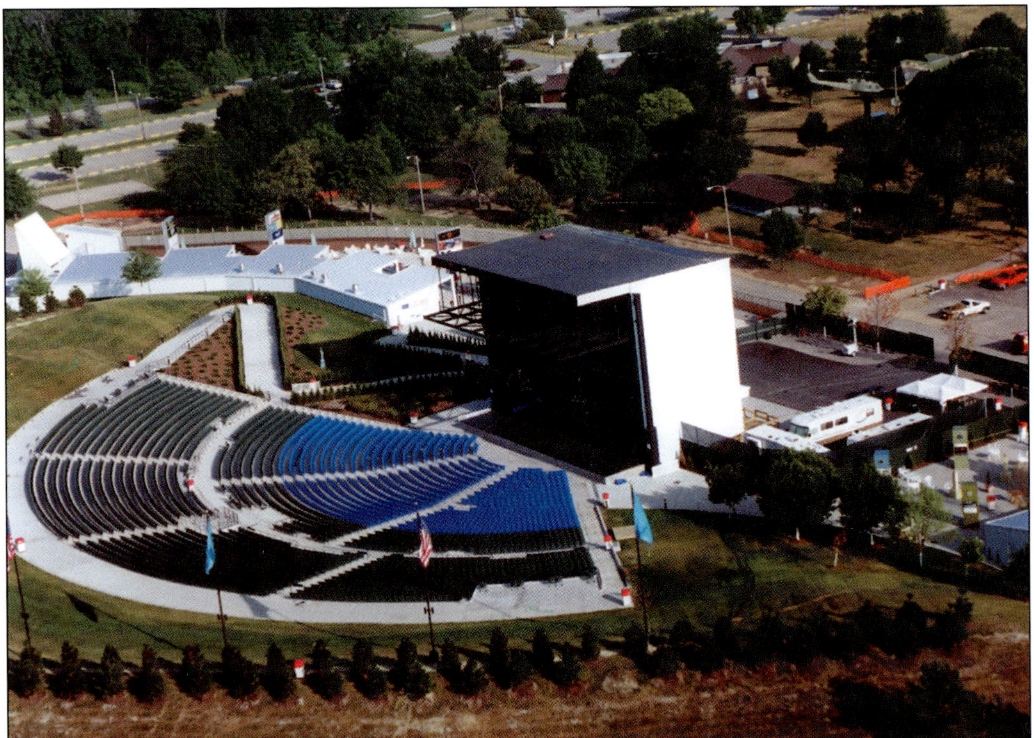

Freedom Hill Amphitheatre, pictured here around 2001, has had a colorful past. It was originally a sanitary landfill from the 1960s, then Dollier-Galinee County Park (named after frontier priests), then an amphitheater using dirt excavated from the construction of I-696 to create the hill. Improvements over the years, a presidential visit, dances, ethnic festivals, lawsuits over noise, and major performers beginning with Conway Twitty and continuing with the big-name acts of today have made this outdoor venue on Metro Parkway a popular concert destination.

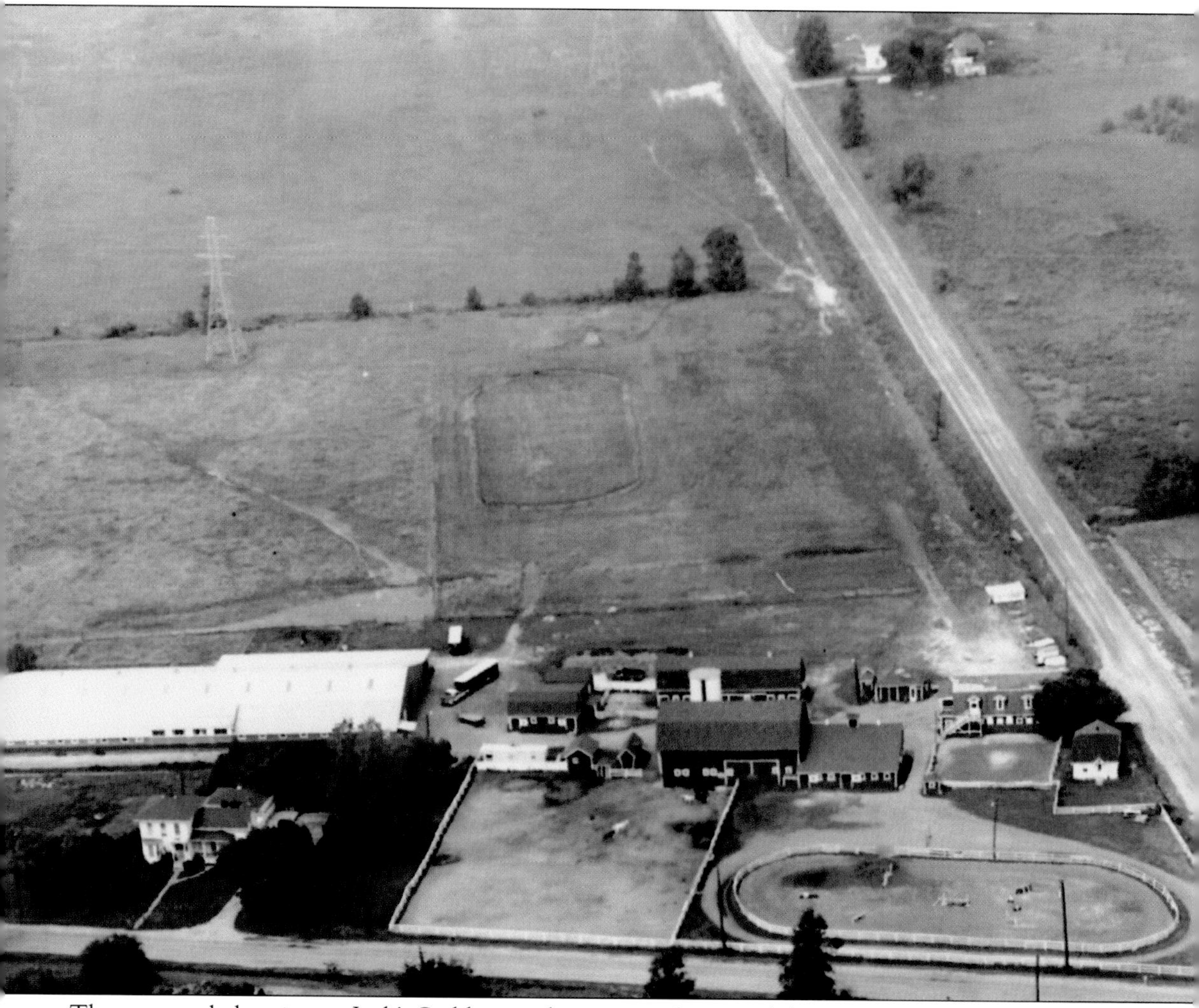

The acreage belonging to Jack's Stables can be seen in this aerial shot from the 1970s. Located on the northwest corner of Clinton River and Schoenherr Roads, the property was originally part of the John Upton farm, then the Charles Upton farm, in the 1800s. In the 20th century, a number of different horse stables, used for recreational riding and competition, occupied the property—Jack's Stables, J & R Stables, and Sterling Stables. The original farmhouse can be seen at lower left, along with many different barns and corrals. Sterling Heights residents remember seeing riders traveling the sides of the roads in the area. This property has since been developed into a condominium complex. Another stable in the city is Springbrook, on Ryan Road south of 19 Mile Road. It is still in operation.